Rainer Geißler, Horst Pöttker (eds.)
Media – Migration – Integration

The series "Medienumbrüche | Media Upheavals" is edited by Peter Gendolla.

RAINER GEISSLER, HORST PÖTTKER (EDS.)

Media – Migration – Integration

European and North American Perspectives

[transcript] Medienumbrüche I Media Upheavals I Volume 33

The Collaborative Research Center 615 at the University of Siegen with funding by the Deutsche Forschungsgemeinschaft (German Research Foundation) produced this book.

Bibliographic information published by the Deutsche Nationalbibliothek
The Deutsche Nationalbibliothek lists this publication in the Deutsche Nationalbibliografie; detailed bibliographic data are available in the Internet at http://dnb.d-nb.de

Cover layout: Kordula Röckenhaus, Bielefeld
Cover illustration: © photocase 2008
Typeset by Anne Weibert and Sarah Hubrich
Printed by Majuskel Medienproduktion GmbH, Wetzlar
ISBN 978-3-8376-1032-1

Distributed in North America by

Transaction Publishers
New Brunswick (U.S.A.) and London (U.K.)

Transaction Publishers   Tel.: (732) 445-2280
Rutgers University   Fax: (732) 445-3138
35 Berrue Circle   for orders (U.S. only):
Piscataway, NJ 08854   toll free 888-999-6778

Content

Rainer Geißler/Horst Pöttker

Preface 7

Horst Pöttker

**Successful Integration? Media and Polish Migration in the
German Empire at the Turn of the 20th Century** 9

Rainer Geißler/Sonja Weber-Menges

**Media Reception and Ideas on Media Integration among
Turkish, Italian and Russo-German Migrants in Germany** 27

Heinz Bonfadelli

Media Use by Ethnic Minority Youth in Switzerland 45

Petra Herczeg

**Migrants and Ethnic Minorities in Austria:
Assimilation, Integration and the Media** 71

Leen d'Haenens

Whither Cultural Diversity on the Dutch TV Screen? 97

Souley Hassane

Mainstream Media vs. Ethnic Minority Media: Integration in Crisis ...117

Augie Fleras

**Ethnic and Aboriginal Media in Canada: Crossing Borders,
Constructing Buffers, Creating Bonds, Building Bridges** 143

Kenneth Starck

**Perpetuating Prejudice: Media Portrayal of
Arabs and Arab Americans** 181

Svetlana Serebryakova

Issues of Migration in Newspapers of the Stavropol' Area 213

**Worst Case and Best Practice in European and North American
Media Integration: What Can We Learn from One Another?**
Round Table Discussion 219

The Authors 245

Rainer Geißler/Horst Pöttker

Preface

"Media, Migration, Integration – European and North American Perspectives" This was the title of a conference held at the University of Dortmund on June 21 and 22, 2007. The presentations and discussions from the conference are documented in this volume. The conference was part of a research project entitled "Media Integration of Ethnic Minorities in Germany, the U.S., and Canada", a project undertaken by the Universities of Dortmund and Siegen in 2002, long before German politics and media began to heatedly debate the topic of integration. That project, in turn, was one element of a research unit located at the University of Siegen and sponsored by the German Research Foundation (DFG): "Media Upheavals, Media Cultures, and Media Aesthetics at the Beginning of the 20th and in Transition to the 21st Century" (*Medienumbrüche. Medienkulturen und Medienästhetik zu Beginn des 20. und im Übergang zum 21. Jahrhundert*).

In June 2004, the first conference within the context of the project "Media Integration" took place in Siegen. The papers presented at this conference were made accessible to a broader audience through their appearance in the volume "Integration durch Massenmedien. Mass Media Integration", published by Transcript Verlag in 2006. The insights gained during the first phase of the research project were published in 2005 in a fundamental manual now recognized as a standard reference work in the field (*Massenmedien und die Integration ethnischer Minderheiten in Deutschland. Problemaufriss – Forschungsstand – Bibliografie*). Another volume presenting findings specific to the second phase of the project will follow in 2009.

At the conference in Siegen in 2004, we were intrigued by the idea of bringing together, on the one hand, scholars concerned with the conditions and consequences of communication in the mass media and, on the other, media practitioners[1]. In this way we were able to explore both the opportunities and the risks of mass media communication for integration in societies attracting large numbers of immigrants. Even at that time, in addition to a number of participants from German universities and editorial staffs, speakers from Canada, the U.S., and the Netherlands also took part.

---

1   Rainer Geißler/Horst Pöttker (Hg.): Integration durcch Massenmedien/Mass Media Integration. Medien und Migration im internationalen Vergleich. Media and Migration: A Comparative Perspective. (Medienumbrüche, Bd. 17). Bielefeld: transcript 2006

For the second conference, which is documented in this volume, international developments were our central theme. Our focus was not on a uniform theoretical approach, but, rather, on enriching the debate by combining perspectives from various countries on both sides of the Atlantic with sizable immigrant populations.

At the same time, it was important for us to be able to maintain a certain continuity within our discussion. For this reason, we were especially pleased to have recruited three speakers, Leen d'Haenens (the Netherlands), Augie Fleras (Canada), and Kenneth Starck (U.S.A.), who were also at the conference in Siegen in 2004. Petra Herczeg (Austria), Svetlana Serebryakova (Russia), Souley Hassane (France), and Heinz Bonfadelli (Switzerland) allowed us to considerably enhance the scope of international perspectives this time. Fortunately, journalists in authoritative positions, such as Jona Teichmann (WDR) and Rainer Rosenberg (ORF), spontaneously agreed to take part in the concluding debate. It is perhaps an indication of some form of cosmopolitan progress in the social sciences and in cultural studies that not only for this publication, but also during the entire proceedings of the conference on German soil we were able to consistently make use of English as a lingua franca.

The editors wish to express their gratitude not only to the speakers and participants at the conference, but also to all of those without whose help this book could never have been completed: the German Research Foundation (DFG), the offices of the presidents of Dortmund and Siegen Universities, the Siegen research center "Media Upheavals, Media Cultures, and Media Aesthetics at the Beginning of the 20th and in Transition to the 21st Century" as represented by its spokesperson, Professor Peter Gendolla, the academic staff and student assistants on the research project "Media Integration of Ethnic Minorities in Germany, the U.S., and Canada", and special thanks to the journalist Anne Weibert, who took on the responsibility of preparing this volume for publication, to Thomas La Presti, who helped us with proofreading the English texts, and to the members of our secretarial staff in Dortmund and Siegen, Angelika Schomann and Christa Still. We are immeasurably indebted to our two colleagues and friends in North America, Professor Augie Fleras (University of Waterloo, Canada) and Professor Kenneth Starck (University of Iowa, U.S.A., currently at Zayed University, FAR/UAE), whose intellectual support we have had the privilege to rely upon for many years.

Rainer Geißler, Horst Pöttker
Dortmund and Siegen, September 2008

Horst Pöttker

Successful Integration? Media and Polish Migration in the German Empire at the Turn of the 20th Century

For some time now, German politicians have claimed that their country is cosmopolitan, that it open-mindedly accepts immigrants of foreign descent and culture and encourages their integration into society. Such claims have become popular since politicians discovered that Germany has been a country distinguished by immigration for years and since they discovered their country's need for immigrants in order to maintain its economic and political position in the world despite a blatantly low birth rate. Current proclamations of German willingness to and capacity for integration often cite Polish migrants as a perfect example. In the decades prior to World War I, these people emigrated to the growing industrial region along the rivers Rhine and Ruhr, and their descendants today may, at best, be recognized by their Slavonic last names. But is this really an appropriate example? An answer may be found by looking at the role that the media – at that time, primarily the press – played in the development of the relationship between the German majority and the Polish minority in society.

1. Theoretical background

In his seminal work on the Polish population (Kleßmann 1978) in the Rhine-Ruhr area from the 1870s to 1945, social historian Christoph Kleßmann focuses his analysis on the integration of the Polish minority. In addition to factors beneficial to integration – in particular, the fact that the so called *Ruhr Poles*, many of whom did not emigrate from a foreign country, but from the Eastern regions of the then German Empire, were of German citizenship – Kleßmann also notes an impressive number of circumstances and tendencies detrimental to integration, such as Polish nationalism, which was fueled by territorial divisions and the lack of statehood during the 19th century. But Kleßmann restricted himself to an analytical classification of integrative and adverse factors, without considering the success or failure of this integration process. The approach here is more practically oriented and is concerned with the following issue: With regard to the Polish minority, is it apt to talk about a process of successful integration? Statistics on the number of Polish migrants and their descendants who remained in Germany will be one crucial criterion. Further considerations raise an issue that is of special significance for media practice today: If the history of the Poles in the Rhine-Ruhr area is to be thought of as a case of successful integration, principles and practices might be found in both the mainstream and ethnic press of the time that might be worth emulating today. But if that history proves to be an example of an unsuccessful integration process, we should focus on structures and practices that journalism and the media should avoid if they are to encourage and further the integration process.

Within a tradition stemming from Émile Durkheim's influential work (Durkheim 1977, 306-316), *social integration* forms the basic concept for our understanding of integration: It is a desired social process that links the segments of a society (individuals, institutions, groups) by means of their particular awareness to a united societal whole, in which both similarities and unity on the one hand, and differences and conflict, on the other, are of importance. It can readily be seen that this definition, not concerned with cultural differences among the various parts of the societal whole, differs fundamentally from the concept of *assimilation*, which asserts cultural homogeneity as a precondition for societal unity. This difference becomes even more evident with the concept of *intercultural media integration*. For here, the intensity and content involved in communication between the different cultural segments of a society, the knowledge – as a result of this communication – which different societal sectors have of each other, participation in societal institutions, and the acceptance of basic cultural values serve as indicators of successful integration (Geißler/Pöttker 2005, 41).

This definition is not only in contrast to the concept of assimilation, but also to ideas that with regard to migrants and ethnic minorities are not concerned with the issue of societal unity, but, instead, focus on (individual or cultural) identity. As the concept of intercultural media integration consciously focuses not on homogeneity, but on mutual knowledge and communication about differences, high priority is assigned to discovering what makes society possible without questioning the identity of the individual or group. Behind this idea is the premise that societal structures which destroy the identities of individuals or groups cannot themselves persist for a long period of time.

Within the scope of the approach described in this article, research methods are closely related to the specific research issues. Section 2 is designed to determine the degree of success in the integration of the *Ruhr Poles*. Thus, data, documents, and literature are subject to analysis here. The two following sections (3 and 4) deal with reports in the German local press and in the Polish ethnic press (in the selective translation by the monitoring German authorities) and summarize the tentative findings of our ongoing quantitative and qualitative analysis of the specific historical newspapers. Finally, the last section contains an interpretation of these findings and applies a perspective of interaction theory to the initial assessment of the *Ruhr Poles'* integration process.

2.   Polish migrants in the Ruhr area – an example of successful integration?

From the establishment of the German Reich in 1871 to the beginning of World War I, the amount of black coal mined in the Ruhr area increased tenfold, while the personnel of the mines increased sevenfold. This seemingly miraculous growth in industrialization would have been impossible, if hundreds of thousands of Poles had not emigrated from the four eastern provinces of the then German Empire – Posen, Silesia, Eastern and Western Prussia – to the mining region in Westphalia in hope of enjoying a better standard of living. Much like today, even at that time an exact count of ethnic minorities and migrant groups was difficult, simply because an exact definition of who is a "migrant" or "person of migration background", is not at all self-evident. More than 99 percent of the Polish migrants back then were German citizens. Apart from their own – or their parents' – place of birth, and apart from somewhat imprecise and variable criteria such as language or religion, the two groups of German majority and Polish minority did not exhibit much divergence. In accordance with the German and Polish seminal works on the subject by Christoph Kleßmann and Krystyna Murzynowska (Murzynowska 1979) – which essentially refer to the same historical sources – one can draw the following approximate picture:

Year	People of Polish origin	Polish-Speaking People (Kleßmann 1978)	Polish-Speaking People (Murzynowska 1979)
1870	10		
1880	40		
1890	122	32	36
1900	333	127	143
1910	497	274	304 (Prussian statistics) 406 (Provincial statistics)
1912			457

Table 1: Poles from the Eastern German Provinces in the Ruhr area (in thousands). (Kleßmann 1978, 37, 260 and Murzynowska 1979, 25, 30-31)

Around 1870, about 10,000 migrants from Eastern Prussia lived in the Ruhr area; by 1880 this number had increased to 40,000. In 1890 there were about

120,000 migrants; by the turn of the century there were about 330,000 to 340,000. Shortly before World War I, the number reached its peak of 500,000. Figures for Polish-speaking people are lower. According to Kleßmann, they amount to 127,000 in 1900, 274,000 in 1910 (Kleßmann 1978, 37, 260), whereas Murzynowska makes use of the official Prussian statistics (143,000 in 1900, 304,000 in 1910), but also refers to provincial statistics (406,000 in 1910 and 457,000 in 1912) (Murzynowska 1979, 30). Taking the migration movement of the years 1910 to 1914 into account, the number of people of Polish migration background in the Prussian provinces *Rhineland* and *Westphalia* amounted to between 450,000 and 550,000 right before the beginning of World War I.

The regional distribution of Polish migrants in the Ruhr area was not uniform. The city of Bottrop was the center of the earliest Polish worker migration in the 1870s. Later on, the Polish population was concentrated in the regions around Dortmund, Bochum, Gelsenkirchen and Essen, whereas the proportion of Poles in the corresponding rural districts was always higher than in large cities.

	1890 absolute	1890 %	1910 absolute	1910 %
Recklinghausen City	716	5.1	12,404	23.1
Recklinghausen County	3,988	5.8	40,847	15.7
Dortmund City	626	0.7	9,722	4.5
Dortmund County	1,699	2.2	26,024	12.2
Bochum City	1,120	2.4	6,269	4.6
Bochum County	2,038	2.7	10,834	9.0
Gelsenkirchen City	1,930	6.9	15,065	8.9
Gelsenkirchen County	7,964	7.1	25,383	17.7
Herne City	2,121	15.2	12,364	21.6
Hamborn City	27	0.6	17,432	17.1
Essen City	211	0.3	3,805	1.3
Essen County	1,887	1.2	17,699	6.4

Table 2: Polish population (except Masurians and bilinguals) in Ruhr area districts with the highest Polish population density. (Kleßmann 1978, 267)

As to the social structure of the Polish minority, it is noteworthy that, in the beginning, primarily unmarried young men or miners unaccompanied by their families migrated to the Ruhr area. The rapid increase in the number of women shows that many men were soon followed by their wives and families (Kleßmann 1978, 41). By the time of World War I, the numerical proportion of men and women had almost reached the same level, the proportion of women increasing from 40% in 1890 to 80% in 1910 (Murzynowska 1979, 36). At the same time, the proportion of Poles who were born in the Ruhr area increased to one third (Murzynowska 1979, 33). Much like the demographic trends among ethnic migrants today, the birth rate – which was higher than average in the German Empire among miners in any case – was especially high among the Polish and the Masurians (Kleßmann 1978, 42).

Year	Men	Women	Women per 100 Men
1890	25,539	10,145	39.5
1900	88,745	53,969	60.8
1905	120,266	84,421	70.2
1910	171,892	131,930	76.7

Table 3: Numerical proportion of men and women among the Polish population in the Ruhr area. (Murzynowska 1979, 36)

The overall picture that these statistics present indicates that the majority of *Ruhr Poles* did not intend to return to the Eastern agrarian areas, which were characterized by large land holdings, rural stagnation, and large-scale unemployment. Instead, the migrants desired to seek their fortune in the prospering mining regions along the Rhine and Ruhr. A willingness to integrate was especially high among the Protestant, mostly conservative and monarchist Masurians from Eastern Prussia. But it also seems that many of the predominantly Roman Catholic immigrants from Posen, Western Prussia and Silesia were just as determined to make their living in the industrialized West.

Most of them put this decision into practice, but many did not settle permanently in the industrial region along the Rhine and Ruhr, as the statistics demonstrate. According to Kleßmann and Murzynowska, who again made use of the Prussian statistics, the number of only or mostly Polish-speaking migrants in the Ruhr area sank significantly from 304,000 to 82,000 between 1910 and 1925 (Kleßmann 1978, 261). This cannot exclusively or even to a great extent be attributed to the acquisition of the German language in the meantime. In the same period, the number of bilinguals only increased by 29,000, from 25,000 to 54,000, whereas the number of people exclusively speaking the Polish language dropped dramatically from 249,000 to 15,000, almost tenfold the increase in bilinguals.[1]

The number of people of Polish migration background in the Ruhr area had decreased significantly by the mid-1920s, although exact specifications on the extent of migration, further migration, and return to the homeland are "virtually impossible" (Kleßmann 1978, 152) due to the discrepancies, even

---

1   Calculations on the basis of statistics from Kleßmann 1978, p. 261.

contradictions, between the statistical sources. Restitution offered by the Polish state is often seen as a major reason for the return to the homeland of many Poles who had settled in the Ruhr area and were, for the most part, willing to become integrated: Poles of German citizenship who were older than 18 years old were guaranteed a right to Polish citizenship. The time period for exercising this right expired on January 10th, 1922. Those persons who had decided to take up residence in Poland by then were allowed to relocate with their movable estate free from duties (Kleßmann 1978, 156).

Both German and Polish sources estimate that between 300,000 and 400,000 people of Polish migration background lived in the Ruhr area in 1921. Officials in organizations of the *Ruhr Poles* estimated that about two thirds of them would make use of this right to Polish citizenship (Kleßmann 1978, 157). De facto, according to the Polish embassy, the total number of Poles in the Ruhr area had decreased to 230,000 by 1923; the Polish consulate estimates the number to have sunk to 150,000 by 1929.[2] But the return to the homeland facilitated by the right to Polish citizenship was much lower than had been expected by either the Polish or the German authorities. According to statistics cited by Kleßmann, a total number of 30,000 to 40,000 people in the entire Ruhr area made use of this privilege, a relatively low figure that "might be traced back to the Polish government's request to only opt for Poland if one intended to actually return to the country by January 10th, 1923; all others were advised to keep their German citizenship" (Kleßmann 1978, 159). Incidentally, the Polish government did not provide much support for returning migrants, so that their number was actually lower than the number of people who had exercised their right to Polish citizenship.

Year	Polish Population in the Ruhr Area	Migration until then	Further Migration to the Polish Homeland	Further Migration: to France Britain, U.S.A
1914	500	50	20	30
1921	350	150	80	70
1923	230	270	70	200
1929	150	350	40	310

Table 4: Migration of the Polish Minority from the Ruhr Area in the 1920s (in thousands). (Estimates according to: Kleßmann 1978, esp. p. 161-168)

The rapid decrease in the number of *Ruhr Poles* in the 1920s seems to have been caused primarily by the migration movement of discontented miners and

---

2   Kleßmann 1978, 156: With a view to these statistics, one should keep in mind that by the 1920s "criteria on who is a Pole, a Masurian, or to be considered a German", had begun to blur both on the Polish and on the German side.

their families. Many of these people moved to Lorraine and other mining areas both in France and Belgium. Others, whose numbers can hardly be reliably estimated, went to the United States. In light of Kleßmann's stipulation that the number of well-integrated Poles remaining in Germany was only one third of the pre-war figure (Kleßmann 1978, 193), one can conclude that during the 1920s an estimated 250,000 Poles migrated from the Ruhr area to other highly industrialized countries such as Britain, France or the United States.

Several factors appear as possible causes of this further migration: the overall dire macroeconomic situation in Germany, the mining crisis, the Ruhr occupation, and the active recruitment by French mining syndicates which, under the auspices of the French military in the Ruhr area, had their own recruitment office in Duisburg in 1921 (Kleßmann 1978, 162). Yet, there were already "about 12,000 Polish miners from the Ruhr area in the cities of Barlin, Lens, Lalange, Dechy and D'Arenberg in northern France prior to World War I" (Kleßmann 1978, 161) – that is, at a time of economic growth which was not beset by the dire circumstances that prevailed in defeated post-war Germany. Hence, there must be other reasons for the widespread further migration among the *Ruhr Poles*, qualified miners who were not readily replaceable in the short term. Kleßmann provides a significant clue when he notes a "fatal circular mechanism" related to the successful recruitment efforts of the French mining syndicates: "Apparently, the hostility experienced in interacting with the German population led numerous Poles to give way to the campaigning of the occupying powers, and every single case of further migration which became known simply reinforced the general feeling of distrust towards the Poles" (Kleßmann 1978, 164). The portrayal of the Polish minority in the German press prior to World War I and the response in the Polish ethnic press can shed some light on the reasons for this distrust on the part of the German population.

3.   The Polish minority in the German local press prior to World War I

No comprehensive systematic analysis exists of the image of the Polish minority communicated to the German majority by German local and regional newspapers. Whenever such sources are cited in historical studies on the *Ruhr Poles* (e.g., Burghardt 2000), only individual articles serve to illustrate specific aspects.

The *Recklinghäuser Zeitung* lends itself well to an exemplary systematic content analysis, for Recklinghausen was the city with the largest Polish minority in the Ruhr area. The newspaper was published daily by the company

J. Baur. If the Polish minority was to be a topic for the local press at all, this would certainly have been the case in Recklinghausen.

There are no exact figures on the circulation of the *Recklinghäuser Zeitung* during this period; an advertisement from November 1912 mentions a total of 12.516 subscribers (*Recklinghäuser Zeitung*, vol. 82., 16th November 1912, p. 1). How many of these subscribers were of Polish descent could become apparent when the Baur archives have been made available, but it can be assumed that the number was low, as the migrants had established a press of their own in the Polish language. According to the advertisement mentioned above, there was only a low amount of mail delivery in the predominantly Polish neighborhoods such as southern Recklinghausen and the mining settlement of "König Ludwig". The Recklinghäuser Zeitung, which claimed to be the most widespread newspaper of the region, was more or less frequently and intensively read by at least one third, but no more than half of the 250.000 German residents of Recklinghausen. For the process of integration as defined above, the newspaper's reports on the Polish part of the population – as a basis for the German majority's knowledge of and attitude towards the *Ruhr Poles* – are of fundamental significance.

In the context of our research, the *Recklinghäuser Zeitung* has now become the subject of a systematic and precise content analysis. Even the acquisition of the historical newspaper material ensures that we are the first to undertake this task, for the Baur publishing company in Recklinghausen has a very restrictive policy on providing access to the historical material (although the period in question is not generally considered to be controversial). The required volumes from the turn of the century were not – as might have been suspected – to be found at the Institute for Newspaper Research, but, instead, in the Baur archives in Recklinghausen. They were filed on microfilm and could not readily be printed out, which presented significant obstacles to analyzing such an extensive amount of material. For a first analysis of the material acquired under great technical difficulties, we can take recourse to a randomly selected 30-day period in 1912, a year which was not yet dominated by dramatic developments in domestic or foreign affairs. To determine whether or not journalistic coverage related to the *Ruhr Poles* was beneficial to that group's integration process, reports affecting everyday life would seem to have the greatest relevance – the everyday life of both the Polish minority and the German majority, as well as the professional everyday life of the journalists.

The most significant impression to be gained from this analysis is that the Polish minority – despite its size of 20% of the total population – is only rarely a topic in the voluminous local section of the *Recklinghäuser Zeitung*. Apart from the occasional appearance of obviously Slavic names in news about accidents and crime, there is little mention of the Polish minority in the newspaper's local section City and District Recklinghausen. To cite an example, news from January 18th can be briefly quoted here:

> Waltrop, January 18th. At the coal mine Waltrop, miner Karl Zicharski had an accident at work yesterday. He broke his leg and had to be hospitalized.

The sources show no journalistic coverage of problems related to the Polish minority, nor is even the presence of the minority a topic. In the same issue, the reader could learn from the local part of the newspaper:

> König Ludwig, January 19th. Sources have said that on Sunday, January 21st, there will be a large gathering of adherents of the Roman Catholic faith in the hall of "Haus Hartmann" (guesthouse "Glückauf"). Information will be presented on the most pressing social problems. There will also be a discussion on how underprivileged families can achieve success, prosperity, and personal fulfilment. A competent guest speaker has been engaged for this occasion. As these issues are especially significant, it is expected that no Roman Catholic man, woman or girl will miss this important meeting.

Since four fifths of all miners at the coal mine "König Ludwig" were of Polish descent, some readers will have presumed from this news that this was a gathering of Polish people (regardless of whether this was actually the case). It seems that here the description "Roman Catholic" was being used as a substitute for "Polish", that journalists undertook every effort to avoid mentioning the ethnic designation. Reports on events from the southern – and predominantly Polish – area of Recklinghausen frequently made use of the word "Catholic", without explicitly mentioning the Polish minority, so that readers could only infer the ethnic background of the people involved when, for example, a new children's home was opened (*Recklinghäuser Zeitung*, vol. 82, 3rd April 1912, p. 2), or the training ground of a fire brigade was made accessible for sporting activities "on Sunday afternoons for the Catholic youths' club" (*Recklinghäuser Zeitung*, vol. 82, 3rd April 1912, p. 2). For journalists, direct mention of the ethnic background seems to have been taboo.

The migrant group was only immediately recognizable if this was unavoidable, as, for example, in news from the civil registry office, or the semiofficial and voluminous coverage of the city council's meetings, or of committee elections, in which Poles competed with their own candidates. The civil registry office in Southern Recklinghausen reports the following births on April 3rd, 1912:

A son: Railway worker Andreas Zalcsinski, Miner Wilhelm Jentoch, Miner Aegidius Lurzsak, Miner Adalbert Kowalzewski, Miner Johann Matcia, Miner Johann Madry, Bookseller Stanislaus Starkicwicz;

A daughter: Miner Vinz. Garca, Woodworker Johann Janczyk, Railway worker Peter Reckhemke, Painter Rudolf Kieszlich, Miner Joh. Machinski, Locksmith Wilhelm Koch, Miner Josef Giezek, Miner Joh. Elsner, Miner Franz Szudra, Miner Franz Stachorski, Miner Andreas Bartkiewicz.

This official piece of news accurately reflects the ethnic composition of the district, whereas such accuracy was lacking in other journalistic coverage of the time. A further example has to do with elections:

On December 6th and 7th of last year, elections were held for all of the assessors to the mining court of Eastern Recklinghausen. Voter participation among workers was about 50%. Among the workers who were elected, five were from the German Miner's Alliance, three from the Polish Alliance, and one from the Christian Alliance. None of the court's former assessors was re-elected. (*Recklinghäuser Zeitung*, vol. 82, 3rd April 1912, p. 3)

But the direct reference to Polish migrants usually went no further. The refusal to explicitly specify the involvement of Poles in local reporting extended to descriptions of alleged criminals, accident victims, and suicides, without clarifying ethnic or migrant backgrounds and, in this way, helped perpetuate a German tradition in journalism. Reports on crimes, then, rarely mentioned Poles in any direct way. This could be interpreted as having been beneficial to the integration process. Still, in many cases the question remains whether readers were able to infer from contexts that Poles were indeed the group being reported on.

At the turn of the 20th century, film emerged as a new medium, and printing techniques facilitated the incorporation of graphics and photography into texts. Increasingly, visualization played a role in sources of public information and entertainment. For this reason, our analysis of the *Recklinghäuser Zeitung* also takes visual features into account. Perhaps this would be where Polish migrants made their appearance. The *Recklinghäuser Zeitung* did not print photographs in 1912, but all of the sections, especially the one on "International Politics", included graphics and drawings. In the 24 issues[3] of the 30-day period in 1912 analyzed here, 95 drawings, 14 maps, and a total of

---

3   The *Recklinghäuser Zeitung* appeared six times per week.

109 illustrations could be found, an average of 4.5 visual elements per issue. None of these illustrations dealt with issues concerning the Polish segment of the population or with Polish migration as such. Hence, the refusal to mention the group also extends to the visual elements of the newspaper. The only exceptions were advertisements, in which Slavic names occasionally appeared. Thus, journalists themselves did not violate the taboo, although perhaps they should have – to facilitate transparency and promote societal communication, which could have furthered the integration process. Instead, if the taboo was ignored, this was done by the administration, by political institutions, and by some of the migrants themselves, who were interested in buying publicity to further their economic interests.

In light of such meagre findings, it seems necessary to look for reports of events in which some mention of the Polish minority was practically inevitable. Among these events were the "Riots of Herne", during which in June 1899 Polish miners were among the protesters against an increase in miners' insurance premiums which would particularly affect young, unskilled workers. Other such events include the large-scale miner strikes in 1889, 1905 and 1912. In 1889, still at an early phase of migration in which Polish nationalism had not yet developed among the migrants from the Eastern provinces, the *Wochenblatt für den Kreis Recklinghausen* (the weekly predecessor of the *Recklinghäuser Zeitung*) published reports in language that tended to malign the Polish minority and to provoke feelings against them. This might have been related to the subject matter, as the newspaper reported on conflicts between Polish workers who were on strike and German strike breakers:

> Bottrop, May 8th. Close to the new pit of the coal mine "Prosper", there has been a row between miners. While returning from their shift, twenty of the local miners were assaulted by about 80 Polish workers who were loitering. (*Wochenblatt für den Kreis Recklinghausen*, vol. 55, 11th May 1889, p. 3)

Four days later, a similar report appeared:

> Bottrop, May 12th. A number of German miners was attacked by a large group of their Polish colleagues on a countryside road. The Poles were outraged because their German colleagues had not immediately joined them in their strike. An attacker identified by the name of Bernatzi was shot in the back, but was not critically injured. A landowner who lived nearby had fired off his shotgun to alarm the military. (*Wochenblatt für den Kreis Recklinghausen*, vol. 57, 13th May 1889, p. 2)

This early connection of violence to an immigrated minority in the local press is noteworthy, as the connection was taken up again and expanded during the "Riots of Herne" ten years later. At that time, the regional and national press, in particular the conservative *Rhein-Westfälische Zeitung*, warned against a "foreign infiltration" and a threat to German orderliness by the allegedly strike- and crime-affiliated Polish migrants (Kleßmann 1978, 75-82). Regional and national newspapers could afford to treat the Polish minority as a subject involving political conflict. In contrast to the Recklinghäuser Zeitung, such papers did not have to serve a large audience composed of several, if not all, social classes. This may be the main reason for the omission of the conflict-laden topic in the local reports of the *Recklinghäuser Zeitung*.

4. The press of the Ruhr Poles and its instrumentalization by the German administration

Polish migrants in the Ruhr area could choose from many different Polish-language newspapers, most of which were published in one of the four Eastern provinces and then mailed to their readers. In Rhineland-Westphalia, the *Gazeta grudziadzka* from Graudenz was the most frequently read newspaper, which in 1911 had 5,000 subscribers in the main postal district of Dortmund alone. Other Polish papers with a high circulation were published in the Ruhr area itself, such as the oldest and most important among them, the *Wiarus Polski*, which was published in Bochum. Kleßmann describes the paper as the "central organ and organizational focus of Poles in the Ruhr area" (Kleßmann 1974). Another radical paper with Polish nationalist tendencies was the *Narodowiec*, with 2,700 subscribers and a total circulation of 3,000. Also, there were religious newspapers with a strict Roman Catholic orientation, such as *Tygodnik Maryanski*, and trade union papers, such as *Glos Gornika*. It is noteworthy that there was a definite lack of a unionist, social democratic tendency among the newspapers that were published in the Ruhr area, as well as among the miners themselves.

At the dawn of World War I, the total circulation of newspapers for Polish readers in the Ruhr area amounted to between 50,000 and 70,000. For a total Polish population of about 500,000, this number seems small – compared to the German segment of the population, in which case there was one newspaper for every third person. Yet, this number should be seen in light of the fact that the migrant population was mostly of rural background and often had only little formal schooling. Apparently, among Polish migrants there was a strong need to communicate in their familiar language – a need which certainly contributed to the formation of a culturally defined group identity.

Still, language itself was not the most salient issue, as attempts on the part of German publishers to set up a Polish-language newspaper demonstrated. The preference for the established, radical Polish press as opposed to these German attempts at Polish-language publications can be seen, for example, in the history of *Wiarus Polski* and the paper modeled after it, the *Narodowiec*, which not only outlasted World War I, but also followed the mass of Polish miners who migrated further to industrial regions in France and Belgium. Apart from an interruption because of the German occupation, the *Viarus* was published in Lille from 1923 to 1961 (Kleßmann 1974, 397); the *Narodowiec* followed migrating Polish miners to Lens, where it continued to be published up to the end of the 1970s. When so many migrants leave a country, not in order to relocate in their homeland, but to move to another foreign country, and their newspapers (are forced to) follow them, it is certainly not appropriate to speak of a minority's successful integration into the society at large.

Title	Place of Publication	Frequency	Tendency	Circulation	Subscriptions
In the Ruhr Area					
Wiarus Polski	Bochum	daily	radical nationalist	9,000	8,500
Tygodnik Maryanski	Bochum	weekly	religious	5,000	4,500
Glos Gornika	Bochum	2 x per month	unionist nationalist	30,000	
Gazeta Gornicza	Bochum	weekly	unionist social dem.	3,000	
Narodowiec	Herne	daily	radical nationalist	3,500	2,700
From the East					**OPD DO**
Gazeta Grudziadzka	Graudenz				5,200
Postęp	Posen				400
Katolicki	Posen				500
Sokol	Posen				1,000
Total of subscriptions DO/MS/D					**21,200**

Table 5: Large-scale Polish Newspapers ("Ethno-Press") in the Ruhr-Area, 1911. [OPD = Oberpostdirektion Dortmund]. (Source: Kleßmann 1978, p. 280f., 282)

But just as certainly, the ethnic newspapers mentioned above did not contribute to the integration process of the *Ruhr Poles*. They campaigned against almost any aspect of intercultural integration: against learning the German language, buying goods in German shops, interethnic marriages – especially between Polish men and German women, subscribing to and reading German newspapers. In a word, they were against all the various forms of intercultural communication and contact between the Polish minority and the German majority in everyday life (Cf. Der Polizei-Präsident, Abt. II.: Übersetzungen aus westfälischen und anderen polnischen Zeitungen. Jg. 1912, No. 41, 11. Oktober 1912, p. 383ff).

Moreover, their reporting provides further substantiation that there was a significant amount of further migration of Poles to Lorraine prior to World War I. On October 9th, 1912 the *Viarus Polski* published the following "warning":

> Many Poles, especially from Silesia, leave their homes for France without prior information. But what is waiting for them there is misfortune, as the French mines only employ workers from the Rhineland and Westphalia. Salaries are not higher than in Westphalia. But, since we are allowed Polish teachers and Polish pastors, freedom of speech is granted. Also, the clubs are allowed every freedom they require. (…) Work is not so harmful to health, as the coal is free of gas. But the salary fluctuates. (Der Polizei-Präsident, Abt. II.: Übersetzungen aus westfälischen und anderen polnischen Zeitungen. Jg. 1912, No. 41, 11. Oktober 1912, p. 388)

This quote clearly indicates that the further migration of Poles to France and the failure of their integration into German society were linked to the pressure to assimilate that they had had to face in Germany. The Roman Catholic Polish nationalism of the newspapers mentioned can also be understood as a reaction to the pressure to assimilate brought forward from the German side.

It is not without a certain irony that in German-language research contexts all of the statements about the Polish ethnic press – those made by Christoph Kleßmann and others, and even the assertions in this paper– are based on the historical translations of the German authorities. These translations were probably not inauthentic, although this possibility should also be taken into consideration.

What is more disturbing than the philological accuracy of the texts is their selection. It is possible that the apparently strong nationalist tendency of the successful Polish newspapers *Viarus Polski* and *Narodowiec* would prove to be less prominent, if recourse were taken to the Polish originals instead of to the selective translations. In this regard, a great amount of intercultural content analysis remains to be done.

5.   Conclusion: Why did the integration of the Ruhr Poles fail?

The analysis of both the German majority newspapers and the Polish minority newspapers indicates that the Polish ethnic identity, which was linked to the Slavic mother tongue, the Roman Catholic faith, and to Polish national history, was not accepted in the German majority culture. Indeed, it seems that the existence of this ethnic identity was hardly noticed. Apparently, the dissatisfaction that led many of the Poles to migrate further was less a matter of salary and economic affairs than of obstacles to their customary cultural practices in their new environment. In the case of the *Ruhr Poles* prior to World War I, cultural differences between the ethnic minority and the majority were ignored by local newspapers like the *Recklinghäuser Zeitung* on the one hand, and explicitly denied by political parties, authorities and the regional and national press on the other. The effect was the same. Disregard for the collective minority identity evoked counter-reactions, as had been the case with the press of the Polish minority: adherence to a cultural identity which had been declared illegitimate was proclaimed; the ignorance exhibited by the majority culture was interpreted as an attack from external sources and thus reinforced the communicative barriers between majority and minority.

These barriers and the resulting alienation of the minority, and the eventual failure of the integration process, certainly were effected by interdependencies between the actions of both the majority and the minority. Yet, which of the phenomena was the initial one is a debatable matter: the pressure to assimilate and Germanize the *Ruhr Pole* minority or their Polish nationalist separatism. All of the known sources indicate that no political nationalism among the Polish migrants existed during the first decade of migration from the East to the industrial region in Rhineland-Westphalia. Indications of organized Polish nationalist movements first emerged in the 1890s, approximately at the time when German authorities started to monitor the Polish ethnic press in the Ruhr area. Both the German (local) press (e.g., *Recklinghäuser Zeitung*) and the Polish ethnic press (e.g., *Wiarus Polski*) contributed to the failure of the process of integration. To further intercultural integration, the German local press should have taken note of the Poles in the Ruhr area, informed the majority about their particular way of life, and thus prepared the way for public acceptance of this lifestyle. The Polish ethnic press, on the other hand, should have helped interest its readers in the German majority culture instead of promoting uncompromising and exclusive positions. Neither of these developments actually took place. Hence, the effect of the media on the process of intercultural integration was detrimental rather than encouraging.

The question remains, what media and journalism might learn from this historical counterexample in terms of a possible contribution to the process of intercultural integration. Any generalizations that could be drawn from this example would perhaps be very limited: Poland's territorial divisions and the lack of a national government for more than a century provided fertile breeding ground for separatist and nationalist tendencies in the Polish migrant community. Under more favorable conditions, the detrimental effect on integration could have been less serious. On the other hand, this historical example also involves positive factors, such as the German citizenship of many of the migrants. At least this combination of both positive and negative factors would seem to make generalization to a certain extent justifiable.

In this sense, then, the largely unsuccessful integration process of the Ruhr Poles can be instructive for the media in two ways. First, the example demonstrates that if the media ignore immigrant communities and their ethnic differences, this will not promote integration. On the other hand, it is apparent that intercultural integration is furthered if journalists take their job seriously and comprehensively report on the everyday life of ethnic minorities with accurate and authentic material. Second, it is detrimental to intercultural integration if ethnic media only perceive hostile elements in the majority culture and attempt to prevent their minority audience from communicating and interacting with the majority in positive ways. Moreover, journalists working in ethnic media can contribute to integration if they make sincere efforts to provide publicity for their audience's concerns. For migrant audiences, this also means that the accommodating society should naturally have a place in this media constellation.

6. References

Burghardt, Werner (2000): "Die polnischen Arbeiter sind...fleißig und haben einen ausgeprägten Erwerbssinn..." – Zur Geschichte polnischer Berg-arbeiter in Recklinghausen 1884-1924. In: Bresser, Klaus/Thüer, Chris-toph, eds.: Recklinghausen im Industriezeitalter. Recklinghausen, pp. 401-423

Durkheim, Émile (1977): Über die Teilung der sozialen Arbeit. Frankfurt a.M.

Geißler, Rainer/Pöttker, Horst, eds. (2005): Massenmedien und die Integration ethnischer Minderheiten in Deutschland. Problemaufriss – Forschungs-stand – Bibliographie. Bielefeld

Kleßmann, Christoph (1974): "Der 'Viarus Polski' – Zentralorgan und Organisationszentrum der Polen im Ruhrgebiet 1891-1923." In: Beiträge zur Geschichte Dortmunds und der Grafschaft Mark, vol. 69, pp. 383-397

Kleßmann, Christoph (1978): Polnische Bergarbeiter im Ruhrgebiet 1870-1945: soziale Integration und nationale Subkultur einer Minderheit in der deutschen Industriegesellschaft. Göttingen

Murzynowska, Krystyna (1979): Die polnischen Erwerbsauswanderer im Ruhrgebiet während der Jahre 1880-1914. Dortmund (Polish Original 1972)

Der Polizei-Präsident, Abt. II., ed. (1912): Uebersetzungen aus westfaelischen und anderen polnischen Zeitungen. Vol.. 41, 11th October 1912, pp. 383ff

Rainer Geißler/Sonja Weber-Menges

Media Reception and Ideas on Media Integration among Turkish, Italian and Russo-German Migrants in Germany

This article is a small part, a fragment, of the work from an extensive research project on the role of the media in the integration of migrants. This project is being conducted by a team of sociologists and communications scholars at the Universities of Siegen and Dortmund. The project's title is: Media Integration of Ethnic Minorities. With regard to both analytical and normative considerations, the fundamental concept behind our inquiry is "media integration". After the description of this concept we will present some empirical findings on the media use of Turkish, Italian and Russo-German migrants and on the issue of which views these migrants hold with respect to certain aspects of media integration.

1. Key Concepts: Integration and Media Integration

1.1 What is Integration? Intercultural Integration: a Middle Course between Assimilation and Segregation

Any attempt to systematically clarify the role of the mass media in integration will first have to concern itself with the fundamental conception of 'integration'. What does the 'integration' of 'migrants' actually mean? Anyone doing work on this theme will quickly discover that 'integration' is a distinctly complex, multilayered concept subject to contradictory interpretations. At the outset, the concept of integration is of a double-sided nature: it is an analytical and systematic concept on the one hand, yet at the same time also a normative political concept. Not only is integration an instrument of scientific analysis, but the concept also always entails desirable goals, desirable developments, and a desirable final state. Thus, anyone doing academic research on integration is always – intentionally or not – in the midst of a political debate. (In this sense, for instance, concepts such as 'integration policy' or 'integration spokesperson' have become more and more widespread on the German political scene in recent years, even though for more than two decades concepts such as 'policy on foreigners' and 'commissioner for foreigners' had been used exclusively.) In light of its political implications, it is no surprise that the concept is very controversial – both in politics and in the academic disciplines (Geißler 2004).

Up to this point, an *assimilative* version of integration has been predominant in German research on migration. Here, integration is equated with assimilation. In his expert's report for the independent committee on immigration established by the national government (*Süßmuth-Kommission*), Hartmut Esser (2001) asserts, "Social integration into the accommodating society is [...] actually *only* possible in the form of *assimilation*" (emphasis in the original). For Esser, the opposite pole to integration (in the sense of assimilation) is the *segregation* of migrants – a simple juxtaposition of majority and minorities, a state of mutual isolation that leads to an 'ethnic class' (or, more precisely, an ethnic 'lower class'). In this view, segregated and thus excluded groups are not able to participate appropriately in the social life of the core society. For this theory of integration, an integration into the social structure – i.e., equal opportunities in the educational system, on the labor market, and in access to significant institutions (e.g., access to mass media) – can only succeed if minorities become culturally assimilated. In Canada, assimilative versions of integration have belonged to the past for some time now; they are no longer applicable today. 'Assimilation' is a concept of the "assimilationist era" (Fleras/Elliot 1992, p. 67), which has been overcome for more than three decades.

Nor do we still work with the dichotomous contradiction between assimilative integration and segregation; instead, we extend the conceptual dichotomy to a trichotomy. Alongside the concept of assimilative integration we place the concept of *intercultural* integration. Intercultural integration marks a middle course between assimilation and segregation. The concept of intercultural integration shares certain common features with, but also exhibits significant differences to, the concept of assimilative integration. Common to both is the normative idea of appropriate integration of migrants into the accommodating society: equal opportunities for the majority and for minorities in access to education, the labor market, and important institutions. The aim of both conceptions is to prevent the formation of "ethclasses" (Gordon 1964), to impede the ethnicization of structures promoting inequality. Nevertheless, both concepts have to do with totally different ideas of socio-*cultural* integration. Whereas the assimilative concept has as its goal the cognitive, social, and identity-related assimilation (= adaptation) of minorities to the majority culture, the concept of intercultural integration seeks a proper balance between the equal rights of minorities to maintain a certain cultural difference and the demands of the majority for (partial) acculturation and adaptation.

Intercultural integration follows from an important fundamental principle of Canadian multiculturalism. In his classic work on multiculturalism in Canada entitled "Engaging Diversity", Augie Fleras expresses this idea with the bipolar formula of "unity-within-diversity", or "diversity-within-unity"

(Fleras/Elliot 2002). The pole of "diversity" is associated with migrants' rights to socio-cultural difference, rights to maintain and thus to engage in their particular cultural traditions, their language, their ethnic communities. The pole of "unity" places limits on these rights and demands a certain adaptation of the migrants – that they learn the language of the country they have emigrated to and other abilities important for being able to get along in the accommodating society: knowledge of laws and basic values of this society, orientation to these and identification with them, openness for interethnic and intercultural contacts beyond the borders of the ethnic community.

The concept of "intercultural integration" challenges the people involved – the majority and the minorities – to seek and find a suitable balance between the desires of the minorities to have their cultural and social distinctions respected and the desires of the majority to have a common legal, cultural, and social framework that is indispensable for living together. Within this context, it is certainly a problem to establish or, more precisely, to negotiate (Kastoryano 2002) what Fleras/Elliot (2002, 9) call the "multicultural line" between unity and diversity, that is, an answer to the questions: Where does the right to difference end? Where does the obligation to adapt begin? The concrete design of this "multicultural line" is a dynamic, never-ending process; it is the subject of societal and political debates and the result of political, often enough also of court decisions.

If both models of integration – the assimilative one and the intercultural one – are applied to reality, evidence of both can certainly be found. Both assimilative and intercultural integrative processes take place. Apparently, *assimilation* is a *long-term operation* that takes place over the course of several generations, and intercultural integration appears to be a preliminary stage to assimilation. Nevertheless, we prefer to consider intercultural integration as an important goal of integration policy and as a significant heuristic concept for migration research. Intercultural integration is more humane than assimilation. It lessens the pressure to assimilate, which, in Germany, has been shown to be experienced by migrants as an unreasonable demand (Rauer/Schmidtke 2001). Intercultural integration also takes into account the feelings of many migrants who do not wish to relinquish the cultural and social roots of their ethnic heritage and their corresponding sense of identity.

Perhaps one should actually call the humane middle course between assimilation and segregation "multicultural" integration, as the concept is strongly oriented to the philosophy and policy of Canadian multiculturalism. But for two reasons we prefer the term "intercultural" integration. On the one hand, a heated debate on multicultural society in Germany has filled the concept of "multicultural" with other, negative content ('simple juxtaposition' of ethnic groups, 'parallel societies', 'ethnic ghettos') and for many people the term has become a politically highly emotive word (cf. Mintzel 1997). Thus, this term would lead to misunderstandings, especially since only a small number of Germans are familiar with the principles of Canadian multiculturalism. On the other hand, the prefix 'inter-' expresses better what the concept actually intends: living together, having common ground, and engaging in exchange. The prefix 'multi-' can, indeed, be associated with 'simple juxtaposition' or 'parallel'.

1.2 What is Media Integration? Intercultural Media Integration: a Middle Course between Media Assimilation and Media Segregation

The results of these general reflections on the topic of integration are now to be more directly related to problems involved in issues of media and migration. To this end, we have developed a concept of media integration, which we define as follows: the integration of ethnic minorities into the media system and into a public sphere produced and sustained by the mass media.

The observations made below take into account the fact that in Germany – as in other societies attractive for immigrants – there is an ethnically pluralistic media system and an ethnically pluralistic public sphere. In other words, in addition to the predominant German mainstream mass media (majority media), which are primarily produced by Germans in the German language, there are ethno-media that are produced by the ethnic minorities themselves and are usually in their own language, only rarely in German or bilingual.

With recourse to the typology developed above, it would now seem appropriate to differentiate three types of media integration or non-integration: media segregation and assimilative media integration (media assimilation) as the two external poles, and intercultural media integration as a middle course between the two extremes. These three 'ideal types' are to be characterized briefly in what follows.

1.2.1 Media Segregation

Media segregation is the opposite of media integration. It occurs whenever ethnic minorities primarily consume ethno-media and in this way allow ethnic segments of a public sphere to exist that are isolated from the accommodating society and its dominant public sphere. Often, the ethno-media are produced in the countries of origin and for the indigenous population. If they are produced in the accommodating society, they are to a great extent or even exclusively oriented to the original culture. In extreme cases, they contain no information at all about Germany, nor do they provide assistance in dealing with integration problems in the society at large. Typical media-segregated audiences are, for example, Turks who live in Germany and exclusively watch Turkish television programs or read Turkish newspapers that were made in Turkey for the Turkish population there.

In the German media system, ethnic minorities are less apparent as producers than as consumers. As far as media content is concerned, they are thematized relatively rarely and, if so, as 'foreigners', as people who don't belong. Their representation is distorted in a negative way. They are dealt with, e.g., as 'problem groups', as groups that live in Germany but tend to pose problems for society more than anything else.

1.2.2   Assimilative Media Integration

The opposite pole of media segregation is assimilative media integration. Here, at the level of social structures ethnic minorities are 'institutionally' integrated, i.e., they are appropriately represented in the functionally significant institution of the mass media – as journalists, managers, controlling authorities (e.g. on television boards) or as proprietors. Since the assimilative model presumes that ethnic minorities are also 'adapted' in socio-cultural respects, such minorities no longer represent any ethnically specific problems or interests in the German media system. There is no ethnically specific coverage in the mass media since the ethnic minorities no longer exist as socio-culturally specific groups. They have been fully absorbed and assimilated into the diversity of the German majority culture – with respect to cognitive, social, and identity models (see above). There are no distinct ethnic segments of the public sphere because there are no ethno-media and because the ethnic minorities use German media in patterns similar to those of the Germans themselves (e.g., dependent on their level of education).

It is obvious that both of the models outlined so far only relate to very limited sections of the real mass media situation in Germany as a country attracting immigrants. They are not useful as normative models that would contain desirable goals. Media segregation prevents the desirable integration of ethnic minorities, and assimilative media integration is at odds with the mental disposition of a large number of migrants who do not wish to break all bonds with their homelands. Apparently, the integrative requirements of the accommodating society and the specific socio-cultural needs of the migrants can best be brought into an appropriate balance with the third model.

1.2.3 Intercultural Media Integration

In the assimilative model, the ethnic media and public spheres are missing; in the segregationist model, the majority and the minorities and their respective media and public spheres are isolated from one another. In contrast, in the intercultural, integrative model, the majority and the minorities are intermeshed; intercultural communication takes place. The specific characteristics of this model relate to media production, their content, and their use.

-   Production. At first glance, the situation in mass media production seems very similar to that of the assimilative model: an appropriate, if possible, proportional participation (with respect to the percentage of ethnic groups in the entire population) of ethnic minorities in German majority media. Yet, the proportional representation in the intercultural model implies a totally different fundamental conception of the socio-cultural integration of migrants and of their role in the mass media. Here, representatives of ethnic minorities are not socio-culturally assimilated; instead, they represent the ethnic groups with certain specific problems and interests. Structurally, their situation can be compared to that of representatives of the two sexes in their societal roles. They help to bring about a pluralistic, democratic public sphere, and, in doing so, they contribute specific information and specific knowledge about their ethnic groups and their problems. They personify an important part of the multi-dimensional, democratic pluralism in the German media system: its ethnic dimension, which ranks at the same level as other dimensions, such as those of pressure groups, the sexes, age groups, or religious organizations. In this model, ethno-media also exist in addition to the ethnically pluralistic German media. Migrants with knowledge of the accommodating society produce such media themselves or at least participate in their production in order to ensure that the content is designed in a way that promotes intercultural integration.

-   Content. First of all, the representation of ethnic minorities in the majority mass media is oriented to the role the German media play in promoting active acceptance. To increase an awareness of the inter-dependence between the majority and the minorities, they provide ex-planations for the *necessity of immigration*, for the demographic and economic significance and benefits of migrants, but also for Germany's international obligations to admit refugees for humanitarian reasons. At the same time, they draw attention to the necessary intercultural inte-gration and to integration at the level of social structures. Equal opportunity, the necessity of a minimum form of acculturation, but also tolerance toward legitimate ethnic particularities in accordance with the principle of 'unity within diversity' (see above) are the guidelines for reporting and commentaries.

Furthermore, the representation of ethnic minorities also embodies the ethnic dimension of *media pluralism*. The mass media impart relevant knowledge of the varying groups that live and cooperate with one another to the respective other groups. Since the Germans – for language-related reasons – only rarely make use of ethno-media, the majority media are practically their sole media resource for information on the nature and problems of the ethnic minorities. Conversely, the ethnic minorities are only then able to participate in social and political affairs in Germany in an informed and knowledgeable way if they relatively regularly use German media in order to learn about and understand German current affairs and their contexts. One stimulus to regular media consumption is already provided by the circumstance that the ethnic minorities recognize their own interests and problems in the coverage of the majority media.

The characteristics of media content that is integrative in an intercultural way can also be expressed negatively: Germanocentric media that only allow ethnic minorities inadequate coverage, that ignore their mental dispositions and their problems, or in whose reporting discrimination and ethnic negativism predominate (e.g., 'foreigners' as groups that are primarily a source of problems for the German population) contradict the model of intercultural integration. Still, this does not mean that problems with migration and integration in the accommodating society should be taboo. On the contrary, such problems are – much like problems concerning relationships between the sexes or between the generations – a part of the pluralistic public discourse. But they should not dominate this discourse.

For non-assimilated minorities, ethno-media are a necessary complement to the German majority media. Their main target groups are the bicultural, often bilingual segments of the ethnic minorities whose desires for contact with their original culture and language and for information on the specific situation and specific problems of their ethnic group in the larger society cannot be adequately satisfied by the German mass media. In light of the ethnic diversity and the increasing internal socio-cultural differentiation of the individual ethnic groups, meeting such requirements is beyond the capabilities of the German mass media. In the pluralistic German media system, ethno-media have functions similar to those of specific media for women, youth, or certain religious communities. Of major importance is the *integrative nature of the content presented*. Segregationist content – as in an exclusive focus on the original culture or a confrontation between a 'superior' original culture and the culture of the accommodating society that is presented in a distorted, negative way – is not in accordance with this model.

- Media Use. It is unrealistic to expect Germans to make use of the ethno-media. For this reason, an appropriate representation of ethnic minorities in the German mass media is extremely important. On the other hand, it is absolutely indispensable for the intercultural integration of ethnic minorities that such minorities make use of the German mass media. With no knowledge of current affairs and their contexts in the society at large, integration into the social structures – appropriately taking advantage of opportunities in politics, on the labor market, in the educational system, and in other significant institutions (see above) – is not possible. Thus, the attractiveness of the German mass media for ethnic minorities is an important prerequisite for their intercultural integration. In addition, non-assimilated minorities with a bicultural orientation will also make use of the ethno-media of their original culture. Through such groups, the dominant German public sphere becomes and remains interconnected with the ethnic sub-spheres.

2. Media Reception and Ideas on Media Integration among Turkish, Italian and Russo-German Migrants in Germany

2.1 Methodology

We will now present some select tentative findings of a comprehensive study on media use and integration of migrants (including their children) from Turkey, Italy, and Russia. Over 1,000 persons from Italy, approximately 700 persons from Turkey (excluding Kurds), and approximately 1,000 persons from Russia were interviewed. Here, we will simply present the findings for over 500 Russo-Germans (not those for Russian Jews or for other Russians). Only members of pure migrant families were interviewed, that is, no children

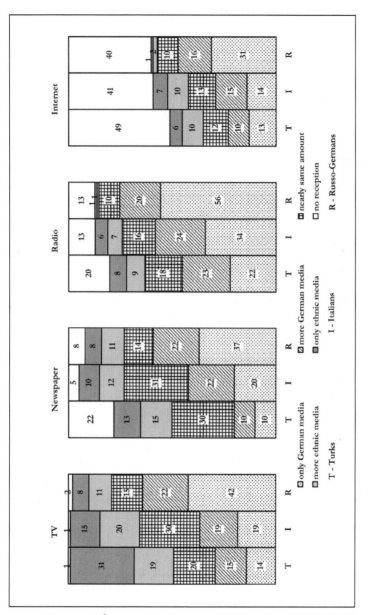

Figure 1: Media Reception[1]. T = Turks; I = Italians; R = Russo-Germans.

1   Source: Sonja Weber-Menges - Survey on Media Reception and Integration of Migrants (preliminary results). N = 673 migrants from Turkey, 1023 from Italy and 512 Russo-German migrants.

from mixed families consisting of natives and migrants were surveyed. We have excluded these because their patterns of behavior and attitudes are almost identical to those of the natives. The sample is representative for North Rhine-Westphalia. It can probably be assumed that to a certain extent the findings would also apply to all of western Germany.

2.2   Media use

Media use depends on two important factors: on the media-related wants and needs of the migrants, but also on the programs that are offered. Furthermore, for all three groups media use is dependent on age, knowledge of the German language, and the length of the person's stay in Germany. The older the migrants are, the less fluent they are in German, and the shorter the time they have lived in Germany, the more frequently they make use of their own ethnic media (figure 1).

Nevertheless, any fear of large-scale ethnic media ghettos in Germany is unfounded. Media ghettos, that is, the exclusive use of ethnic media, with no German media made use of, are marked red on the diagram. Only small minorities of migrants exclusively make use of ethnic media. The largest one is the Turkish TV ghetto, with 31%. One of the reasons for this is that some of the women from Turkey are illiterate and do not have a very good command of the German language, either. Apart from this Turkish TV ghetto, media ghettos only involve between 6 and 10 percent of the migrants and, in one finding, 15 percent (an Italian TV ghetto).

Large portions of the Russo-German population are assimilated in their use of media, that is, they make use only of German media (marked green on the diagram). This is true only of relatively small minorities of the Italians and Turks. However, the group of those who are assimilated is somewhat larger than those whose behavior corresponds to a media ghetto.

The majority of the migrants makes use of both German and ethnic media and is, thus, interculturally integrated.

2.3   Views on ethnic media

Only very few migrants have the impression that their ethnic media – for the Turks, Turkish media, for the Italians, Italian media, and for the Russo-Germans, Russian media – have segregating effects and report on Germany and the Germans in a negative way (figure 2).

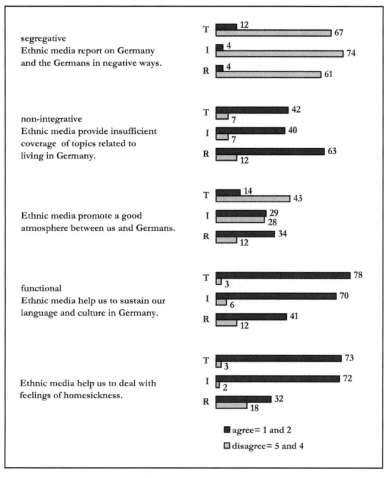

Figure 2: Views on ethnic media.[2]
T = Turks; I = Italians; R = Russo-Germans. Response measured on a scale of 1 to 5 (strongly disagree = 1, strongly agree = 5); here: agree = 5 and 4; disagree = 1 and 2.

But neither do they observe integrating effects in the media content. Only a few think that ethno-media promote a good atmosphere between migrants and Germans. Almost half of the Turks responded negatively to this question.

Yet, ethnic media do fulfill other important functions which presumably support the intercultural integration of migrants. For Turkish and Italian migrants, they represent an important linguistic, cultural, and emotional tie to their homeland, a function that is significant only for a minority of the Russo-

2   Source: Sonja Weber-Menges - Survey on Media Reception and Integration of Migrants (preliminary results). N = 673 migrants from Turkey, 1023 from Italy and 512 Russo-German migrants.

Germans. As a rule, Russo-Germans had conceived of themselves as a minority in Russia and, for this reason, they are not as attached to their homeland as Italian migrants are to Italy or Turkish migrants to Turkey. Many Russo-Germans feel as if they have "returned home" to the land of their ancestors and feel no need to maintain ties to the country they have emigrated from.

2.4   Views on the German media

Views on the German media prove to be quite negative (figure 3). These media meet with the greatest skepticism on the part of Turkish migrants; Russo-Germans evaluate them somewhat more positively; the Italians' position is somewhere in between. Turks and Italians criticize the absence of topics that would be interesting to migrants and the cliché-like representation of migrants – especially the Italians find that their image in the media involves stereotypes. All three groups complain of predominantly negative reports on migration and migrants, for example, the representation of migrants as criminals. The Turks voiced this criticism most frequently. With respect to the issue of whether the German mass media promote a good atmosphere between migrants and Germans, these media were judged to be just as deficient as the ethno-media. Turkish migrants were the most critical here – with reference to both German and Turkish media. With reference to one issue, Russo-Germans in particular, to a lesser extent the Italians, and even less the Turks, perceive media content with an integrating effect – German media help migrants to cope with everyday life in Germany.

2.5   Migrants' ideas on how to improve media integration

Which suggestions do migrants make on how to improve media integration? Do their ideas correspond to our concept of media integration (figure 4)?

A clear majority of the Turks (76%) and of the Italians (70%) interviewed would like to see more coverage and more positive reports on migrants and their culture and activities, their celebrations and festivities, their clubs and organizations. Only a small minority of both groups rejects such intensified coverage because they suspect a lack of interest in such topics on the part of the Germans or because they think that these things are none of the Germans' business. Russo-Germans are more reserved towards such improvements. In any case, 40 percent say that they have no opinion on this. Apparently, the interests of the Russo-Germans are more strongly represented in the German media than are those of the other two groups.

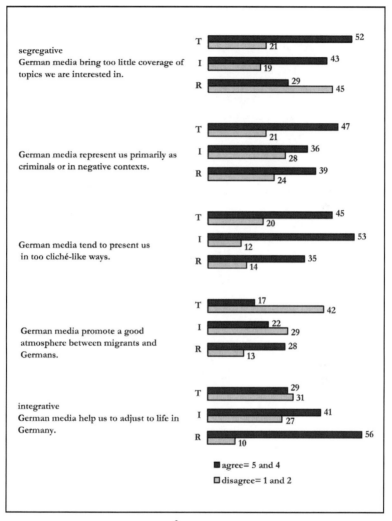

Figure 3: Views on the German media.[3]
T = Turks; I = Italians; R = Russo-Germans. Response measured on a scale of 1 to 5 (strongly disagree = 1, strongly agree = 5); here: agree = 5 and 4; disagree = 1 and 2.

3   Source: Sonja Weber-Menges - Survey on Media Reception and Integration of Migrants (preliminary results). N = 673 migrants from Turkey, 1023 from Italy and 512 Russo-German migrants.

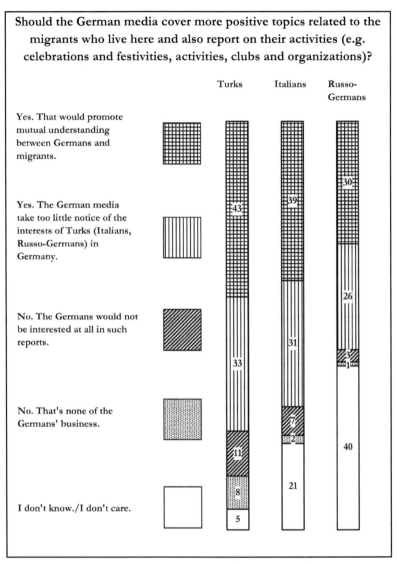

Figure 4: More positive coverage.[4]

The three groups also agree on how the representation of migrants and media integration could be improved (figure 5). The demand for more migrants among the media personnel was raised most frequently. We postulated this as early as five years ago as an important condition for media integration.

---

4   Source: Sonja Weber-Menges - Survey on Media Reception and Integration of Migrants (preliminary results). N = 673 migrants from Turkey, 1023 from Italy and 512 Russo-German migrants.

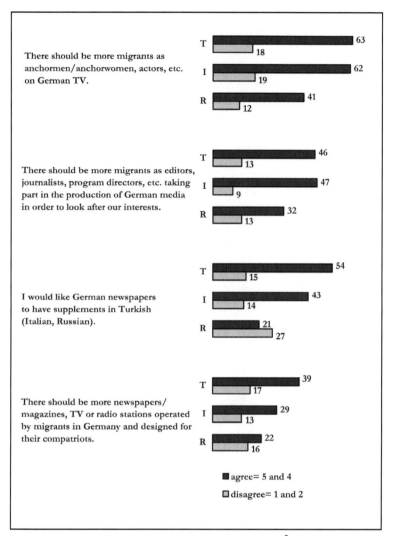

Figure 5: Improving media integration – migrant's suggestions.[5]
T = Turks; I = Italians; R = Russo-Germans. Response measured on a scale of 1 to 5 (strongly disagree = 1, strongly agree = 5); here: agree = 5 and 4; disagree = 1 and 2.

In the last two years, this position has also been increasingly taken up in Germany by politicians and decision makers at the public broadcasting companies – most recently at a joint conference of the German broadcasters ARD and ZDF in Mainz.

---

5   Source: Sonja Weber-Menges - Survey on Media Reception and Integration of Migrants (preliminary results). N = 673 migrants from Turkey, 1023 from Italy and 512 Russo-German migrants.

Foreign-language supplements to German daily newspapers are also considered desirable, especially among the Turks. On the other hand, there is little interest in "genuine ethnic media" produced by migrants themselves in Germany. In general, Russo-Germans voice a demand for increased participation in the production of the German mass media less frequently than migrants from Turkey and Italy.

3.   Summary

Of the three complexes media use, media content, and media production, the use made of the media corresponds most closely to our model of media integration. The majority of migrants makes use of both German and ethnic media. Thus, the German public sphere and ethnic sub-spheres are in general interconnected with one another. Only small minorities live in media ghettos.

In contrast, media content – of both German and ethnic media – meets with a great deal of skepticism on the part of migrants. Mass media programs are judged to be substantially lacking in integrating effects. This sort of criticism is most common among Turks, most rare among Russo-Germans. Large segments of the Russo-German population have undergone assimilative media integration. Such differences can be plausibly explained by the hypothesis of cultural conflict: the more remote from one another the cultures of migrant and indigenous groups are, the more complications are involved in media integration.

Migrants also note a distinct lack of integrating effects in the production of German mainstream mass media. For these groups, increased participation of migrants in media production is an important demand to counteract the dominance of negative images in the media's representation of migrants.

4.   References

Esser, Hartmut (2001): Integration und ethnische Schichtung. Mannheim: Mannheimer Zentrum für Europäische Sozialforschung. Arbeitspapier Nr. 40

Fleras, Augie/Elliot, Jean Leonard (1992): Multiculturalism in Canada. The Challenge of Diversity. Scarborough, Ontario

Fleras, Augie/Elliot, Jean Leonard (2002): Engaging Diversity. Multiculturalism in Canada. 2nd edition Toronto

Geißler, Rainer (2004): "Einheit-in-Verschiedenheit. Interkulturelle Integration von Migranten – ein Mittelweg zwischen Assimilation und Segregation." In: Berliner Journal für Soziologie 14, pp. 287-298

Gordon, Milton M. (1964): Assimilation in American Life. The Role of Race, Religion and National Origins. New York

Kastoryano, Riva (2002): Negotiating Identities. States and Immigrants in France and Germany. Princeton

Mintzel, Alf (1997): Multikulturelle Gesellschaften in Europa und Nord-amerika. Passau

Rauer, Valentin/Schmidtke, Oliver (2001): "Integration' als Exklusion zum medialen und alltagspraktischen Umgang mit einem umstrittenen Konzept." In: Berliner Journal für Soziologie 11, pp. 277-296

Heinz Bonfadelli

Media Use by Ethnic Minority Youth in Switzerland

1. Introduction

Migration is a well-known phenomenon all over the world. Although people have always been moving, migration flows have reached a new quantitative and qualitative dimension since the 19th and 20th centuries. Europe, above all Western Europe, has become one of the targets of larger flows of immigration, especially since World War II. In Switzerland, for example, every third resident belongs to an ethnic minority or has an immigrant background, i.e. is a descendant of at least one parent from a country other than Switzerland. Migration developments and the resulting coexistence of different ethnic groups involve conflicts like racism and inequalities on a structural as well as a social level. Such conflicts in multicultural settings have triggered debates on the integrative function that different spheres of society should fulfill.

The modern *mass media* play a far-reaching and complex role in today's multicultural society. They may be of relevance to the *social integration of ethnic minorities* in that they are, for example, an important source of information about politics, culture, and everyday life in society. Mass media can provide day-to-day news and convey social norms and values, thus offering members of ethnic minorities the opportunity to participate in the (national) society of the host country by creating a common knowledge base and a basis for interpersonal communication. But they can also contribute to *segregation* in many ways, for instance, by stressing *negative images and stereotypes of immigrant groups* (Schudson 1994; Cottle 2000). Young people, whether of migrant background or not, use local and national, but also global media representations and symbols of popular culture (Lull 2001) on an individual level. They identify with or distinguish themselves from such representations and symbols; or they use them to construct multifaceted forms of *hybrid identities* actively and in creative ways (e.g. Barker 1997; Ogan 2001; Nilan/ Feixa 2006).

Communication research started taking more interest in the field of ethnic minorities and mass media during the 1970s. *Research issues* are usually tackled from different academic disciplines in an interdisciplinary setting. Depending on the approach chosen, the studies investigate different aspects. One line of research concentrates on *media content* (Poole 2000; Hafez 2000; Esser 2000; ter Wal 2004; Müller 2005a; Nacos/Torres-Reyna 2007; Hafez/Richter 2007;

Bonfadelli 2007), above all on the *representation of immigrants* and the *presence of negative stereotypes* in mass media, hypothesizing that there is a connection between how media deal with ethnic minorities and the degree of their integration into the host society. From the *media production perspective*, ethnic diversity in media organizations has been of interest (Riggins 1992; Husband 1994; Geissler 2003). Another topic of public debate and research focuses on *strategies and programs of public broadcasters* towards migrants and of ethnic minority media as programs produced by and addressed to ethnic minorities (Becker 1998; Busch 1999; Kosnick 2000; Christensen 2001; Camauër 2003; Weber-Menges 2006; Leurdijk 2006).

Since mass media can exert an influence on the integration of ethnic minority groups only if they are used, an in-depth investigation into the aspects of the ethnic minorities' media use is crucial. Although the relevance of media use for social integration had been recognized before, communication studies scholars began to carry out thorough research on this issue only in the last two decades. Because communication technologies such as the internet, cable and satellite television have changed the media system by creating new transnationalized communicational and cultural spaces, the number of studies dealing with issues of media use and migration has increased. Still, research findings in this subfield are, generally speaking, somewhat fragmentary (see Carøe Christiansen 2004; Müller 2005b; Piga 2007).

2. Theoretical Perspectives

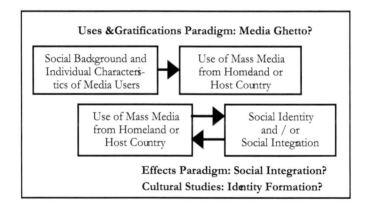

Figure 1: Media Use and Ethnic Minorities: Various Research Traditions

Three theoretical perspectives (Bonfadelli/Bucher/Piga 2007; Bucher/ Bonfadelli 2007) guiding most of the research concerning media use of ethnic minorities can be identified (see Figure 1): a model based on uses and gratifications, a focus on media effects, and a cultural studies approach.

2.1 Uses & Gratifications Paradigm

The uses and functions of media are the focus of this line of research and therefore represent the dependent variable in the so-called uses and gratifications paradigm. The main research issues are: To what extent do ethnic minorities use and prefer print and electronic media from their countries of origin (homeland) and abstain from using the indigenous media in their country of residence? Why is this the case, or how can this be explained? Various dimensions, such as education, socioeconomic status, language skills (linguistic fluency), religious affiliation or ethnic identity, are referred to in order to explain these phenomena. A leading hypothesis claims that ethnic minorities in most European countries prefer to use print and electronic media from their homeland and are, as a result, trapped in a so-called "media ghetto". Whereas earlier studies looked at the different media types consumed separately, more recent ones apply typologies of media use (see table 1) that link homeland and host country media (Adoni/Caspi/Cohen 2002). However, sometimes it is not sufficiently clear whether these labels only point to patterns of media consumption or also indicate different types of attitudes towards acculturation.

		Use of Media from Host Country	
		Low	High
Use of Media from Home Country	Low	**Detached / Alienated**	**Adaptors / Integrated**
	High	**Separatists / Bonding**	**Dualists / Bridging**

Table 1: Typology of Media Use by Migrants (based on Adoni/Caspi/Cohen, 2002)

In his qualitative study, Hafez (2002) developed a *typology* also based on the use of minority media from the country of origin and of majority media from the host country, but added considerations of acceptance and trust related to the political system and culture. As a consequence, he differentiated the so-called "separatists" (see Table 1) into three subtypes. For the "diaspora"-type (see Table 2), the dominant use of minority media from the homeland has to do with pragmatic reasons – mainly lack of language skills – but it is combined with a feeling of trust towards the political conditions of the host country. "Political exile" means that cultural bonding with the country of origin is still strongly combined with mistrust towards the political system of the new country. According to this scheme, the "cultural exile"-type of user bonds with the culture of the country of origin and trusts the political institutions of the new country. In contrast to this classification of "separatist" users, "biculturalism" means that both media of the host country and those of the country of origin are used. The result is a reflective in-between position that manifests itself in a critical stance towards the culture and media of the homeland and of the new country. Finally, the "assimilation"-type is similar to the "adaptor" type in Table 1: These people show a high consumption of majority media and have developed positive attitudes towards the culture and political system of their host country, perceiving it now as their new home country.

USER TYPE	MEDIA ORIENTATION	ORIENTATION TOWARDS CULTURE AND POLITICS
1. Political Exile	Dominant use of minority media from country of origin	Cultural, political bonding to home country and mistrust in politics of new country
2. Cultural Exile		Cultural bonding to home country but trust in political system of new country
3. Diaspora		Pragmatic use of media from home country and political trust in new country
4. Biculturalism	Mixed use of minority media from home country and majority media from host country	Reflective and critical stance on country and media of origin but on new country as well
5. Assimilation	Dominant use of majority media from host country	Positive attitudes to culture and political system of new country

Table 2: Typology of Media Use by Migrants (based on Hafez 2002)

Besides these differentiations concerning media use as dependent variables, there has also been some theoretical development related to the *independent variables* influencing media behavior. Whereas earlier studies considered ethnicity to be the most influential causal factor and compared ethnic minority groups with the main population of a country, more recent studies (e.g. Weiß/Trebbe 2001) argue in a more differentiated way, analyze the mediating influence of social factors like everyday situation, language skills and extent of integration, socioeconomic status, education or gender, and attempt to incorporate these factors into more advanced theoretical models (see Figure 2).

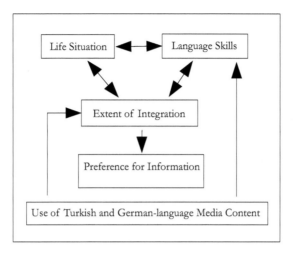

Figure 2: Theoretical Model of Media Use (based on Weiß/Trebbe 2001)

A further major research concern is to determine the *impact of ethnicity compared to other social divisions*. Recently, the concept of "social capital" has been discussed in the context of media use, political participation and the integration of migrants (e.g. Jacobs/Tillie 2004). It is assumed that being embedded in social networks – an indicator of social capital – is an important factor influencing the level of media use and, furthermore, the level of trust in the political system.

2.2   Media Effects Paradigm

In comparison with the uses and gratifications approach, the media effects paradigm (Bonfadelli 2004) focuses not on media use itself, but on social integration on a macro level. In a complementary way, then, the cultural studies paradigm deals with cultural identity on a micro level. According to most functionalist theories, media perform unplanned and long-term socialization and integration functions for a society by bridging different social and ethnic groups and assimilating different people into a common civil culture (Schudson, 1994; Peeters/d'Haenens 2005). In this view, then, the use of majority host country media by ethnic minorities will result in better social and cultural integration. On the other hand, it is hypothesized that the persistent use of media from the homeland and in the language of origin will help maintain individuals' old cultural identity and will thus have detrimental effects on integration. One normative consequence would be that ethnic minority groups should use the majority media available in the new host country in its language to fully integrate into the new socio-cultural context.

Immigrants still using their homeland media in their language of origin are regarded as not integrated and labeled as separatists in the typology of Adoni et al. (2002) and are still considered bonded to the culture of origin.

This general assumption of the mass media's positive integration function for migrants has at least been further differentiated or even put to question by various middle-range theories that attempt to explain the possible effects of mass communication in general or, in particular, in the migration context in detail, and that have been empirically tested (Bonfadelli 2004). Both *agenda-setting theory* and the *media-framing perspective* postulate that media coverage focusing on controversial or negative incidents or key events like 9/11 in New York in 2001 or the attacks by skinheads and neo-Nazis on asylum centers in Hoyerswerda (17.9.1991) can represent migrants as a problem or threat to society and influence the public agenda in this way (Brosius/Eps 1993; Scheufele/Brosius 1999). This applies especially when migrants are framed negatively and in a stereotyped way, as many content analyses demonstrate (Greenberg et al. 2002, on the German media see Müller 2005a). Another problem are the long-term media effects of the widespread and constant use of *metaphors and phrases with negative connotations* like "the boat is full" and "floods of refugees" or "Islamic terrorism" etc. that delegitimize the minority groups themselves (Poole 2000; Schiffer 2005). Critical discourse analysts like Teun van Dijk (1991) postulate increasing racism in society as a result of such media content.

Cultivation theory takes as its starting point the results of such content analyses and claims that television cultivates stereotyped images of minority groups in the long term, especially in the minds of so-called 'heavy viewers' (Gerbner et al. 2002). These 'mainstream' perceptions of social reality can even lead to an increased fear concerning minority groups. Nevertheless, it should be remembered that debates on national identity in Europe or America are not new or unique and that foreigners or minority groups in general have always been regarded suspiciously by the dominant majority groups, even without the influence of media coverage (e.g. Huntington 2004).

Furthermore, since most empirical surveys are not longitudinal, but, instead, based on just one point in time, there is a *methodological problem involved in demonstrating causality* between media use and media effects as dependent variables. From the uses and gratifications perspective, the supposed media effects like social integration can also be interpreted as independent variables. In other words, it is not clear whether better social integration is really the result of media use or if preferred use of domestic media is the result of a higher level of social integration.

2.3   Cultural Studies Perspective

The cultural studies paradigm (Hall 1980; Hepp 1999) is contrary to the "media-centric" effects paradigm, since for the former the media user is the focus of interest and analysis. Media use, then, is seen as a purposeful selection of media, and the reception process is considered to be an active construction of meaning. This perspective does not simply assume an alternative between adapting to the new country's culture through consuming host media on the one hand and bonding to the old country of origin and remaining culturally isolated by using homeland media on the other (Peeters/d'Haenens 2005). Instead, a third possibility is also taken into consideration.

In this sense, members of ethnic minorities are seen to be able to use varying kinds of media, their homeland media and the media of the new host country. This dualistic position is not regarded as deficient or as a danger for the development of a cultural identity. Being able to participate in both cultures and using media from both countries and in both languages enables members of ethnic minority groups to bridge the norms and values of different cultures and to actively develop new forms of a so-called reflective hybrid identity. To promote mutual respect, social participation, and cultural integration, today's pluralistic societies even seem to require that everyone attain an understanding of the everyday life, norms and values of other cultural groups. To this end, the mass media play a significant role by providing not only homogeneous images of the so-called home country in a national perspective, but by disseminating information and knowledge about the different minority groups and their everyday culture (Barker 1997). On the basis of these theoretical premises, new forms of cultural identities can be postulated.

A first type of cultural identity is locally bounded and based on difference. Distinct traditions are kept separately in time and space. For instance, Swiss citizens perceive themselves as Swiss, or Turkish migrants living in Switzerland perceive themselves as Turks. They live in Turkish neighborhoods and interact and communicate mostly with Turks. A second type of cultural identity is similar concerning local "boundedness" and difference, but the separate traditions of Swiss and Turkish identity can be juxtaposed in the same person, insofar as different identities are expressed, depending on the situation. For example, the person behaves as a Turk with Turkish friends, but behaves like a Swiss in settings with Swiss people. A third type of identity is the result of the assimilation into a new culture and the absorption of new values and norms. This is the case for a youngster with Turkish parents who grows up in Switzerland, behaves like a Swiss, and has a corresponding self-image. Fourth, besides these locally bounded identities there are translocal and shifting

51

identities as a result of a new global media culture. For example, young people in different countries conceive of themselves and behave as "hip hoppers" in contrast to "heavy metal" fans through their identification with certain global media symbols (see Lull 2001). Shared concerns and belief systems on a worldwide level also help to form transnational global identities based on similarity, as, for instance, with globalization critics, environmentalist movements, or fundamentalist religious groups.

	DIFFERENCE	SIMILARITY
Locally Bounded	1. Distinct traditions, kept separately in time and space. Turkish or Swiss identity. 2. Separate traditions are juxtaposed in time and space. Hybrid identity as Turkish and Swiss and appropriate switch from one to the other in certain situations.	3. Assimilation into the new culture and absorption of new values and norms. Parents are Turkish, but child's self-image is Swiss.
Translocal Shifting	4. New global forms of identity based on distinct taste/style cultures like "hip hop" or "heavy metal".	5. New forms of identity · based on shared concerns like "anti-global" movement

Table 3: New Forms of Cultural Identities (adapted from Barker 1997: 616)

3. A Swiss Survey of Media Use by Adolescents: Research Issues and Research Design

So far, research on the media use of ethnic minorities in Switzerland has been rare. The only relatively comprehensive survey about media use of immigrants was conducted in 1995 by the research unit of the Public Broadcasting Corporation SRG (Anker/Ermutlu/Steinmann 1995). With several research projects, the Institute of Mass Communication and Media Research at the University of Zurich (IPMZ) is engaged in filling this knowledge gap. One project that began in 2003 and was recently completed is concerned with the function of media in constructing social identity in a multicultural setting. It focuses on a comparison of two groups, adolescents from the indigenous Swiss population and those of migrant background (Bonfadelli/ Bucher 2006; Bucher/Bonfadelli 2007). Some of the findings from this research will be presented below. Other projects were concerned with analyzing media representations of Islam in Swiss newspapers (Bonfadelli 2007).

3.1   Research Issues

The research project referred to above was funded by the Swiss National Science Foundation (NRP 52: Childhood, Youth and Intergenerational Relationships) and examined the relationship between culture-specific characteristics (in addition to other socio-demographic factors) and the function and role the media and ICT play in identity-formation processes for children and adolescents living in a multicultural setting. In particular, our study specifically addressed the following questions:

-   What role do mass media and ICT (access, usage, functions, favourite programmes etc.) play in the lives of Swiss youth in comparison to young people from an immigrant background?

-   To what extent is media use determined by characteristics of cultural background (country of origin, religion) in comparison to socio-demographic factors (gender, education or social background of family)?

-   What role do media and ICT play in the formation of identity for the inter-generational setting of immigrant life?

3.2   Methods

The project approaches the issue "media, migration and youth" from an *interdisciplinary perspective* and is divided into two closely linked studies consisting of:

-   *A quantitative study* (Heinz Bonfadelli & Priska Bucher, University of Zurich), which analyzes the use of both old and new media, cultural identity and attitudes toward other cultures among immigrant youths by comparing them with a similar sample of indigenous youths (both parents born and raised in Switzerland). Eighty-eight classes in the greater Zurich metropolitan area with a high rate (>25%) of children of immigrant background were visited during the summer of 2004. The sample of 1486 students is composed of 49% female and 51% male students and is also well balanced regarding age (12-16 years). About a third of the students are indigenous Swiss; two thirds are students of immigrant background.

-   *A qualitative study* (Heinz Moser & Thomas Hermann & Christa Hanetseder, School of Education, Zurich) was based on different strategies of ethnographic fieldwork and in-depth interviews with members of 8 Turkish/Kurdish families. The methodological approach is based on cultural studies, ethnography and visual methods. The in-depth interviewing, in particular, offered insights into the relationship between media and cultural identity and thus further differentiated the findings from the quantitative investigation. This fieldwork highlights the function that media and ICT play in processes of identity formation in an inter-generational setting (see Hermann/Hanetseder 2007).

4.   Results

4.1   Structural Inequalities: Parents and Children

A first issue deals with structural inequalities on the basis of background data concerning the socio-economic status of the parents and the educational level of the adolescents. Our comparative data demonstrate very pronounced structural inequalities (Table 4): On the one hand, the social status of the Swiss families is higher, and on the other hand, the educational level of Swiss adolescents is significantly higher in comparison to adolescents from a migrant background.

Socio-Economic Status of Family			
Percentages	Low	Medium	High
Swiss Youth	6	62	32
Migrants	34	40	26
Educational Level of Adolescents (Only Secondary School)			
Percentages	Low	Medium	High
Swiss Youth	5	44	51
Migrants	24	46	30

Table 4: Socio-Economic Status of Families and Educational Level of Adolescents

But inequalities exist independent of family background: Our data demonstrate that, in general, more adolescents from a migration background have a lower educational level, whereas more Swiss adolescents have higher levels of education. This can be observed independently of the socio-economic status or the educational background of their parents. Moreover, the influence of ethnic background is especially strong among adolescents coming from ex-Yugoslavia, whereas ethnic background seems to be much weaker among adolescents coming from Italy.

4.2   Values, political interest and occupational expectations

When asked about the most important values for living a comfortable life, about 97% of the students mentioned "good friends". The same importance was attributed to the item "not to be unemployed". About 92% of the young people considered a good education and an interesting job important for leading a rewarding life. Here, there were no differences between Swiss students and students from a migration background. As to the items "to have a lot of money" and "to believe in something", only 35% and 45%, respectively, of the young Swiss as opposed to about 60% and 70%, respectively, of the youths from a migrant background ranked these as important. Noteworthy with respect to all questions regarding attitudes is that the answers of adolescents of Italian origin are similar to those of the Swiss young people, whereas the responses of adolescents from other countries of origin differ to a greater extent.

%	Swiss	Migrants	Italy	Turkey	Ex-Yugoslavia
Yes, quite sure	35	29	32	30	26
Yes, maybe	55	58	56	56	61
No, probably not	9	11	10	13	11
No, certainly not	1	2	2	1	2
Note: Switzerland: N=499; Migrants: N=969; Italy: N=166; Turkey: N=136; Ex-Yugoslavia: N=350.					

Table 5: Do You Believe That You Can Achieve Your Own Occupational Goals?

About 20% of the young people claim to have no interest in political affairs; 24% of the Swiss adolescents and 33% of those from a migration background mention that Swiss politics are important. With respect to the politics of the country of origin or of other countries, the interest of students from a migration background is even stronger: 43% and 44%, respectively, regard these matters as significant, whereas only 17% of Swiss youths consider politics of other countries to be important. There is a significant connection between education and political interest in the Swiss segment, whereas this is not the case in the segment from a migration background. Political interest also depends on media use: Young people who frequently read (newspapers and/or books) are politically more interested.

Future occupational chances and opportunities as appraised by the young immigrants are quite similar to the assessments of Swiss adolescents. Most of the students think they will find a satisfying job. This is most certainly a positive finding, especially in light of the generally high fear of becoming unemployed (see Table 4).

4.3 Cultural Orientations and Multiculturalism

A typology of cultural orientation was constructed on the basis of several indicator questions, such as preferred language of media use, main language used in the family and with friends, ethnic background of friends, perceptions of group membership, interest in events occurring in Switzerland or in the home country, etc. (see table 6). A majority of the adolescents from a migrant background were classified as "Swiss-oriented" (45%) in comparison with only 24% "homeland-oriented"; 24% have a "dualist" orientation; and a minority of 7% seems to be detached from both, their country of origin and from Switzerland. There are no significant differences between young people from Italy, Turkey or ex-Yugoslavia; but parents from each ethnic group are significantly more homeland-oriented, according to the perceptions of their children: ex-Yugoslavia (45%), Italy (48%) and Turkey (57%).

% 'yes'	Switzerland	Italy	Turkey	Ex-Yugoslavia
If someone immigrates to Switzerland, he/she has to assimilate	64	51	37	53
People from different countries living in Switzerland make Swiss society more interesting	39	44	66	70
Swiss people can learn something from immigrants	38	63	62	79
It's not bad if not all people are similar; Swiss people are quite diverse, too	62	72	72	77
If Swiss people and immigrants from other countries respected each other, there would be no problems	79	80	82	80

Table 6: Attitudes Towards Multiculturalism in Switzerland

Compared to their peers of migration background, Swiss youths have a more skeptical view of multicultural society (Table 6): They agree more that immigrants have to assimilate and they negate more that a mix of cultures can be interesting and that Swiss people can learn something from immigrants. Only regarding the item: "If Swiss people and immigrants respected each other, there would be no problems", does a large majority of those questioned agree, irrespective of the country of origin.

4.4   Media Access

One basic prerequisite for media use is, of course, media access. For this reason, we asked young people which media are available in general at home and, especially, in their own bedrooms. In light of media access at home, migration background is more significant than social background with respect to print media, satellite TV, and new media. Swiss families seem to have better equipment in their living rooms than do families from a migration background. But a somewhat different result is observable if one looks at the media available in the youths' bedrooms (Table 7).

Mentioned (%)	Swiss	Migrants	Italy	Turkey	Ex-Yugoslavia
Newspaper Subscribed	89	61	64	63	55
Magazine Subscribed	65	46	48	56	45
TV	99	98	99	99	97
Satellite TV	24	61	56	71	74
Video Equipment	85	80	84	74	78
DVD	75	64	70	59	53
Radio	77	68	74	66	63
Stereo Equipment	70	63	65	53	59
Computer	81	52	60	40	38
Internet	80	49	57	34	38
Playstation	52	40	43	34	34

Table 7: Media Access at Home, Except Own Bedroom

Interestingly, adolescents' own access to new media is higher among the immigrants. This means that parents from an immigrant background offer their children access to ICT, but without using this technology themselves. But the ownership of print media (books, subscriptions to newspapers and magazines) is significantly lower among families and children from an immigrant background.

In addition to migration background, gender and level of education also prove to be important predictors for media access. Having one's own access to electronic media is strongly dependent on gender: boys have better access to computers and the internet than girls do. Furthermore, the number of books youths actually own is closely related to the personal level of education and to the social background of the family; but there are negative correlations with the availability of a TV in one's own bedroom.

Mentioned (%)	Swiss	Migrants	Italy	Turkey	Ex-Yugoslavia
Magazine Subscribed	24	17	11	10	21
Ø Number of books	37	23	22	24	16
TV	32	46	50	39	52
Satellite TV	6	6	8	5	8
DVD	27	39	36	46	44
Video Equipment	18	23	25	22	25
Radio	89	74	78	69	72
Stereo	87	78	83	81	74
PC	45	56	51	68	61
Internet	30	49	40	64	56
Playstation	25	37	40	43	41

Table 8: Media Access in Own Bedroom

4.5 Digital Divide

Internet Access (%)		Own Room	In Family	No Access
Migration Background	No	30	62	8
	Yes	49	38	13
Sex	Male	47	44	9
	Female	37	49	14
Age	12-13 Years	34	55	11
	14 Years	41	48	11
	15 Years	45	46	11
	16-18 Years	48	40	12
SES	high	40	53	7
	medium	40	49	10
	low	48	34	18
Education (Only Secondary School)	high	41	54	4
	medium	46	42	12
	low	46	32	22

Table 9: Dimensions of Digital Divide

In the public debate on the digital divide, one can find hypotheses assuming a lack of access to the internet on the part of migrants. A closer look at access to the internet in Switzerland (Table 9) demonstrates that there is not only a gap concerning ethnical background, but also concerning gender, age, the socioeconomic status, and educational background of the family. Taken together, boys, older adolescents, and those coming from more affluent families have better access to the internet, at least within the family.

4.6   Media Use

Not surprisingly in light of similar studies in other countries (d'Haenens 2003; Weiß/Trebbe 2001), Swiss adolescents listen to the radio more frequently and for more hours per week than adolescents from an immigrant background. Young people of immigrant background spend more hours watching TV, whereas the frequency of watching TV does not differ from the TV habits of their Swiss peers. The segment of those who do not use the internet at all is higher among the immigrants, but, on the average, young people of immigrant background spend more time online than their Swiss counterparts. Whereas there are no differences between Swiss youth and others concerning the use of magazines and newspapers, students of immigrant background read books significantly less frequently and fewer hours per week than Swiss adolescents.

in %	Swiss		Migrants		Italy		Turkey		Ex-Yugoslavia	
Newspaper	47	7	44	11	36	12	38	15	46	13
Books	43	5	33	11	31	13	34	7	33	13
Magazines	41	5	30	13	27	15	22	16	30	13
TV	89	3	96	0	99	0	94	2	95	0
Video	25	11	35	8	36	9	27	10	41	3
DVD	28	10	41	8	39	8	37	7	47	8
Computer	53	4	60	7	48	10	60	7	63	9
Internet	67	7	71	11	61	19	72	14	73	8
Radio	70	5	50	14	55	10	35	19	49	17
Music (CD)	89	1	90	1	89	1	96	1	91	1
Playstation	31	30	34	27	33	22	40	19	30	30

Table 10: Frequency of Media Use ("At Least Several Times per Week" vs. "Never")

With respect to the use of other media, there are no significant differences between Swiss pupils and others. Immigrant families do not have as many computers as their Swiss counterparts; but in the bedrooms of youths of immigrant background more computers are to be found than in the bedrooms of the Swiss.

Migration background is a more important predictor than other factors with regard to reading, how frequently books are read, watching TV and listening to the radio. With reference to reading books and using audio-visual media, there is a correlation between migration background and reading frequency, but education level and gender are more important predictors.

	Swiss	Migrants	Italy	Turkey	Ex-Yugoslavia
Newspaper	1h30	1h30	1h40	1h30	1h20
Books	3h10	2h40	2h30	3h00	2h10
Magazines	2h00	1h40	1h40	1h45	1h40
TV	10h15	13h00	13h20	12h15	13h35
Video	2h15	2h40	2h10	2h35	3h25
DVD	2h45	2h50	2h55	3h10	2h30
Computer offline	5h10	6h00	7h 25	5h25	6h15
Internet	8h25	10h30	9h35	10h20	11h00
Radio	6h30	3h50	4h35	2h15	3h20
Music (CD)	10h30	10h20	11h35	9h40	9h30
Playstation	3h35	3h35	4h00	3h25	3h00
Total	**54h45**	**56h35**	**59h25**	**54h00**	**56h25**

Table 11: Media Use in Hours per Week

For the use of computers and the internet, there is no significant difference between Swiss adolescents and others, but education is responsible for the largest part of the variance. Gender is a good predictor for the offline-use of computers – boys use computers more frequently than girls – but girls use the internet as often as their male peers, especially to communicate with school friends.

4.7   Preferences for Media Content

There are no differences between Swiss adolescents and migrants with respect to the appeal of entertaining TV programs, as much of the media content in such programs is chosen in accordance with youth-specific interests. But as for TV information programs, it is obvious that young migrant people prefer to watch news on private stations, whereas Swiss youths more often mention programs from the public broadcaster. As to print media, there are similar interests regarding the best liked genres, yet it should be emphasized that the wide variety of different types of print media is better utilized by Swiss pupils. Youth-specific and topic-oriented interests are characteristic for the internet. In addition, young people of immigrant background also use the internet for e-mails and chats to keep in touch with relatives and friends in the country of origin. To sum up, the globalized sphere of international TV programs, e.g., MTV, media symbols and formats targeted at young people are highly visible, especially in the open-ended questions dealing with favorite media content.

4.8 Media as a Topic of Conversation

Modern mass media also play an important role as a topic of conversation in the everyday life of young people. Hence, we asked the adolescents which media they talk about with which persons (Table 12).

Partners mentioned in %	Mother		Father		Siblings		Colleagues	
	CH	M	CH	M	CH	M	CH	M
TV	46	44	37	37	54	50	83	79
Video	30	25	30	23	55	55	74	71
Radio	39	20	27	21	23	18	30	28
Music	33	29	30	21	55	53	84	86
Books	41	26	21	16	23	24	31	26
Newspaper	54	39	51	41	20	21	30	33
Magazines	26	18	19	16	31	28	53	47
Computer-Games	9	5	14	9	37	38	58	61
PC Graphics/Photos	13	10	28	19	13	24	23	32
PC Programming	7	6	36	23	17	29	26	40
Internet Pages	19	16	27	19	35	35	68	71
Internet Chats	6	6	5	5	21	21	57	69

Table 12: Partners for Conversations about Different Media

In families from a migrant background, there is less conversation between children and parents about the print media than in Swiss families. But young immigrants talk with their siblings or peers just as much as Swiss youths do.

Adolescents of migrant background talk about new media (internet, programming etc.) primarily to friends and siblings, whereas Swiss pupils also mention the father as an important interlocutor; this is probably a result of the different occupational background of Swiss fathers and their computer and internet skills.

The limited amount of discussions on the media between young people and their parents in migrant families also seems to be a consequence of language differences in the media content used: Parents of migrant families use media more frequently in their mother tongue, whereas their children often use them in German, which complicates conversations about media.

5. Main Findings

In response to our questions concerning access to and use of media, the major findings (to a great extent corroborated by similar findings in other research) were as follows:

- Except for TV and satellite TV, the *ownership of media devices* is more widespread in Swiss families than in families from an immigrant background. At the same time, it can be stated that youths' own access to new media is higher among the immigrants; but immigrant families do not own as many computers as their Swiss counterparts. As we have seen above, this means that parents of immigrant background offer their children access to ICT, but without using it themselves. In addition, ownership of print media (books, subscriptions to newspapers & magazines) is lower among families of immigrant background.

- Young people of immigrant background spend more hours watching TV, whereas how frequently they watch TV does not differ from the TV habits of the native Swiss. The segment of those who do not use the internet at all is higher among the immigrants, but, on the average, young people from an immigrant background spend more time online than Swiss youngsters. Although there are no differences between Swiss youths and others concerning the use of magazines and newspapers, students of immigrant background read books less frequently and fewer hours per week.

- With regard to identity-formation processes, our qualitative data illustrate how young people actively use friends or relatives or role models from the world of football or music in order to define their own style, by means of which they express themselves. Media play an important part for them, both for keeping in touch with peers and relatives or for discussing news from the world of sports or show business.

- Migrant youths often do not fully belong to both the Swiss culture and the culture of origin. They develop the deepest roots in the place where they live and in relationships to a broad – sometimes international – network of relatives, friends and peers. In such a situation, a political aim of straightforward assimilation is highly counterproductive.

- Contrary to the widely held belief that young people of migrant background live in a kind of "parallel society" and/or "media ghetto", our study indicates that *migrant youths are not a homogeneous group*, but are characterized by a diversity of individual personalities, social backgrounds and manifold patterns of media use. As a consequence, policy measures, school projects or media coverage should take this existing social and cultural diversity more into account.

- Yet, there is mutual influence as well. Young people of both Swiss and migrant backgrounds share many media and cultural preferences typical of people their age – above all, globalized youth-oriented television and music programs, youth magazines and internet sites.

- Young people of migration background (and their parents, too) have high aspirations regarding their chances of education and future occupation. These claims and efforts remain in conflict with the existing educational inequalities of children from other countries of origin and with other mother tongues. Despite these 'hurdles', the majority of young people of migrant background is surprisingly satisfied.

6. Conclusions

Our multidisciplinary research project attempted to achieve several objectives concerning theory, methods and data, and is intended to be of practical relevance for various fields, such as the social sciences, school and family education as well as journalistic practice.

On a theoretical level, the project tried *to enrich the theoretical foundations* of a culturally oriented migration theory by linking concepts of media use with the perspective of a globalized community of young immigrant media users. Using concepts like "hybrid identities", we referred to socialization theory and stressed aspects like "active media use", "self-socialization" or the dissolution of traditional identity concepts.

An important *methodological objective* of the project was to develop an instrument to gather quantitative as well as qualitative data concerning the role and functions of traditional media (print and electronic) and new media (computer and internet) for children and youths of immigrant backgrounds. In addition, a special focus of the qualitative research was the involvement of visual data in the research process.

Furthermore, the project's aim was to accumulate knowledge based on empirical data for the first time in Switzerland about the complex relationship between identity-formation processes and media use in the lives of young people of migrant background. The research findings demonstrate differences in media habits between young people of Swiss background and those from a migrant background. But besides ethnicity, we observed even greater differences in various areas of media consumption concerning factors like personal level of education, social status of the family, or gender. As a consequence, a *complex multifactor model* is needed to fully understand the use and effects of media in the lives of young people. Based on empirical data, the project attempts to sensitize social science research in Switzerland for the issue of 'migration and media' and to establish a network of experts for media and migration in the context of our two international workshops.

In particular, the results of the quantitative study stress differences between migrant and Swiss young people and should give school teachers a better understanding of the media behavior of their pupils in order to prepare the ground for developing specific courses of action in schools or for measures directed towards families to provide better equal opportunities to both groups. Together with the results of the qualitative investigation, the ways media use and consumption are related to the identity-formation processes of youths from an immigrant background have become manifest.

The project demonstrates manifold influences of the media on migrants who live in a state between integration into a new socio-cultural environment, bonding relations to their old diaspora communities, and the conflicting demands of bridging these different cultures. Under these circumstances, it is necessary to find new perspectives for successful integration. The concept of hybrid identity, which integrates "here" and "there" in the construction of identities, provides new impulses for the politics of immigrant integration. It accepts that integration is not a process of fundamental change of identity – which, in fact, would be a process of alienation. In contrast to conservative approaches, hybrid identities should be interpreted as positive resources for the development of a particular position or attitude in a multicultural society.

In this context, we are aware of the risks involved when segregating behavior overwhelms integrative aspects. Integration as a process between a mere adoption of so-called "Swissness" and the conservation of migrant mentalities is a difficult path we have to follow. With respect to this sensitive task, we have attempted to show how and where integrative aspects need to be strengthened in our youth policies and in schools, and how we can learn from the cultural resources of immigrants.

Our findings can also be of significance for media professionals, as they demonstrate the importance of media for the integration of young people from a migration background and indicate the opportunity to anchor media coverage on a more realistic and thus less stereotypical basis. The findings also point to the need for immigrants themselves to be represented in the media in a more diversified and more accurate manner.

7.   References

Adoni, Hanna/Caspi, Dan/Cohen, Akiba (2002): Media, Minorities and Hybrid Identities. The Arab and Russian Communities in Israel. Cresskill, NJ

Anker, Heinrich/Ermutlu, Manolya/Steinmann, Matthias (1995): Die Mediennutzung der Ausländerinnen in der Schweiz. Ergebnisse einer schriftlichen Umfrage in der ganzen Schweiz vom März/April 1995. Bern

Barker, Chris (1997): "Television and the reflexive project of the self: soaps, teenage talk and hybrid identities." In: British Journal of Sociology, 48(4), pp. 611-628

Becker, Jörg (1998): "Multiculturalism in German broadcasting." In: Media Development, 45(3), pp. 8-21.

Bonfadelli, Heinz (2007): "Die Darstellung ethnischer Minderheiten in den Massenmedien." In: Bonfadelli, Heinz/Moser, Heinz, eds.: Medien und Migration. Europa als multikultureller Raum? Wiesbaden, pp. 95-116

Bonfadelli, Heinz (2004): Medienwirkungsforschung I: Grundlagen und theoretische Perspektiven. Konstanz

Bonfadelli, Heinz/Bucher, Priska/Piga, Andrea (2007): "Use of old and new media by ethnic minority youth in Europe with a special emphasis on Switzerland." In: Communications, 32(2), pp. 141-170

Brosius, Hans-Bernd/Eps, Peter (1993): "Verändern Schlüsselereignisse journalistische Selektionskriterien?" In: Rundfunk und Fernsehen, 41, 4/1993, pp. 512-530

Bucher, Priska/Bonfadelli, Heinz (2007): "Mediennutzung von Jugendlichen mit Migrationshintergrund in der Schweiz." In: Bonfadelli, Heinz/Moser, Heinz, eds.: Medien und Migration. Europa als multikultureller Raum? Wiesbaden, pp. 119-145

Busch, Brigitta (1999): "Von Minderheitenmedien zu Medien in multiligualen & multikulturellen Situationen." In: Medien Journal, 23(2), pp. 3-12

Camauër, Leonar (2003): "Ethnic Minorities and their Media in Sweden. On Overview of the Media Landscape and State of Minority Media Policy." In: Nordicom Review, 24(2), pp. 69-88

Carøe Christiansen, Connie (2004): "News Media Consumption among Immigrants in Europe." In: Ethnicities, 4(2), pp. 185-207

Christensen, Christian (2001): "Minorities, Multiculturalism and Theories of Public Service." In: Kivikuru, Ullamaija, ed.: Contesting the Frontiers. Media and Dimensions of Identity. Göteborg

Cottle, Simon, ed. (2000): Ethnic Minorities and the Media. Changing Cultural Boundaries. Buckingham, New York

Esser, Frank (2000): "Massenmedien und Fremdenfeindlichkeit im Ländervergleich. Eine Analyse internationaler Nachrichtenmagazine." In: Schatz, Heribert/Holtz-Bacha, Christian/Nieland Jörg-Uwe, eds.: Migranten und Medien. Neue Herausforderungen an die Integrationsfunktion von Presse und Rundfunk. Wiesbaden, pp. 82-105

Geissler, Rainer (2003): „Multikulturalismus in Kanada – Modell für Deutschland?" In: Aus Politik und Zeitgeschichte, Bd. 26, pp. 19-25

Gerbner, George/Gross, Larry/Morgan, Michael/Signorielli, Nancy/Shanahan, James (2002): "Growing Up With Television: Cultivation Processes." In: Bryant, Jennings/Zillmann, Dolf, eds.: Media Effects. Advances in Theory and Research. Mahwah, NJ., pp. 43-67

Greenberg, Bradley S./Mastro, Dana/Brand, Jeffrey (2002): "Minorities and the Mass Media: Television into the 21st Century." In: Bryant, Jennings/Zillmann, Dolf, eds.: Media Effects. Advances in Theory and Research. Mahwah, NJ., pp. 333-351

Hafez, Kai (2002): Die politische Dimension der Auslandberichterstattung. Das Nahost- und Islambild der deutschen überregionalen Presse. Vols. 1+2. Baden-Baden

Hafez, Kai (2000): "Imbalances of Middle East Coverage: A Quantitative Analysis of German Press." In: Hafez, Kai, ed.: Islam and the West in the Mass Media. Fragmentes Images in a Globalizing World. Cresskill, NJ, pp. 181-197

Hafez, Kai/Richter, Carola (2007): "Das Islambild von ARD und ZDF." In: Aus Politik und Zeitgeschichte, 26-27, pp. 40-46

Hall, Stuart (1980): "Encoding/Decoding." In: Hall, Stuart et al., eds.: Culture, Media, Language. Working Papers in Cultural Studies 1972-79. London/New York, pp. 128-138

Hepp, Andreas (1999): Cultural Studies und Medienanalyse. Opladen/ Wiesbaden

Hermann, Thomas/Hanetseder, Christa (2007): "Jugendliche mit Migrationshintergrund: heimatliche, locale und globale Verortungen." In: Bonfadelli, Heinz/Moser, Heinz, eds.: Medien und Migration. Europa als multikultureller Raum? Wiesbaden, pp. 237-271

Huntington, Samuel P. (2004): Who Are We? America's Great Debate. London

Husband, Charles, ed. (1994): A Richer Vision: The Development of Ethnic Minority Media in Western Democracies. Communication and Development Series, London

Jacobs, Dirk/Tillie, Jean (2004): "Introduction: Social capital and political integration of migrants." In: Journal of Ethnic and Migration Studies, 30(3), pp. 419-427

Kosnick, Kira (2000): "Building bridges. Media for migrants and the public-service mission in Germany." In: Cultural Studies, 3(3), pp. 319-342

Leurdijk, Andra (2006): "In search of a common ground. Strategies of multicultural television producers in Europe." In: Cultural Studies, 9(1), pp. 25-46

Lull, James (2001): "Superculture for the communication age." In: Lull, James, ed.: Culture in the Communication Age. London, pp. 132-163

Müller, Daniel (2005a): "Die Darstellung ethnischer Minderheiten in Deutschland." In: Geißler, Rainer/Pöttker, Horst, eds.: Massenmedien und die Integration ethnischer Minderheiten in Deutschland. Problemaufriss, Forschungsstand, Bibliographie. Bielefeld, pp. 83-126

Müller, Daniel (2005b): "Die Mediennutzung ethnischer Minderheiten." In: Geißler, Rainer/Pöttker, Horst, eds.: Massenmedien und die Integration ethnischer Minderheiten in Deutschland. Problemaufriss, Forschungsstand, Bibliographie. Bielefeld, pp. 359-387

Nacos, Brigitte L./Torres-Reyna, Oscar (2007): Fueling Our Fears. Stereotyping, Media Coverage, and Public Opinion of Muslim Americans. Lanham etc.

Nilan, Pam/Feixa, Carles, eds. (2006): Global Youth? Hybrid identities, plural worlds. London/New York

Ogan, Christine (2001): Communication and Identity in Diaspora. Turkish Migrants in Amsterdam and Their Use of Media. Lanham.

Peeters, Allerd L./d'Haenens, Leen (2005): "Bridging or Bonding? Relationships between integration and media use among ethnic minorities in the Netherlands." In: Communications, 30(5), pp. 201-231

Piga, Andrea (2007): "Mediennutzung von Migranten. Ein Forschungsüberblick." In: Bonfadelli, Heinz/Moser, Heinz, eds.: Medien und Migration. Europa als multikultureller Raum? Wiesbaden, pp. 209-234

Poole, Elisabeth (2000): "Framing Islam: An Analysis of Newspaper Coverage of Islam in the British Press." In: Hafez, Kai, ed.: Islam and the West in the Mass Media. Fragmented Images in a Globalizing World. Cresskil, NJ, pp. 157-179

Riggins, Stephen H., ed. (1992): Ethnic Minority Media. An International Perspective. Newbury Park/London/New Delhi

Scheufele, Bertram/Brosius, Hans-Bernd (1999): "The Frame Remains the Same? Stabilität und Kontinuität journalistischer Selektionskriterien am Beispiel der Berichterstattung über Anschläge auf Ausländer und Asylbewerber." In: Rundfunk und Fernsehen, 47, 3/1999, pp. 409-432

Schiffer, Sabine (2005): Die Darstellung des Islams in der Presse. Sprache, Bilder, Suggestionen. Eine Auswahl von Techniken und Beispielen. Würzburg

Schudson, Michael (1994): "Culture and the Integration of National Societies." In: Crane, Diana, ed.: The Sociology of Culture. Oxford, pp. 21-43

ter Wal, Jessica (2004): European Day of Media Monitoring. Quantitative analysis of daily press and TV contents in the 15 EU Member states. European Research Centre on Migration and Ethnic Relations. Utrecht

Van Dijk, Teun A. (1991): Racism and the Press. London/New York

Weber-Menges, Sonja (2006): "Ethnomedien in Deutschland." In: Geißler, Rainer/Pöttker, Horst, eds.: Integration durch Massenmedien/Mass Media-Integration. Bielefeld, pp. 121-145

Weiß, Hans-Jürgen/Trebbe, Joachim (2001): Mediennutzung und Integration der türkischen Bevölkerung in Deutschland. Ergebnisse einer Umfrage des Presse- und Informationsamtes der Bundesregierung. Potsdam

Petra Herczeg

Migrants and Ethnic Minorities in Austria: Assimilation, Integration and the Media

Fremd ist der Fremde nur in der Fremde -
A stranger is strange only in a strange land
(Karl Valentin)

This paper explores issues concerning the media situation of ethnic minorities and migrants in Austria. It is based on the premise that ethnic minority groups that have been present in the country for centuries and contemporary migrants encounter similar problems in preserving their languages and culture within the society at large. This situation results from an asymmetrical relationship between majority and minority. In contrast to migrants, semi-autonomous minorities are well-integrated into Austrian society. Yet, there are a number of parallels between ethnic minorities and migrants in reference to the ways they are dealt with by agents such as the media, politicians and the general public. The Austrian media landscape reflects the conflict-ridden situation of ethnic minorities and migrants.

1. Introduction

In the perception of the general public, ethnic minorities and migrants have something in common: both groups have problems with their image. At best, their image is neutral; but very often, esteem for both segments of society is slight, and thus, they have a negative image among the population.

In Austria, semi-autonomous minorities are a fairly local phenomenon in certain parts of the country. The largest minority includes approximately 30,000 members, but in spite of this small number ethnic minorities have always been a "conflict-ridden" issue in Austrian politics and media.

Croats in Burgenland and Slovenes in Carinthia have been officially recognised in Austria since 1955. Yet, the key issue has always been — and still is — the implementation of Article 7 of the Austrian State Treaty of 1955, which grants minorities the right to educational opportunities in their own language and the right to use their own topographic designations and (road) signs officially and to use their native language in public institutions.

The controversies about the installation of bilingual road signs in the Slovenian and German languages in Carinthia ("Ortstafelkonflikt") have clearly illustrated to what extent emotions and opinions are expressed in the politically oriented public sphere and conveyed by the media.

The number of migrants in Austria is about ten times higher than that of the semi-autonomous minorities. Migrants comprise nearly 15 percent of the Austrian population and are at the centre of media attention and public debate. There are approximately 1.2 million residents who are either foreign citizens or persons born abroad who have acquired Austrian citizenship (Federal Institute of Statistics Austria 2007).

2.   Problems in Defining "Heimat" and "Identity"

In addition to Croats and Slovenes, groups which have lived in Burgenland and Carinthia for centuries, the "Volksgruppen Gesetz" of 1976 officially recognized Czechs, Slovaks and Hungarians as semi-autonomous ethnic minorities. The criteria for such recognition were: Austrian citizenship, non-German mother tongue, existence of a separate nation and the principle of "Beheimatung", which can be described as maintaining a distinct traditional lifestyle in certain regions of the country. Not until 1993 were Roma and Sinti officially recognized as a semi-autonomous minority. Previously, such recognition had been refused on the grounds that Roma and Sinti were not a "native minority" ("keine bodenständige Minderheit").

After the end of the Second World War, Austrian politicians and nearly all of the national opinion leaders were engaged in building an "Austrian identity", which was intended to have nothing to do with the "Volksnation" of the Nazis. The somewhat unexpected official recognition of the Roma as an Austrian ethnic group in 1993 was facilitated by concerns for Austria's international reputation. After many years of fruitless effort, the organisations of the Roma under the leadership of Rudolf Sarközi and representatives of the Centre for Ethnic Groups succeeded in eliminating any reservations against official recognition. At the same time Austria attempted not to compromise itself in the aftermath of the "Waldheim debate". Because of the discussion about the role of the former UN secretary general and newly elected Austrian president in the Nazi past, the Austrian government took care not to send out the wrong signals by not recognizing an ethnic group which had nearly been totally annihilated by the Nazis. At the same time Austria was promoting the implementation of regulations in favour of ethnic minorities within the CSCE and did not want to make its role there seem questionable because of problems connected to the country's internal affairs (Baumgartner 2000).

2.1 Ethnicity as a Nation-Building Paradigm

Austria was anxious to perceive itself as "eine gute politisch-konsensuale Staatsnation" (Wodak et al 1995, 7), as an uncontested nation oriented to the state and not to a specific (in this case, German) people. Languages were not to play a part in the development of a new Austrian identity (de Cillia 1995, 4). Yet, during this entire period Austrian language policies actually aimed at the assimilation of members of minority groups and their languages. When members of ethnic minorities demand their rights, the majority's perception of itself as an in-group can be reinforced, and this can lead to an exaggerated idealization of the in-group (Treibel 1993, 334f), with the consequence that ethnic and national affiliations are exploited.

In this context, the majority identifies itself as "we"/"us", while members of minority groups become "them"/"others". In the public sphere, only "major" languages are perceived; the "minor" languages of ethnic minorities are only noticed if issues concerning ethnic groups are reported on. The majority population is poorly informed about minority issues and sees minorities mainly as troublemakers who are constantly making demands and never seem satisfied. The demands of ethnic groups seem to annoy the general public. Various ethnic groups are often perceived as a single consistent group characterized by its own rituals, languages, and cultural expressions. The public image of ethnic groups, especially that shown on television, is dominated by clichés that present such groups primarily in folkloristic contexts.

A glance at the situation of the language minorities in Burgenland shows that, on the one hand, they have acquired a special legal status and that efforts have been made to officially preserve regional languages, but that language assimilation is a dominant trend, so that only small and somewhat concerned groups of minority language users persevere (Baumgartner 2000). Even after 20 years, Perchinig's description of Austrian public debates on minorities is still accurate. He maintains that much of the debate centers on the criterion of language, and that no new arguments related to objective or subjective criteria of belonging to a minority have been found. For one side ("objective") "assimilation" primarily consists in abandoning the minority language; for the other side assimilation means the abandonment of "self-identification as part of the minority" (Perchinig 1988, 134).

Ethnic identity (a sense of belonging to a particular group) expresses itself in the use of a common language and of cultural codes, in acting together as a group and in sharing a common history (Fillitz 2003, 24). Ethnic identity, one of the most complex concepts of sociological theory, is to be understood as a process and not as a constant. Max Weber defined ethnic groups on a symbolic level as "those human groups that entertain a subjective belief in their common descent because of similarities of physical type or customs or both, or because of memories of colonization and migration; this belief must be important for the propagation of group formation; conversely, it does not matter whether or not an objective blood relationship exists. Ethnic membership (*Gemeinsamkeit*) differs from the kinship group precisely by being a presumed identity, not a group with concrete social action, like the latter." (Weber 1978, 389)

2.2 Subjective Perception and Reality

Perceiving oneself as belonging to a group does not necessarily correspond to objective circumstances. Reasons for differentiating the group from others are of secondary import and can be based on tradition or on "disposition". As one example, Weber mentions language communities, which can produce ethnic communities for a variety of reasons – e.g., due to specific economic or political conditions. Ethnicity provides an opportunity for socialisation and collectivisation (Ornig 2006, 34). For semi-autonomous groups this is an ambiguous situation, because, on the one hand, the individual has to decide if he or she wants to belong to an ethnic group, and, on the other, there is the issue of what kind of values and concepts the ethnic group is perceived as representing. This applies to the situation of both semi-autonomous and fully assimilated minorities. Ethnic identities are created by communication within one's own group and in distinction to others.

"For ethnicity to come about, the groups must have a minimum of contact with each other, and they have to entertain ideas of each other as being culturally different from themselves. If these conditions are not fulfilled, there is no ethnicity, for ethnicity is essentially an aspect of a relationship, not a property of a group" (Eriksen 1993, 11-12).

Ethnic identities are integrated into power relations which are characterized by asymmetrical communicative relations. Since 1945, this has also been evident in Austrian history (Weiss 2000, 25). The official politics in the road sign controversy provide an example, as it was not until 2000 that bilingual road signs for Croats and Hungarians were installed in Burgenland, despite the fact that the Austrian State Treaty of 1955 explicitly included an obligation to set up such signs.

3.   The Situation of Migrants from the 1960s to the Present

There had been few migrants in Austria before the late 1960s, when the so-called "Gastarbeiter" ("guest workers"), primarily from ex-Yugoslavia and Turkey, began to come to the country. Between 1961 and 1972, 265,000 immigrants came to Austria. For the most part, they were employed in heavy labour and, at any rate, did work that was not appealing to Austrians. They were not integrated into Austrian society and had a negative image within the Austrian population.

To counteract negative reactions on the part of the general public and the media, the government started an awareness campaign to increase the acceptance of migrants. Posters showed a little boy and a big man, with the boy asking the man, "I haaß Kolaric, du haaßt Kolaric – warum sogn's zu dir Tschusch?" ("My name is Kolaric, your name is Kolaric – why do they call you bad names?") This campaign alluded to the fact that many Viennese citizens are descendents of Slavic immigrants, which could be readily demonstrated by reading the names in a Viennese telephone directory.

This first distinctive wave of migration in the second half of the twentieth century was followed by constant immigration: the former guest workers attempted to bring their families to Austria, and their focus of interest shifted to Austria. Now, second and third generations of people of immigrant background live in the country.

A second wave of migration arrived with the dissolution of former communist regimes in Eastern Europe. This migration could be seen as a return to the regional migration typical of the 19th and early 20th centuries in Austria, involving people from the Czech Republic, the Slovak Republic, Hungary, Poland and Romania (Hintermann 2000, 10). Between 1989 and 1993, the number of persons with foreign citizenship living in Austria increased from 387,000 to 690,000.

Especially during the war in the Balkans, the number of citizens of former Yugoslavia emigrating to Austria increased, as did immigration from Turkey and other countries. In the early 1990s, about 90,000 refugees from the Bosnian war came to Austria. Approximately half of them remained there. According to official statistics, about 155,000 persons of Bosnian origin now live in Austria. About 41,000 are now Austrian citizens. Hence, tens of thousands of Bosnian refugees have been integrated into Austrian society.

3.1   Migrants in the Media

Xenophobia has become a major issue in the media, after initial moves in this direction were undertaken by the right-wing Freedom Party and then popularized by the *Neue Kronen Zeitung*, a tabloid that has the highest circulation of all of the newspapers in Austria (the *Neue Kronen Zeitung* is read by 43.8 percent of all Austrians of age 14 and older – a total readership of 3,031,000).

Surveys indicate that even today somewhat diffuse attitudes towards "foreigners" among the Austrian public remain and that migrants are primarily perceived "as a problem". A new discourse has appeared in the mass media: "…different migrant groups were portrayed as a threat to the social system, to security, and the economic stability of Austria. The stereotypes created in the early 1990s were still prevalent in today's newspapers and broadcasts." (Joskowicz, EUMC[1] 2002, 311). This discourse was dominated by references to economic arguments ("Wirtschaftsflüchtlinge") and during the Bosnian war in 1993 the *Neue Kronen Zeitung* reported "primarily about the discussion about refugees in Austrian politics and the impact that the refugees would have on the economy, and did not consider the perspectives of refugees at all" (Joskowicz, EUMC 2002, 318). In 1993, the Freedom Party's anti-immigrant petition ("Österreich zuerst" – "Austria first") was propagated by the tabloid *Neue Kronen Zeitung*. The quality press opposed the petition. One typical way this tabloid engaged in opinion making can be seen in the fact that it practically ignored one of the largest demonstrations ever held in Austria, the "Lichtermeer" ("Sea of lights") against the FPÖ anti-foreigner campaign.

As mentioned above, immigration from Turkey and also from African and Asian countries increased simultaneously with a third phase of migration. This led to further stereotypical reporting on migrants' issues and to corresponding perceptions on the part of the general public. In her comparative analysis ("Alte und neue Minderheiten - zum Einstellungswandel in Österreich 1984 – 1998"), Hilde Weiss demonstrates that the category of "Ausländer"/ "foreigners" is very imprecise, as foreigners can be "illegal aliens, refugees, persons working in Austria for shorter or longer periods, with or without Austrian citizenship, immigrants of the first, second or third generation, tourists, Europeans or only non-Europeans coming from the western hemisphere or elsewhere, etc." (Weiss 2000, 26).

Furthermore, the EUMC Report demonstrates that at the end of the 1990s, mainly black migrants have been reported on in a negative way, primarily as drug traffickers and in connection with other drug-related crimes.

---

1   EUMC was renamed in March 2007 in EU Agency for Fundamental Rights (FRA) and is based in Vienna.

One particular example is the reporting on the deportation of Marcus Omofuma. The tragic death of Marcus Omofuma led to much coverage in the press: "After being tied up and gagged with adhesive tape by the police, Mr. Omofuma died in an airplane during his deportation from Austria. In the *Neue Kronen Zeitung*, his name was always abbreviated as 'Marcus O.' – a form that is used for alleged perpetrators suggesting that he was a criminal. Already earlier, Africans had been systematically depicted as drug traffickers in the *Neue Kronen Zeitung*." (Joskowicz, EUMC 2002, 321-322)

The tabloid press and surveys on the potential 'risks' of migration have often warned of a "mass immigration" from eastern and central eastern European countries, which, however, has not become a reality.

3.2   The Image of Ethnic Minorities and of Migrants

In the comparative survey mentioned above, a survey on the development of Austrians' attitudes towards so-called "new" and "old minorities" in the period between 1984 and 1998, Weiss discovered that the continuity of stereotypes and attitudes towards the "old" minorities was "impressive". Even "traditional" minorities such as Slovenes, Croats and Jews did not manage to acquire a better image and remained on nearly the same level as 14 years before. What was new was that the ethnic groups that had only recently arrived were assessed in much more negative ways (Weiss 2000, 34f). Only in one respect did acceptance increase: the Austrian population became more tolerant towards a better legal status regulating equal social security and length of residence. On the whole, acceptance of the rights of the semi-autonomous minorities actually decreased somewhat (Weiss 2000, 35). This might be related to a majority opinion that Austrian ethnic minorities have been assimilated and thus are only expected to demonstrate their ethnicity in relation to certain cultural and folkloristic aspects.

Under the assumption that migrants are integrated into society if they have access to social life as "access to work, education, habitation, health, justice, politics, mass media and religion..."(Bommes 2007, 3), it is clear that migrants and ethnic minorities are perceived as not striving for integration if they demand their rights or call attention to politicians' or the general public's disregard for their problems. The majority sees participation in public life only as a process of adaptation. In debates in the media and elsewhere, distinctions between terms such as "assimilation", "integration" or "segregation" are largely ignored.

In 2004, one significant result of a survey undertaken by the GfK Austria Market Research GmbH on the attitudes of the Austrian population towards migration and integration was that nearly a quarter of the Austrian population makes no distinction between "refugees" and "immigrants". People from lower social classes, persons with little formal education, and older people were especially prone to see no distinction here. Twenty percent of the Austrian population stated that they most definitely did not want to have foreigners as neighbours. The groups rated as least popular were Roma and Sinti. Citizens of former Yugoslavia, Romania and Bulgaria but also immigrants from Russia or China were perceived to be well prepared for integration. A categorical rejection of integration and the lowest level of willingness to become integrated were attributed to "Moslem" groups, i.e., Turks, Iranians, Afghans and people from North Africa (Brettschneider 2007, 22f).

Fassmann notes that especially in politics people presume that "the meaning of integration can be defined precisely (...) but 'integration' is only a vague concept for various analytic and normative concepts of integration and can mean many different things. Integration can mean anything from total adaptation to a loose way of incorporating social groups into a larger society" (Fassmann 2006, 225). In the debate on integration in the media and which role the media have to play in this context, the concept of media integration can be seen in three ways: "media segregation and assimilative media integration (media assimilation) as the two external poles and intercultural media integration as a middle course between the two extremes" (Geißler/Pöttker 2006, 21).

The dilemma involved in dealing with both semi-autonomous minorities and fully assimilated groups is evident in the diffuse use of the concepts. But in contrast to the "new" minorities, the main issue for the semi-autonomous minorities is not integration into society. The main problem is how language and culture can be preserved and passed on to future generations. The preservation of minorities' languages involves not only individual responsibility, but also a collective responsibility, and complex issues related to multilingualism.[2]

---

2 A personal note about my student days: When fellow students asked me about my background, I answered that I was from "Burgenland" and told them that I was Burgenland-Croatian and had been raised as a bilingual. Often enough, the response was astonishment, accompanied by compliments on how well I spoke German. I could only reply that we Croatians had been in the area for 500 years and, considering that, I was actually in pretty good shape. More seriously, though, it was obvious that my fellow students were ill-informed about Austrian ethnic groups.

3.3   The Current Situation of Migrants

In 2005, a new law regulating the status of foreigners in Austria went into effect. Certain aspects of this new law have been a subject of heated debate: allowing for force-feeding of hunger strikers or required proof of persecution or danger for asylum seekers and mandatory participation in language courses, as demanded by the so-called new "integration agreement". The aims of this contract are outlined on the website of the Austrian Integration Fund (http://www.integrationsfonds.at). The main goal of the Integration Agreement is that "migrants and asylum beneficiaries [...] learn enough German to participate in the social, economic and cultural life of the host country."

Obviously, migrants must be able to communicate in the language spoken in the host country to facilitate integration. Yet, this should not require the abandonment of the mother tongue, since the knowledge and use of one's native language are significant factors affecting the self-confidence and identity of a person. But in the Austrian public sphere, the ways of representing languages other than German are inadequate, even though Austria is a multilingual country.

Often, migrants have been held responsible for the poor results attributed to the Austrian education system in the PISA report of 2003. Not only the right-wing FPÖ attempted to depict such results as an effect of "mass migration", but also the media often focused on the problems involved in teaching migrants' children. One major issue of this debate was whether one-year pre-school attendance should be mandatory for migrants' children to insure better knowledge of the German language. In contrast, a view of migrants' languages as cultural resources that can only be activated if a society is able to offer suitable conditions has, for the most part, been disregarded (Bourdieu 1983).

3.4   The Discourse on the Deportation of Asylum Seekers in 2007

To what extent the mass media can contribute to the integration of individuals is a subject of much debate. As Geißler and Pöttker have demonstrated (Geißler/Pöttker 2006), the media have a function related to social integration, insofar as they provide the public with relevant topics. According to Pöttker, one of the major responsibilities of journalism is to mediate between social segments in this complex domain. Mediating between distinct ways of life and practical knowledge creates an open-ended sphere that allows for participation in society as a whole (Pöttker 2000, 377-378).

In the autumn of 2007, a large-scale debate on integration arose among the general public and in the media when refugees who had been living in Austria for several years were to be deported. Laws on foreigners require the deportation of asylum seekers even if the processing of their applications has been going on for years. All members of the government agreed that there was no need to change the laws on foreigners and that no general right to permanent residence should be put into effect.

The media reported that families who had been staying in Austria for years were to be split up and deported. The refugees involved were described as well-integrated and, together with their children, as forming part of the community. The dominant viewpoint in mass media reports can be expressed with the headline: "Thousands in danger of being deported. Uncertainty a cause of anxiety for long-term asylum seekers" (*Der Standard* 5th Oct 2007).

Individual cases have been portrayed in the mass media. On 3 October 2007, under the headline: "Deported" the *Salzburger Nachrichten* printed a photograph of the Milici family holding hands, with the six children lined up between their parents according to their age. The caption read: "The township of Peggau in Styria fought against the deportation of family Milici in vain. On Tuesday, the eight members of the family were deported. … According to mayor Werner Rois, in the past two years the members of the family had become fully integrated. Many of the co-residents are shocked that humanitarian aspects are not taken into consideration in such cases. On Monday, the mayor and other people from Peggau demonstrated in front of the centre for deportation in Vienna."

One case especially caught the attention of the mass media: Fifteen-year-old Arigona Zogaj went into hiding to avoid her impending deportation. Her father and brothers and sisters had already been deported; her mother had had a nervous breakdown and had been hospitalized. Arigona stated in a letter that she was in danger of committing suicide and that she would only resurface when her younger brothers and sisters had returned to Austria.

In contrast to its usual anti-foreigner slant in reporting, even the tabloid *Kronen Zeitung* started a campaign supporting Arigona Zogaj. The publisher of the "Neue Kronen Zeitung", Hans Dichand, wrote under his pen-name "Cato": "Which of the politicians would dare to act this way? In this case, a condemned humanity must be given priority to the letter of the law" (*Neue Kronen Zeitung* 3rd Oct 2007).

Arigona took an active role and sent a video from her hiding place with a message to the Austrian Minister of the Interior and to the general public. The video was broadcast by the ORF news programme "Zeit im Bild". It shows a girl sitting against the wall of a bare room, looking directly into the camera and saying that she is very badly off and repeating that she is in danger of committing suicide. The aesthetics of the image reminds one of videos of hostages, in which "prisoners" of terrorists appeal to the public to free them. Here, liberation would mean the right to remain in the country.

With tears in her eyes Arigona appealed to minister Günther Platter to allow her brothers and sisters to return. She repeated that she would rather die than return to Kosovo, where she would have no future. In the 5-minute video, Arigona stressed, "I cannot understand at all why Mr. Platter does not allow us to stay in Austria. We did not do anything wrong. I miss my family very much…"

This example illustrates that in public discourses a distinction between "integration" and "assimilation" is becoming blurred. This family consents to complete adaptation, which is regarded by the public as successful integration, but for some of the political actors the legal basis for their continued residence is lacking. For this reason, the Austrian Minister of the Interior publicly interpreted the girl's desperate appeal as attempted extortion and refused to revise his point of view. This interpretation, with the contention that the state could not allow itself to be blackmailed, had the effect of criminalizing the case. These circumstances parallel a tendency to construct negative images of victims reported on in a considerable number of research studies – with the distinction that this time it was politicians and not the mass media that exhibited this tendency (see e.g. Müller 2005, 112; Bonfadelli 2007a).

Commentaries were in widespread agreement in denouncing the "inhumane procedure" in handling this case. In his analysis in the "Salzburger Nachrichten", Andreas Koller wrote:

> The secrecy of the political basis for decisions (the list of criteria regulating deportations - P.H.) results in the inhumanity of the political practice. Government bureaucracy acting in secret nearly inevitably leads to the abuse of power and to despotism. For this reason, the fathers of our democracy established instruments to monitor and control government bureaucracies. One of these instruments is the parliament, another the freedom of the press, a third a critical public. Austrian policy on foreigners is carried out under the observation of these three monitoring authorities. At least, that is the way it seems. Humane treatment only takes place if some extraordinarily dramatic fate (a girl who goes into hiding or a six-year-old is threatened with deportation) is portrayed. *(Salzburger Nachrichten,* 4th Oct 2007)

The general public sympathized with the fate of the girl and her family. The fellow residents of the township organized a demonstration with ca. 500

participants, including artists and politicians. The president of the Austrian parliament, Barbara Prammer (of the Social Democratic Party), made a speech.

Pöttker defines integration as a desirable process which interconnects various segments of society (Pöttker 2005, 40-41), a process involving both similarity and the harmonization of segments of society on the one hand and a wide variety of specific conditions on the other. Below, the criteria affecting integration cited by Pöttker are applied to the factors involved in the public perception of Arigona's predicament.

- *Intensity and contents of communication between segments of society:* Various groups of communicators take action and influence Arigona's situation: a minister of the interior who refuses to reconsider his position on the one hand and on the other the mass media and the general public (which consists of many and varied groups) and the victims, who are represented by Arigona.

- *One result of the extent of communication and of mutual knowledge of varied segments of society:* For the most part, communicated knowledge referred to the fact that this family was integrated into a variety of social communities. Arigona's country of origin is seen as a place without any hope or perspective, where life is not possible. Her appeal culminates in the statement that she and her family "did no wrong". What is meant is that she and her family acted in conformance with widely accepted habits and norms, in other words, that they had become assimilated.

- *Extent of participation on the part of societal institutions:* Institutional participation is demonstrated in Arigona's use of a video message to appeal to the public and the media and to draw attention to her needs.

- *Extent of collective acceptance of basic cultural values:* There was a broad consensus among journalists, a number of politicians and businesspersons, and the general public that humanity was to be valued more highly than the letter of the law and that humanitarian action in granting permission to remain in the country was the required solution.

- *Societal consensus on the extent of pluralistic views and resolution of conflicts between heterogeneous segments of society:* The majority society exhibited conflicting views: the interior minister and some official sources on the one hand, the mass media, certain politicians and businesspersons, fellow residents of the family's town on the other. The general public is prepared to accept some Other, if that Other and his or her fate are portrayed in an individualized way.

The case of Arigona also attracted the attention of the international mass media. The story was covered e.g. by the French newspaper "Le Monde", by the "Herald Tribune" and by the "Associated Press". The international reporting touched upon a crucial point relevant to integration:

> The Zogaj family's story has fanned a fiery debate in Austria about deporting well integrated foreigners who seek asylum and often try to stay on illegally when their applications are rejected. It is a debate similar to those in other European countries, where conflicts about immigration are often tied to questions of national identity and humanitarianism." (*Associated Press*, 6th Oct 2007)

Here again, after the Waldheim controversy and the debates focused on the participation of a right-wing party in the government, Austrian politics were portrayed in a negative context on an international scale.

4. Ethnic Groups, Migrants and their Media

To gain attention from the general public, minorities must be present in the mass media. Multilingual programmes on radio and television provide suitable opportunities to achieve this aim. In the awareness of the general public, ethnic groups are often seen in folkloristic contexts, and migrants are often associated with negative media coverage. The relevant surveys demonstrate that the media primarily convey negative images of migrants.

There are no quantitative surveys on the media use of migrants in Austria. This implies that there is no reliable information on migrants' use, for example, of Turkish television programmes or of print media. In a research overview, Piga states (Piga 2007, 226) that the quantitative dimensions of the motivation behind migrants' media use have been studied extensively, but this does not apply to the situation in Austrian. The ORF (Austrian Broadcasting Corporation) is now planning a survey on migrants' use of television in Austria modelled on the ARD/ZDF study „Migranten und Medien 2007". This is a first step in demonstrating that the non-uniform group of migrants is also considered a target group by the Austrian public broadcasting company.

For migrants, the Austrian media landscape is rather limited. On Austrian television, there is only one weekly programme for all groups of migrants: "Heimat, fremde Heimat", a programme broadcast on Sunday afternoons. The aim of the programme, as described by the editorial staff, is "to support togetherness, cultural variety and integration in Austria". Target groups are "Austrians who are interested in ethnic issues, naturalized immigrants, long-term residents of foreign nationalities and members of Austrian ethnic groups". The programme is presented in German; the persons interviewed on the program use their native tongues, and their statements are translated with the use of German subtitles.

Every Sunday evening, the regional radio station of Vienna broadcasts a radio programme of the same name. A wide variety of topics ranging from political developments to folkloristic features are covered here, often with interviews of minority representatives, members of ethnic minorities, and migrants.

In the Austrian media system, the number of migrants involved in production is negligible. Only in the minority department of the ORF can journalists of a migration background be found. The minority department of the ORF is managed by Silvana Meixner, a migrant from Croatia, who is one of the anchorpersons of the television program "Heimat, fremde Heimat". Another anchorperson is Lakis Iordanopoulos, who originally came from Greece to study in Austria and eventually settled here indefinitely.

The opportunity to become involved in the production of media is a crucial point relevant to integration, for in this way the perspectives of minorities can be integrated into the majority media, and minorities involved in media production can ensure that suitable ethnic programs are offered.

The specific forms that media use and gratifications take are closely related to which generation of migrants a person belongs to. German surveys on television use of Turkish migrants indicate that the elder generation attempted to deal with homesickness and to reinforce their relationship with the old country by watching television programmes from Turkey (Aumüller 2007, 39) – a type of media consumption not perpetuated by the younger generations. Ethnic media can support an orientation directed towards the host country. Yet, ethnic media can also inhibit the disposition to integrate if, instead, there is an emphasis on content that promotes segregation (Geißler/Pöttker 2005, 396).

Although there are no similar empirical data available for Austria, the surveys of ethnic media use mentioned above can indicate which problems have to be coped with by other migrants and can demonstrate how ethnic media have been able to build bridges between various cultures. Migrants' integration involves a learning process the results of which can range from complete adaptation (assimilation) to a type of adaptation that allows for cooperation within the framework of the majority society. Only this second type allows for cultural diversity.

Weiss considers whether maintaining ethnically influenced cultural habits is a barrier to integration and raises the question, "Where can the borderline be drawn between the cultural adaptation required for mastering professional and everyday life on the one hand and assimilation on the other?" (Weiss 2007, 14).

Media and integration play interdependent roles in a society. Hafez (2005, 176) notes three different aspects of integration:

- Civic integration, including, for example, participation in political processes;

- Social integration, i.e., material and institutional integration; and

- Cultural integration, which is necessary for forming personal identities and hybrid identities and relates to demands for equal rights for various cultures.

For the process of integration, these three aspects are determining factors on the social and structural levels, but also on the individual level. The Austrian mass media make no effort to cover topics related to migrants' special interests. As mentioned above, there is a lack of specific quantitative surveys on the media use and the media requirements of migrants. This research deficit is perhaps symptomatic for the treatment of minority media issues. Often enough, migrants are reported upon; they do not attain active roles in society's mass media. Consequently, demands have been voiced that members of ethnic minorities should acquire positions in the editorial staff of large-scale media companies, so that their perspectives can be represented in the reports of the media. Such demands, which are not at all new, are still repeated when media issues are debated in the context of integration – a further indication of the standstill media politics has come to with respect to ethnic minorities.

In Austria there is no daily newspaper in the language of an ethnic minority. Hence, the only media specifically catering for such audiences are certain daily programmes of the public broadcaster and the groups' own ethnic media. The Burgenland Croats and the Slovenes, for example, have weekly journals; other ethnic groups publish magazines on a fairly regular basis. The government provides support for all of these media. The EUMC report from 2002 notes: "Newspapers in the Slovenian and Croatian languages are found to limit reporting to topics connected directly with ethnic identity, whereas media in the majority language are the main providers of general information and entertainment for minorities (Busch 1998). The result of this format is that minority media remain more dependent on state funding." (EUMC 2002, 313)

The majority of the population expects that ethnic minorities and migrants articulate themselves in the language of the majority. Language use "is the commonest form of social behaviour, and the form of social behaviour where we rely most on 'common-sense' assumptions" (Fairclough 2001, 2). Fairclough proceeds on the assumption that language is an important factor of power and remarks, "nobody who has an interest in relationships of power in modern society can afford to ignore language" (Fairclough 2001, 3). Language use involves many opportunities to orient relationships between various segments of a society, which also applies to the relationship between the majority and ethnic minorities. How various groups deal with different languages is also a question of ideology.

4.1 A Typology of Transcultural Media

In her master thesis, Wögerer characterized "transcultural media" in Austria and defined these as media which deal with issues like integration or multiculturalism and promote a counter-establishment public sphere or countercultural developments (Wögerer 2004, 82). She compiled a list of transcultural media in Austria and developed a typology for the print media involved. Wögerer describes transcultural media as exhibiting the following features:

- Multi-, inter- and transcultural content;

- Critical or semi-professional journalism;

- Linked to social movements;

- An interest in promoting a counter-establishment public sphere: a form of communication on integration issues not provided by the mainstream media (Wögerer 2004, 84)

Wögerer's typology is oriented toward key issues and specific target groups (Wögerer 2004, 94). This orientation is somewhat problematic, as the typology is not limited to migrants' media or media for ethnic groups. The typology includes the following:

- *Print magazines of associations or magazines aimed at increasing donations for projects related to migrants' issues* – for instance, the "Gute Zeitung" (Wiener Integrationshaus), "Zebratl" (Verein ZEBRA), "Hin & Her" (Caritas) or "ÖIF-Magazin. Integration in Focus" (Austrian Integration Fund).

- *Magazines concerned with migration policies*, in which a theoretical discussion of issues relevant to migration takes place, e.g., "Liga" (Österreichische Liga für Menschenrechte/Austrian League for Human Rights), "Stimme von und für Minderheiten" (Initiative Minderheiten/Initiative Minorities), "Die Bunte Zeitung" (Verein "Die Bunten") and "Mega-phon" (Caritas Graz).

- *Cultural magazines* such as "der.wisch" (Kulturverein Kanafani/Cultural club Kanafani) deal with specific cultural issues and antiracism.

- *Migrants' media aiming at a specific migrant readership.* There are many print media which are in Turkish or target the Turkish community – media such as "Yeni Vatan", "Yeni Hareket", "Öneri", "Aktüel Haber", and "Vienna Post". These periodicals cover the social and political spectrum of opinions among Turkish migrants, are distributed free of charge and financed by advertisements. "Echo. The first and only magazine for the second generation" is edited six times a year. In Vienna, there are also some periodicals available to migrants from former Yugoslavia in their languages. There is no Turkish-language daily produced in Austria itself.

4.2 Semi-autonomous Ethnic Groups and the Public Broadcasting Company

The public broadcasting company ORF is required by law to offer programmes in the native languages of all officially recognized semi-autonomous minorities . The law on public broadcasting from 2001 specifies that the ORF broadcast appropriate programmes for any recognized ethnic minority, but does not make any stipulations about the use of languages. The European Charter for Regional and Minority Languages was ratified by Austria in 2001. Yet, the Charter entails no further requirements related to additional multilingual programmes for semi-autonomous minorities.[3]

Debates on the use of minority and migrants' languages take place within the context of debates on the presence, use, and impacts of languages in the public sphere and can take various forms. At any rate, the EUMC report stated, "members of many migrant groups and minorities are not presented in the media as individuals. This is due partly to the problems arising from the absence of employees from these groups in mainstream media as well as to the lack of strong minority media in Austria" (EUMC 2002, 322).

---

3   I am familiar with the conditions of the production of minority programmes, as I worked on the Burgenland-Croatian editorial staff for radio and television broadcasts for 8 years. Of course, I am also aware that assessment of media work can diverge dramatically, depending upon whether the perspective is an external or internal one. My colleagues and I often encountered significant problems in finding interview partners who were able to expound on certain topics in Croatian. Frequently, the language competence of these speakers – even in their native tongue – proved to be deficient.

4.2.1 Television

At the same time when the nationwide programme "Heimat, fremde Heimat" is broadcast in the region of Burgenland, there is a 25-minute programme for Croats ("Dobar dan Hrvati") and, in Carinthia, a television program for Slovenes ("Dober dan, Koroska"). The programme consists of a mixture of current affairs and more traditional topics, such as villages and local peculiarities or other cultural concerns.

In addition, ORF Burgenland broadcasts a quadri-lingual television programme called "Servus Szia Zdravo del tuha" four times a year. This is an information programme about the ethnic minorities that live in Burgenland. The main focus is on cultural topics, and the programme is also available as a download on the Internet.

4.2.2 Radio

Here, media staff and institutions do not debate the use of minority languages, nor is there any mandatory arrangement of multilingual programmes. Of course, these circumstances have an impact on the media situation of ethnic minorities in Austria. Space prevents the mention of all the relevant programmes broadcast by the ORF in the past. But it should be noted that in 2001, the ORF and two private radio organizations established a combined public and private radio station for ethnic minorities in Carinthia: Radio Dva. Radio Dva offers a Slovene and a partly bilingual (German and Slovene) 24-hour programme, including much music. That is, much of the time on the air does not involve spoken language.

This is symptomatic for the specific situation of programmes for ethnic minorities. Journalists attempt to reach a target group that has a wide variety of different interests and cannot be defined with a quota. One of the effects is that the Slovene language has become nearly extinct in the local majority radio programme, for the broadcasts in Burgenland now only include: 40 minutes daily for the Croatian, 5 minutes for Hungarian minorities and a number of services in the language of the Roma.

With the introduction of private radio stations in Burgenland in 1998, Radio Mora was established as a trilingual radio project involving the languages Croatian, Hungarian and Romani. These three ethnic minorities shared one radio license with a commercial provider. This project was terminated in 2001, when the government stopped providing financial support.

4.2.3   Public Community Radio

For the Austrian ethnic minorities, there has been an increase in the programmes provided by the medium-wave (AM) station Radio 1476 – especially for Czechs, Slovaks, Hungarians and Roma in Vienna. For the most part, these are bilingual news programmes for ethnic groups, but a major focus is on recruiting youths who are encouraged to work for the radio. The hope is that this could lead to a stronger identification with the programme and demonstrate that the use of minority languages in the public sphere is important for the self-confidence of both individuals and groups. Collaborations with schools like the "Komensky Gymnasium", which are supported by the Education Ministry, make all those involved in school life (students, teachers, parents) aware of the significance of taking part in communicative societal action in languages other than that of the majority. Youths can achieve better language and media competence when they engage in making broadcasts and decide to use their mother tongue to convey ideas and concepts through the media. There are specific problems involved in the use of the languages of Sinti and Roma. Even within the minority, knowledge of their languages is not very extensive, so that the Roma Radio Kaktus is, in fact, multilingual: German may be the lingua franca, yet the various languages of European Roma (Romani, Sinti, Lovara-Romani) are also used. Dialects of Romani from Romania, Serbia or Montenegro, such as Gurbet, Dambaz, Erli, are also spoken. Topics frequently dealt with here include the history and persecution of the minorities, but also the struggle against discrimination and poverty. Radio 1476's programmes are also available on the Internet at http://1476.orf.at.

4.3   Alternative Media and Migrants

For the past ten years, one particular project of the ORF medium-wave station "Radio 1476", multilingual "Radio Africa", has been dealing with issues relevant to the African community in Austria and has become a community-building factor. The people collaborating on this project have also established additional Internet services and cooperate with others in broadcasting African television programmes in Vienna.

These examples illustrate that media and their editorial staff are not simply producers of certain programmes, but that they can promote integration by dealing with certain topics and representing migrants in certain ways. As mentioned above, the public broadcasting company is required by law to represent all relevant groups of society, ethnic minorities included. Yet, the much larger group of migrants is neglected by laws on broadcasting and by most of the broadcasting companies.

There is a tradition of dealing with issues relevant to migrants among alternative broadcasters. Since independent radio stations began their operations, various groups of migrants have been able to produce programmes in their own languages. Radio Orange, e.g., (located in Vienna) broadcasts programmes from different editorial groups in the Turkish, Bosnian, Serb, Croatian, Portuguese, Spanish and French languages. Radio Orange also offers courses on the technical and editorial production of radio programmes.

In Linz, Radio FRO (Free Radio Oberösterreich-Upper Austria) has been broadcasting programmes for migrants since 1998. The staff of Radio FRO explains its immediate popularity with compensating for the intervals when Turkish satellite television was not broadcasting. The audience reacted with enthusiasm and felt that Radio FRO was providing important services.

Another alternative, independent radio station in Austria is the "Radiofabrik" (located in Salzburg). This station offers multilingual programmes such as "Bosporus Nights", with a Turkish student who dedicates the programme to his home city of Istanbul and tries to build bridges between Salzburg and Istanbul by the means of jazz, hip hop, pop and rock music and by talking with guests from countries all over the world, with Turkish being the language most often used. Similar programs include "Zenska Soba", a bilingual programme for women in the Bosnian and German languages, "Lusophonica" in Portuguese, and "Vecer u Radio" in Serbo-Croatian with programs related to the natural surroundings, culture and society "of a country that no longer exists". Descriptions of the programmes can be found on the Internet, where listeners can also make their opinions known or vote on options for certain programmes.

On the whole, independent radio stations broadcast programmes in more than 20 languages. In contrast to the print media, such radio stations provide migrant groups with a lower-cost opportunity of making their presence felt in the public sphere and of reaching the members of their particular target groups (Busch/Peissl 2003, 189f). As noted above, one of the dilemmas of the radio producers is the question of how to reach the target groups, which, much like majority target groups, consist of different people with various needs and interests and various approaches to the media.

4.4 Easy Access through the Internet

The Internet can be seen as a new space for communication that can easily be used by ethnic minorities. One such use is illustrated by the ORF's multilingual site (volksgruppen.orf.at), which is linked with editorial staff in Vienna, Eisenstadt, and Klagenfurt. The homepage offers written news and downloads of several ethnic programmes and can be used by interested target groups as a news archive in the languages of the semi-autonomous minorities in Austria.

The platform for minorities in Austria, "Initiative Minderheiten", established "Radio Stimme" ("Radio Voice"), which is broadcast over independent stations in Vienna, Linz, Graz, Innsbruck and the southern areas of Carinthia. The one-hour programme, which is produced twice a month, aims to counteract any form of marginalisation on the basis of a person's origin or political convictions. "Radio Stimme" attempts to develop counterstrategies for a media landscape which does not support minority issues and uses the Internet for newsletters and downloading radio programmes. It also provides its audience with podcasts of its programmes.

A large-scale consensus asserts that variety is characteristic of our media-dominated society. Yet, the question of how different ethnic groups and their needs are to be covered in the media remains. Resolving this issue is a challenge to all of the relevant groups: journalists, politicians, academics, and the general public. Here, a single aspect is both the starting point and the major problem: developing an awareness of minorities and migrants, such that the majority does not judge them as a threat, but, instead, sees them as an opportunity for everyone concerned to experience plurality. Both scientific and journalistic efforts have a contribution to make here. To overcome segregation in the area of communication, a common European media policy is essential. Particularly in this context, integration can only be promoted if societal and democratic interests are accorded priority over economic interests.

5.   Concluding Remarks

A comparison between the situation of ethnic minorities and that of migrants indicates that both groups have similar problems in gaining the attention of the general public. The actual public perception of such groups is often solely related to negative contexts.

The general public expects that ethnic groups exhibit behaviour in conformity with the mores of the society at large and that they do not dispute widely accepted norms.

In general, the media most accessible to ethnic minorities and migrants are alternative and ethnic media.

It is imperative that public policy establish conditions promoting the integration of ethnic minorities and migrants into the public sphere, supporting their presence in mainstream media, and encouraging awareness-raising projects to integrate the different ethnic groups into society.

Many key factors will impact the success of such efforts. But one paramount insight is that a positive image of ethnic minorities and migrants can only arise in the context of societal communication.

6.   Appendix

In the field of sociology or political science, there is no lack of empirical surveys on migrants and ethnic minorities in Austria. Yet, the data available (for example Weiss 2007; Ornig 2006) do not reveal much about the crucial factors of media and media use. There are a considerable number of qualitative surveys on migrants of various backgrounds, but no long-term studies on the relationship between migrants and the media in Austria.

Bonfadelli et al. compiled European research on the media use of ethnic minorities (Bonfadelli et al. 2007b, 143) and concluded that "the research situation in Europe is disparate and varies considerably in the different countries (…) Most of the studies identified and taken into account come from Northern, North-Western or Central European countries like the Netherlands (7), United Kingdom (5) and Germany (4) whereas only very little research from Southern Europe has been found" (Bonfadelli et al. 2007b, 149). In spite of the fact that 15% of the Austrian population are migrants, there is a significant research deficit here. As Trebbe pointed out (Trebbe 2007, 174-175), much needed research on the relationship between migrants and the media in Austria could be oriented to the following questions:

(1) Can different types of integration and/or assimilation with respect to their attitudes towards the German (or: the Austrian – P.H.) society be described and identified? (2) If so, how are these different patterns of integration related to the society of origin? (3) Is there any evidence for different media use patterns within these types of integration? (4) And, finally, can empirical evidence be provided for effects of integration/acculturation strategies on the use of German and Turkish (and other migrant-language – P.H.) media?

7. References

Aumüller, Jutta (2007): "Türkische Fernsehmedien in Deutschland." In: Bonfadelli, Heinz/Moser, Heinz, eds.: Medien und Migration. Europa als multikultureller Raum? Wiesbaden, pp. 21-42

Bauböck, Rainer/Baumgartner, Gerhard/Perchinig, Bernhard/Pintér, Karin, eds. (1988): ...Und Raus Bist Du! Ethnische Minderheiten in der Politik. Wien

Baumgartner, Gerhard/Müllner, Eva/Münz, Rainer, eds. (1989): Identität und Lebenswelt. Ethnische, religiöse und kulturelle Vielfalt im Burgenland. Eisenstadt

Baumgartner, Gerhard (1995): 6 x Österreich: Geschichte und aktuelle Situation der Volksgruppen. Klagenfurt

Baumgartner, Gerhard (2000): "Die Burgenländischen Sprachminderheiten 1945-1999." In: Widder, Roland, ed.: Burgenland - vom Grenzland im Osten zum Tor im Westen. Aus der Reihe "Geschichte der österreichischen Bundesländer seit 1945." Band 6/5. Wien, pp. 15-55.

Blomert, Reinhard/Kuzmics, Helmut/Treibel, Annette, eds. (1993): Transformationen des Wir-Gefühls. Studien zum nationalen Habitus. Frankfurt/Main

Bommes, Michael (2007): Integration – gesellschaftliches Risiko und politisches Symbol. Essay. Bonn: Bundeszentrale für politische Bildung 24/2007, pp. 3-5

Bonfadelli, Heinz/Moser, Heinz, eds. (2007): Medien und Migration. Europa als multikultureller Raum? Wiesbaden

Bonfadelli, Heinz (2007a): "Die Darstellung ethnischer Minderheiten in den Massenmedien." In: Bonfadelli, Heinz/Moser, Heinz, eds.: Medien und Migration. Europa als multikultureller Raum? Wiesbaden, pp. 95-116

Bonfadelli, Heinz/Bucher, Priska/Piga, Andrea (2007b): "Use of old and new media by ethnic minority youth in Europe with a special emphasis on Switzerland." In: Communications. The European Journal of Communication Research 32/2, pp. 141-170

Bourdieu, Pierre (1983): "Ökonomisches Kapital, kulturelles Kapital, soziales Kapital." In: Kreckel, Reinhard, ed.: Soziale Ungleichheiten. Göttingen, pp. 183-198

Bretschneider, Rudolf (2007): "Wir und die Anderen. Die Einstellung der Österreicher/innen zu Migration und Integration: Was die Meinungsforschung zeigt und was für Integration wichtig ist." In: Integration im Fokus (3), pp. 20-25

Busch, Brigitta/Peissl, Helmut (2003): "Sprachenvielfalt im Wohnzimmer. Sprachenpolitik und Medien." In: Busch, Brigitta/de Cillia, Rudolf, eds.: Sprachenpolitik in Österreich. Eine Bestandsaufnahme. Frankfurt/Main et.al., pp. 180-193

De Cillia, Rudolf (1995): "Deutsche Sprache und österreichische Identität." In: Medienimpulse. Beiträge zur Medienpädagogik. (4) Wien, pp. 4-13

Eriksen, Thomas H. (1993): Ethnicity and Nationalism. Anthropological Perspectives. London

Esser, Hartmut (2000): Soziologie. Spezielle Grundlagen. Band 2: Die Konstruktion der Gesellschaft. Frankfurt/New York

Fairclough, Norman (2001): Language and Power. Second Edition. Harlow et.al.

Farrokhzad, Schahrzad (2006): "Exotin, Unterdrückte und Fundamentalistin – Konstruktionen der 'fremden Frau' in deutschen Medien." In: Butterwegge, Christoph/Hentges, Gudrun, eds.: Massenmedien, Migration und Integration. 2. korrigierte & aktualisierte Aufl. Wiesbaden, pp. 55-86

Fassmann, Heinz (2006): "Der Integrationsbegriff: missverständlich und allgegenwärtig – eine Erläuterung." In: Oberlechner, Manfred, ed.: Die missglückte Integration? Wege und Irrwege in Europa. Wien, pp. 225-239

Fillitz, Thomas, ed. (2003): Interkulturelles Lernen. Zwischen institutionellem Rahmen, schulischer Praxis und gesellschaftlichem Kommunikationsprinzip. Innsbruck

Gächter, August (2000): "Migrationsforschung in Österreich. Das Beispiel der EU-Osterweiterung." In: SWS-Rundschau 40, pp. 163-191

Geißler, Rainer/Pöttker, Horst (2005): "Bilanz." In: Geißler, Rainer/Pöttker, Horst, eds.: Massenmedien und die Integration ethnischer Minderheiten in Deutschland. Problemaufriss. Forschungsstand. Bibliographie. Bielefeld, pp. 391-396

Geißler, Rainer/Pöttker, Horst (2006): "Mediale Integration von Migranten. Ein Problemaufriss." In: Geißler, Rainer/Pöttker, Horst, eds.: Integration durch Massenmedien. Mass Media-Integration. Medien und Migration im internationalen Vergleich. Media and Migration: A Comparative Perspective. Bielefeld, pp. 13-42

Hafez, Kai (2005): Mythos Globalisierung. Warum die Medien nicht grenzenlos sind. Wiesbaden

Hintermann, Christiane (2000): "Die 'neue' Zuwanderung nach Österreich – Eine Analyse der Entwicklungen seit Mitte der 80er Jahre." In: SWS-Rundschau 40, pp. 5-23

Joskowicz, Alexander (2002): "Austria OE." In: Racism and Cultural Diversity in the Mass Media. An overview of research and examples of good practice in the EU Member States 1995 - 2000 on behalf of the European Monitoring Centre on Racism and Xenophobia Vienna (EUMC). Wien, pp. 311-326

Matouschek, Bernd/Wodak, Ruth/Januschek, Franz (1995): Notwendige Maßnahmen gegen Fremde? Genese und Formen von rassistischen Diskursen der Differenz. Dt. Erstausgabe. Wien

Müller, Daniel (2005): "Die Darstellung ethnischer Minderheiten in deutschen Massenmedien." In: Geißler, Rainer/Pöttker, Horst, eds.: Massenmedien und die Integration ethnischer Minderheiten in Deutschland. Problemaufriss. Forschungsstand. Bibliographie. Bielefeld, pp. 83-127

Ornig, Nikola (2006): Die Zweite Generation und der Islam in Österreich. Eine Analyse von Chancen und Grenzen des Pluralismus von Religionen und Ethnien. Graz

Perchinig, Bernhard (1988): "Ethnizität, Minderheit, Assimilation: Einige kritische Anmerkungen." In: Bauböck, Rainer/Baumgartner, Gerhard/Perchinig, Bernhard/Pintér, Karin, eds. (1988): ...Und Raus Bist Du! Ethnische Minderheiten in der Politik. Wien, pp. 129-142

Piga, Andrea (2007): "Mediennutzung von Migranten: Ein Forschungsüberblick." In: Bonfadelli, Heinz/Moser, Heinz, eds.: Medien und Migration. Europa als multikultureller Raum? Wiesbaden, pp. 209-234

Pöttker, Horst (2000): "Kompensation von Komplexität. Journalismustheorie als Begründung journalistischer Qualitätsmaßstäbe." In: Löffelholz, Martin, ed.: Theorien des Journalismus. Ein diskursives Handbuch. 1. Aufl. Wiesbaden, pp. 374-390

Pöttker, Horst (2005): "Soziale Integration. Ein Schlüsselbegriff für die Forschung über Medien und ethnische Minderheiten." In: Geißler, Rainer/Pöttker, Horst, eds.: Massenmedien und die Integration ethnischer Minderheiten in Deutschland. Problemaufriss. Forschungsstand. Bibliographie. Bielefeld, pp. 25-45

Trebbe, Joachim (2007): "Types of Integration, Acculturation Strategies and Media Use of Young Turks in Germany." In: Communications. The European Journal of Communication Research 32(2), pp. 171-191

Treibel, Annette (1993): "Transformationen des Wir-Gefühls. Nationale und ethnische Zugehörigkeit in Deutschland" In: Blomert, Reinhard/Kuzmics, Helmut/Treibel, Annette, eds.: Transformationen des Wir-Gefühls. Studien zum nationalen Habitus. Frankfurt/Main, pp. 313-345

Weber, Max (1978): "Economy and Society." Günther Roth and Claus Wittich, eds., trans. Ephraim Fischoff. Vol. 2. Berkeley

Weiss, Hilde, ed. (2007): Leben in zwei Welten. Zur sozialen Integration ausländischer Jugendlicher der zweiten Generation. Wiesbaden

Weiss, Hilde (2000): "Alte und neue Minderheiten. Zum Einstellungswandel in Österreich (1984 – 1998)." In: SWS-Rundschau 40, pp. 25-42

Wögerer, Johanna (2004): Transkulturelle Zeitschriften in Österreich. Printmedien im Diskurs um Migration, Integration und die "multi-kulturelle Gesellschaft". Diplomarbeit. Wien

7.1   Websites

http://www.integrationsfonds.at
http://www.volksgruppen.at
http://1476.orf.at
http://o94.at/

Leen d'Haenens

Whither Cultural Diversity on the Dutch TV Screen?

In this paper, a country which has traditionally played a visible role in the development of multiculturalism in Western Europe will be examined as a discursive and policy exemplar. In accordance with the Media Act (1988), and notwithstanding important shifts in Dutch integration policy in the last three decades paralleled by an overall toughening of the social climate, cultural diversity continues to be given considerable encouragement on public radio and television, both in program provision and in staff composition. The Concession Act (2000), i.e. the first time that the public broadcaster's social and cultural role is laid down by law, encourages public broadcasting services to make more programs for ethnic minorities as target groups. In its task of serving as a model, the Netherlands Program Foundation (NPS) has to devote no less than 20 per cent of its television and 25 per cent of its radio broadcasting time to multicultural subjects. The Netherlands has focused on the public broadcasting system, which in itself is a "pillarized" model shared among about twenty organizations that have obtained a license because they each represent a certain ideological, political, religious, or demographic section of society.

After historically differentiating framing multicultural programming initiatives in the Netherlands, this paper will carefully examine the lessons and best practices that may emerge from the Dutch experience. What does research inform us about how media can best be utilized to sustain and encourage the co-existence and social cohesion of multiple constituency groups living in the Netherlands? Referring to content analysis on the degree of "colour" on Dutch television, in-depth interviews were conducted with program-makers. This research evidence will allow us to analyze the enabling mechanisms and strengths, as well as the obstacles and failures that have been experienced in an effort to build an integrated, cohesive, and transformative media system in which all members of society are recognized to having a right to both fair portrayal practices and employment opportunities.

1. Recent Shifts in The Dutch Integration Policy

Before going any further, we will point out a number of important shifts in emphasis in the Dutch integration policy. Undoubtedly, the events of September 11, 2001, the bombings in London and Madrid, and the more recent events in the Netherlands such as the assassination of Theo van Gogh in Amsterdam in 2004 have affected citizens' level of tolerance. The Dutch integration policy of the 1980s characterized by "freedom from obligation" and the multicultural ideal has made way for key words like "self-sufficiency" and "personal responsibility" in the 1990s. While in the 1980s immigrant groups were expected to promote cultural diversity by preserving their own identity within the current political values of the country (Castles & Miller, 1993), this changed drastically as of the mid-1990s when the emphasis shifted to integration and assimilation.

Immigrants were confronted with the *Newcomers Integration Act* (WIN) as of 1998, stating that each newcomer was obliged to participate in an integration program with Dutch language lessons, courses on social and employment-related familiarization and support, and a test on the degree of integration after one year. Until the end of 2003, the *Employment of Minorities Promotion Act* (SAMEN Act, 1998), which made it compulsory for firms that employed at least 35 people to maintain separate registration of multicultural staff, was one of the most important legal integration instruments. Both acts aimed at improving the position of the newcomers with education and employment measures, but the SAMEN Act (1998) also indirectly promoted the presence of more "colour" in the media and consequently had more impact on the immigrants' cultural rights.

As of March 15, 2006, the *Civic Integration Abroad Act* became law as a consequence of the Dutch Cabinet's Outline Agreement dated May 16, 2003, aiming at the following: "Any person who wishes to settle permanently in the Netherlands must actively take part in society, learn Dutch, be aware of Dutch values and abide by the rules". The Civic Integration Abroad Act is to be seen as a set of additional conditions to the Newcomers Integration Act that one should meet in order to obtain an authorization for temporary stay in the Netherlands, the major change being that newcomers must now have a basic knowledge of Dutch language and society even before coming to the Netherlands.

This gradual stiffening of the law demonstrates that the freedom from obligation of the integration policy during the early 1980s has made way for self-sufficiency and personal responsibility in the new millennium. As a central point in the integration policy the preservation of one's identity has now been replaced with assimilation. This means that adaptation and personal responsibility are considered more important to active citizenship than the preservation of one's own identity and culture. There is a growing emphasis on the independence and self-sufficiency of the individual. Government measures are aimed at equipping immigrants with the knowledge and skills that will promote their independence and self-sufficiency.

The Council for Social Development (2005, 2006) recently released two studies that aim at enhancing social cohesion. Its study *Unity, Diversity, and Ties* is a plea for a new integration model allowing a "culture of difference". The Council recognized the negative consequences of concentration (e.g., the so-called "white flight" of native Dutch fleeing away from the cities, and the "black schools" with high concentration levels of ethnic minority kids) on integration. Since a deconcentration policy would run up against legal, constitutional and practical objections (e.g., one cannot tell people where to live and where not to), the Council pleaded in favor of a new model, based upon unity which creates space for diversity, provided that new ties, along other lines than ethnic ones, be made. The primary issue was to create social cement and to promote the socio-cultural integration of minority groups. As a response to the Council's report the then-Minister for integration and immigration, Rita Verdonk, asked for more concrete definitions of "unity" and "binding" and wondered how to foster "spontaneous meetings and contacts among groups". She also asked the Council to operationalize further the notion of "common frame" and the definition of what belongs to it and what does not. Various examples of this binding policy along other lines than ethnic ones are given in the Council's study *No Longer with the Backs Towards Each Other. A Study about Binding.* The Cabinet's reaction to the Council's recommendations followed an and/and-approach of both geographical spreading, albeit on a voluntary basis, and building new forms of integration along other than ethnic lines. For this policy to be successful, the Cabinet built its new integration campaign around three recommendations of the Council: 1) Strengthening communication of basic democratic values and conduct in education and community work, e.g., by adding integration issues to the curriculum and giving youths the tools to defend themselves against radicalization; 2) Investing in the command of the Dutch language; 3) Fostering access to communal stories through the media, in theatre, and in literature. In this respect the notion of "binding leadership" was highly visible in the much criticized &-campaign [www.en.nl] of the hard-line Minister which amounted to €10 million. However, the political environment will presumably change with the new government.

In June 2006 the Dutch cabinet went through a major crisis, after its smallest coalition partner (D66) said it could no longer reconcile its visions with the country's hard-line immigration and integration minister Verdonk. This resulted in the resignation of the government. Early elections took place in November 2006. A new coalition government made up of the Christian Democrat Appeal (CDA), the Social Democratic Labour Party (PvdA) and the Christian Union came into power in February 2007. The future may well bring a more positive environment for migrants. This new government, which seems to want to return to the consensus politics of the Dutch polder model, has made the decision to halt the deportation of long-term asylum seekers in December 2006 and has initiated a more humane policy that will provide a general pardon for those asylum seekers who arrived in the Netherlands before April1, 2001 and who have made a request to stay.

After this general introduction and overall evaluation of the Dutch integration policy, as well as the societal model that lies underneath it, we will sketch the peculiar structure of the public broadcasting system which is considered apt to represent all social and ideological fractions in society. Parallel to this, the degree to which the Dutch media system succeeds in reflecting the diversity of its population in its media content and workforce will be assessed. This is an issue that has been and still is at the forefront of controversy and concern in the media industry.

By way of illustration, two research initiatives questioning the diversity of the media will be looked into. In an effort to improve the symbolic representation of the "majority" as well as of the "minority" in each other's eyes and to achieve greater social and cultural participation of ethnic minorities in the media, we will assess the way in which the Dutch portray, or omit to portray, symbolic diversity on television. Special emphasis will be put on the public broadcaster's contribution to fostering a more inclusive media portrayal. The first case deals with the responsibility assumed by a pluralist society consisting of both the commercial and public broadcasters to create fair portrayals of age, gender, and ethnicity. The second refers to in-depth interviews with producers of homemade fiction and their views on critical success factors enabling (or not) diverse television content.

2. The Dutch Broadcasting System: The Right Answer to Appeal to All Taste Cultures?

The Netherlands has not chosen a unitary national public broadcasting system (as in most other European countries). Nor does it have a commercial broadcasting model (as in the US or Luxembourg). Rather, it has come up with a prototype of its own, commonly characterized as a "pillarized" model. Neither market nor state-oriented, the Dutch model of broadcasting was developed by its civil society, i.e. social movements that were already well established in most domains of social life (Bardoel, 2001, 2003; Van der Haak & Van Snippenburg, 2001). The ideological foundation for this strategy is rooted in the Calvinist and Catholic social ideologies of "cultural sovereignty" and "subsidiarity": These movements aimed at uniting and emancipating their own social groups while at the same time isolating themselves from external "modernist" influences (i.e., the existing liberal-bourgeois elite and the emerging socialist Labour movement). Although unique, the Dutch system fits well into Hallin & Mancini's (2004) North/Central European or Democratic Corporatist Model in which consensus-seeking by coalition governments usually led to tolerant and moderate pluralism (Bardoel, 2006). Hence, originally this system, built around the notion of external pluralism, was not designed to confront citizens with diverging viewpoints at all, but on the contrary aimed at uniformity, at providing religious and ideological fractions in society with their own truth and their own window to the world in a structure of social segregation or social "apartheid" (Bardoel, 2006).

Over the years the Dutch public service expanded to eight full-license broadcasting companies: five classical networks (representing the Calvinists, the Catholics, the liberal-conservatives, and the liberal-protestants) dating back from the 1920s, while a broadcasting company aimed at a general audience, one evangelical, and one addressing youths became part of the system in 1966, 1971 and 1998 respectively. Netherlands Public Broadcasting (*Publieke Omroep*, NPB) is the new name for the former NOS that serves as the overarching umbrella organization for the national public broadcasting service: its main tasks are to coordinate and direct programming. Nowadays broadcasting time on Dutch public radio and television is shared by 23 private organizations, big broadcasting associations and small licensed broadcasters, that have obtained a broadcasting license because they (re)present a certain religious, social or spiritual fraction in society or have a specific programming task (i.e. NOS, NPS and the educational broadcasters).

Membership numbers as a criterion for the division of broadcast time and money were first introduced in the 1967 Broadcasting Act: a minimum of 150,000 paying members were required for obtaining a full license, with a program guide as the binding agent between the organizations and the members. These guides became instruments in a commercial struggle between the different broadcasting organizations. The former social and ideological ties were thus de facto transformed into a mainly consumer-oriented relationship (Van der Haak & Van Snippenburg, 2001). The Media Act (1988) and the Concession Act (2000) explicitly state that public broadcasting organizations themselves determine the form and content of their programs. Nevertheless, standards are set by imposing the production of a full range of programs comprising information, education, art, culture, and entertainment. For television, minimum percentages for these program categories are also stipulated: information and education (min. 35%); arts (min. 12.5%); culture, including arts (min. 25%); entertainment (max. 25%); European productions (min. 51%); Dutch or Frisian (50%); independent producers (25%); subtitling or hearing impaired (50%). That the public service continues to be an open and dynamic system allowing new organizations to join, is illustrated by MAX, focusing at senior citizens, and Llink, representing new social movements, which entered the public system in September 2005. Those organizations wishing to join the public system must show at least 50,000 signatures of members and demonstrate that they add something new to the existing range of programs, thus increasing the diversity of the public broadcasting service.

In light of this traditional concern for (re)presenting all social and ideological fractions in society, we ask ourselves to what extent provisions are made in order to (re)present the more recent multicultural aspect of society in the Dutch public broadcasters' supply.

3. What About Provisions for Cultural Diversity?

In accordance with the Concession Act[1] (2000), in recent years cultural diversity has been given considerable encouragement on radio and television. This cultural diversity is expressed in the program provision as well as in the composition of the staff behind the scenes. The Concession Act (2000) encourages public broadcasting organizations to make more programs for ethnic minorities as target groups. This is the first time that the social and cultural role of the public broadcasting service has been laid down by law. In its task of serving as a model, the Netherlands Program Foundation (NPS) has to devote no less than 20 per cent of its television broadcasting time and 25 per cent of its radio broadcasting time to multicultural subjects. The idea behind this is that ethnic minorities should no longer have to resort to satellite channels from their country of origin for a media menu that appeals to them, but that they are able to find something to suit their taste in the Dutch public broadcasters' supply. As far as media content is concerned, this has resulted, for example, in public broadcasting services developing a broader program supply aimed at ethnic minorities. The Memorandum "Media and Minorities Policy" of the then-State Secretary of Media and Culture, Van der Ploeg, presented in 1999 (Bink, 2006), paved the way for the minorities passage in the Concession Act. However, these stipulations had yet to convince the policy- and media producers at the public broadcasting corporation. To support this, the public broadcaster launched a bureau for representation and diversity "Meer van Anders" (*More of Something Else*) in 2002. That same year three other organizations involved with media in a culturally diverse society came into

---

1   The Concession Act is part of the Media Act and states that the public broadcasting foundation holds the concession to produce public radio and television programs from 2000 to 2010.

being: MTNL (multicultural television in the four largest cities), FunX (metropolitan, multicultural radio station for youths) and Mixed Media (intermediary for traineeships for immigrant journalists). It appeared that on a national level, projects were being initiated in radio, television, and the press leading to more ethnic groups recognizing themselves in the media.

Visions of broadcasting towards ethnic minorities have undergone major changes in the Netherlands. In the 1950s and 1960s programs were aimed at target groups with educational and informative content about the home country and in the 'own' language. *Paspoort* (Passport) was such a service program supplying news and information in an effort to foster successful integration. Until the 1980s these target audience programs predominated on radio and television. But after realizing that the integration issue was not all that successful, new journalistic programs were produced to onesidedly remedy this failure, by informing ethnic groups in Dutch about the Netherlands, while emphasizing at times their intrinsicalities and their "exoticisms" in comparison with Dutch society and the Dutch: *Meer op zondag* (More on Sunday) was an example. The 1990s, the decade of the emergence of commercial channels, introduced a smarter portrayal of ethnic minority groups on television, albeit as part of foreign (read US) programs. The NPS was set up in 1995 in order to provide more depth and quality, and get rid of the target audience television once and for all. As of the mid-1990s a crosscultural approach was adopted instead, and black actors and presenters became gradually more visible on the TV screen in programs such as *Comedy factory, Dunya and Desie, Bradaz, Urbania*, and children's programs with a multicultural angle[2]. Also in the informative field, different topics such as dating, sexuality, religion, cultural differences, relationships with partners of different origins were brought to the fore. After 9/11 and in the aftermath of the murders of Pim Fortuyn (2002) and Theo van Gogh (2004), the multicultural society's reality has become more grim, which resulted in NPS programs emphasizing the political side of the multicultural society, for instance in programs such as *De meiden van Halal* (The Halal Girls). In short, nowadays there seems to be more variety in the portraits of ethnic minorities shown on Dutch television. On the one hand there is the soft, unproblematic approach of *Urbania*, also adopted in the Europe-wide program *Cityfolk*, staging three city dwellers one of whom is of ethnic minority

---

2   Comedy factory is a TV show with Surinamese presenter Raymann staging national and international stand-up comedians; Dunya & Desie evolves around a Moroccan and a Dutch 15 year-old living in Amsterdam and discussing teenage problems; Bradaz is a comedy about two Surinamese brothers running a music shop; Urbania shows portraits of people living in the multicultural city of Amsterdam.

background. On the other hand in the problem-seeking *Premtime*, a Surinamese presenter looks for discrimination and stigmatization in Dutch society and by doing so, succeeds in portraying this society in a much less stereotypical fashion than it is the case in the regular current affairs programs such as NOVA/*Den Haag Vandaag* (NOVA/The Hague Today).

As far as the employment of ethnic minorities is concerned, in 1995 national and regional public broadcasters and the World Service signed a declaration of intent striving for equal participation by ethnic minorities in all functions and at all levels. This resulted in the "More Colour in the Media" project implemented by Mira Media, a non-profit organization lobbying for more inclusivity. Towards the end of this project, the Stimulating Labor Participation of Minorities Act (SAMEN Act) came into force as a successor to the Act promoting equal employment for immigrant groups, which, however, terminated in December 2003. Since 2002 the public broadcaster's Office for Diversity (formerly the Department of Portrayal), has worked on implementing the Concession Act for improving the visibility of ethnic employees within public broadcasting, both on and off screen. Several Mira Media projects are linked to this aim by acquiring information through immigrant opinion-leaders and their networks and approaching them (i.e., the online database "Perslink") and by training immigrants to become media professionals (i.e., "Multiple Choice").

Notwithstanding these initiatives and good intentions, two consecutive Monitors of Diversity (Sterk/Van Dijck, 2003; Koeman/Peeters/d'Haenens, 2007) showed that overall Dutch television (both public and commercial) is still far from providing a fair and pluralistic account of society. Furthermore, by way of a complementary qualitative professional insider's perspective on the matter, seven program makers were interviewed in-depth about their views on visualizing diversity. This research (Aarden, 2006), of which we are providing a secondary analysis, assesses both the obstacles and opportunities (e.g., media logic, casting, scenario) experienced by the program makers when working at the (re)presentation of constituent groups in society on the Dutch public broadcaster's fiction output.

4. Recent Research Evidence: Two Examples

As of the beginning of 2000, a need for statistics showing the state of affairs concerning questions of representation on Dutch television was felt. This empirical evidence was meant to persuade media professionals to improve their representation of the multicultural society in all its pluriformity and from multiple perspectives. A coding instrument was developed (see also Sterk,

2006) identifying all persons and characters visible on television and labelling them for various categories (gender, ethnicity, age group, and visible disability) as well as their function in the program (anchor, talk show host, leading character, etc.). Ethnicity was operationalized in terms of visibility (skin colour, hair, shape of the eyes, style of clothing, family name, and/or self-identification). Summarizing, the results revealed that the dominant group on Dutch television was white (70%), while 14 percent belonged to the group of ethnic others. At first sight, this result does not seem to be too bad, given the approximate 10 percent in demographics. Nevertheless, the 14 percent included "foreign" ethnic groups, the largest group being "African Americans", mainly appeared in bought US productions aired on Dutch commercial channels, in (pop) concerts or athletic events, and were not particularly representative of the Dutch multicultural fabric. In comparison: Just 2.4 percent of the people shown on public television and 1.1 percent on commercial television were of Surinamese or Antillean origin. People from North African descent were represented with a mere 0.2 percent.

4.1 The Diversity Monitor 2005

The second Monitor of Diversity (by Koeman, Peeters & d'Haenens, 2007) is a follow-up of the first and equally evolves around the extent to which and the way in which social reality is being constructed through the Dutch public broadcaster compared to its commercial counterparts. The Diversity Monitor 2005 analysed a total of nine Dutch television channels, among which were three public channels (*Nederland 1, 2 and 3*) and six commercial channels (*RTL4, RTL5, Yorin, SBS6, Net5* and *Veronica*). These were all the Dutch general interest channels at the time which together reached a market share of 89%. A constructed week has been examined: the seven days were spread over the period from Monday, February 28, up to and including Tuesday, April 5, 2005. This was done in order to reduce the risk of current events influencing the data. Only prime-time programs were included in the sample, which consisted of 104 hours of public-service programs and 124 hours of commercial program output[3]. The number of programs analysed amounted to 481 (i.e., 250 of the public channels and 231 of the commercial channels). These programs were predominantly non-fiction (71%). The commercial channels offer, relatively speaking, more fiction, especially because of the input of *RTL5* and *Net 5*.

---

3   These are net figures, i.e. exclusive of commercials, program announcements and parts of programs already begun.

Parallel to the former version of the Diversity Monitor, this content analysis also looked into the ways in which public service as well as commercial TV stations in the Netherlands assume their social responsibility towards a pluralist society. Research questions were: How "virtuously" are the broadcasters portraying social reality when it comes to the visualization of age, ethnicity and gender?; What TV channels are doing a lesser or better job, and in what program genres?

By means of a quantitative analysis the Diversity Monitor charted the (re)presentation of different groups, with particular focus on gender, age and ethnicity. As stated above, under the terms of the Concession Act of 2000, the Dutch public broadcasting system takes its responsibility very seriously: its mission is to address all groups of society and to (re)present them in the most balanced fashion possible. The policy with which this mission is to be carried out highlights the broadcaster's public responsibility and goes beyond mere conformity with program regulations and financial criteria (see Bardoel, d'Haenens & Peeters, 2005). Still, the question remains to what extent the audience-oriented programming policy of the public-service system is effectively more successful than the consumer-oriented approach of the commercial stations in reflecting the diversity of Dutch society. A further question then is: Does the public system not quite succeed in achieving its goals or do the commercial stations manage to do so even without those specific guidelines?

The results revealed a wide diversity of TV programs in the Netherlands, but diversity as such is no guarantee of a balanced (re)presentation of society at large. The fact is that public and commercial stations make a selection of the material they show their audiences, and this results in a kind of sub-optimal diversity. Moreover, audience groups too tend to make their own selections, so that the diversity on offer is effectively reduced even further. Hence, in light of the combined selection mechanisms of the broadcaster and the public, what the viewer eventually gets is at the most a mirror of his or her own group.

On first viewing the results of our research, neither public nor commercial television in the Netherlands appeared to be particularly representative of Dutch society. Women, children, senior citizens and ethnic minorities are, generally speaking, underrepresented. However, finding out if Dutch television or its public channels and commercial channels create a balanced image of different groups is less simple than it might appear to be. Things are fairly simple as far as the men/women ratio is concerned: Men have a clear majority, whoever the broadcaster and whatever the channel or genre, although Net5 is definitely non-chauvinist and Nederland 2 mainly puts men on screen (e.g. in sports programs). The distribution on the basis of ethnic origin shows the most marked distortion of reality. Eight out of ten persons on Dutch television is classified as "white", two out of ten as "non-white". In the latter category we find slightly more people of Mediterranean and Asiatic descent on public channels, whereas commercial channels have a slightly larger percentage of people with a darker skin ("blacks"). The reason for this difference is that commercial channels have a larger number of American films and series, in which African Americans are more numerous.

The Diversity Monitor therefore mainly traced the differences between the public and commercial channels at the level of the program genre. Women are underrepresented in sports items mainly, and in other programs they are presented as common citizens, cast in "softer" roles or invited to discuss social themes. The most balanced male/female ratio is found in children's programs and in entertainment and fiction. The age structure of the Dutch population is best reflected in children's programs, which are also more "colourful" than other genres. With respect to the representation of black people, fiction has an above-average score, but that is due to fiction programs from the US. Information and children's programs present an above-average number of people of Mediterranean origin. With respect to ethnicity in the various genres there are few differences between commercial and public channels: the information and educational programs of the public channels are the only ones that are slightly more colourful. An examination of the relation between ethnicity and the appearance of individuals produces a striking finding: More than half of the white people (55.7%) appearing on screen take the floor several times or regularly, while most non-white individuals (56.9%) are given only one chance to speak. Yet, migrants are not more explicitly presented as spokespersons for their 'own' group than individuals belonging to the native population. Just like other groups, the non-white group is strongest in subjects related to art, culture and entertainment (18.3%). Apart from these three subjects they are mainly associated with the multicultural society (11.7%) as well as terrorism and war (10.7%). The public-service channel in particular mainly highlights migrants in the context of the multicultural society and integration. The commercial channels, by contrast, present people of colour mainly in programs dealing with art, culture, and entertainment. In fiction programs the main activities of white as well as of non-white characters involve work or are distributed over work and home.

Thanks to the combination of our content analysis with continuous audience measurement figures of the programs under study, we were able to assess the demographic composition of the audience in terms of age and gender. A striking example: for non-fiction programs, the composition of the audience (i.e., percentage of women) correlates with the gender of the presenters (i.e., percentage of women in the presenters' team) as well as with the gender of the other actors figuring in the program (i.e., percentage of women in the items dealt with). When it comes to fiction programs, however, the amount of female viewers does not correlate significantly with the percentage of female actors. Additionally, young audiences show a tendency to watch young presenters and youngsters in non-fiction programs, which is clearly not the case for seniors. Moreover, while young people do not seem to watch seniors (neither in fiction nor in non-fiction), seniors do watch their own age group both in fiction and non-fiction. In general, seniors are relatively underrepresented in public television fiction programs and evidently in competition with numerous younger actors, except for a few striking examples in homemade fiction programs attracting a lot of viewers.

Above are a few indications illustrating that diversity in programming does not automatically lead towards diversity of audience groups. Television is therefore not a mirror of society (partly due to the viewer's choice). It may be true that Dutch viewers make a varied selection of programs and zap, for example, from news to entertainment and drama, but that does not mean that in doing so they come face to face with diverse social groups. If diversity on television is linked to a few ratings which are available, what we find is that the preference of the public is for programs with and about their own group: young people select (foreign) programs in which adolescents and young adults are the key figures, and they do not go for programs featuring over-50s. One more example: men tend to zap away from programs in which women are well represented. Nevertheless, public channels tend to be more "coloured" than their commercial counterparts, but we find this feature particularly in programs staging many other (white) persons or in programs attracting a relatively low number of viewers as well as in children's programs.

4.2   Interviewing the Program Makers: What Remedies Are There?

As both Monitors of Diversity were mere quantitative content analyses that revealed a difference between public and commercial channels, homemade and foreign productions, as well as among program genres, it was deemed interesting to look beyond the program as a mere result and pay particular attention to the production process of Dutch homemade fiction. Therefore, the aim was to look behind the scenes, asking program makers working for public and commercial broadcasters about the choices they tend to make when visualizing diversity on the television screen, as well as the rationales behind their casting decisions and story-line selections[4]. The following research questions were raised: Which factors are influencing the ways in which ethnic diversity is being visualized in the production of homemade fiction series? And in what way do these factors play a role in the production process[5]? Four kinds of fiction series were analysed. Seven program makers (either the scenario writer or the creative producer) of a soap series[6], a police series[7], a comedy series[8], and a children's series[9] were interviewed in-depth. Only two of them were working on a series aired on the commercial broadcaster. This illustrates the more prominent role the public broadcaster is playing in the production of homemade fiction in the Netherlands.

---

4   Such research was carried out by René Aarden for his Master's thesis in Communication Studies at Radboud University Nijmegen under the supervision of the author of this article.

5   This basic knowledge examined in the country of residence consists of two parts: knowledge of the Dutch language and of Dutch society. The former is tested with 50 questions examining sentence repetition, answering short questions, finding opposites, retelling stories. The latter is examined by means of 30 questions covering the 7 topics from the DVD 'Coming to the Netherlands' dealing with geography and living, history, polity, democracy and legislation, Dutch language, education and upbringing, health care, work and income. This DVD is part of the integration package that the individual eager to come to the Netherlands should purchase in order to prepare her- or himself for the integration examination, which takes place in the Dutch embassy or at the consulate-general in one's country or neighboring country. Costs amount to €350 to be paid to the Ministry of Foreign Affairs, prior to examination. The exam can be taken over and over again.

6   As soap operas, Goede tijden slechte tijden/Good Times Bad Times (RTL4) en Onderweg naar morgen/On the Way to Tomorrow (BNN, PSB) were selected. Good Times Bad Times is about relations and problems among and within families. The series lasts already for ten years. Underway to tomorrow started off as a hospital series, but changed its focus to the life of urban youth in their twenties.

7   Van Speijck (Talpa) and Spangen (TROS, PSB) were the police series under study. Van Speijk is about the (petty) crime-related ongoings in the Van Speijk street in Amsterdam. Spangen is a detective series in which murder cases are to be solved.

8   De band/The Band (VARA, PSB) and Kinderen geen bezwaar/Children no Objection (VARA, PSB) were the examples chosen for comedy series. The Band follows the lives of five members of a music band. Children no Objection is a sitcom casting a couple with two kids from a former marriage. He is a house husband and she is a psychiatrist. The boy is in love with the girl and does about everything to attract her attention.

9   Ik ben Willem/I am Willem (VPRO, PSB) was the only homemade children's program produced by the public broadcaster. I am Willem is based on a book, following an eight-year-old boy with divorced parents. Willem lives in Amsterdam with his mom and dad alternately.

Seven factors (Table 1) were found to impact on the reflection of ethnic diversity in television fiction: the program maker, the broadcaster, the genre, the media logic, the actors, the audience, and the subject dealt with.

The following paragraphs will look into each of these factors in more detail and expand on the accompanying rationales brought up by the makers interviewed. *Individual preferences and opinions* unmistakably tend to play a role in the portrayal of ethnic diversity (or the lack thereof). Sometimes the aesthetics of the showing of different cultures mark the decision. At times colour does not play a decisive factor in the decision-making process at all. Other factors do, such as the quality of an actor, which is considered more important at all times. Also the personal living context of the producer does have an impact on the series produced.

Success factors	Rationales
Personal experiences and preferences	1. Determining and emphasizing certain issues. 2. Own living conditions play a role in the writing of the scenario. 3. Own opinions of what is "good" when it comes to the showing of diversity.
Broadcasting organization	1. Contact with contact person/intermediary at the broadcasting organization. 2. Few conditions set out by the broadcasting organization when it comes to diversity.
Genre	1. Each genre has its own possibilities. 2. Each genre is in principle apt to show diversity.
Media logic	1. Too few crew members from ethnic minority background available. 2. Amount of time and money available is determining the possibilities to visualize ethnic diversity.
Audience	1. Connection seen between the colour of the series and the colour of the audience.
Actors	1. Disagreement about the influence of actors on the ethnic diversity of the series. 2. Disagreement about whether a character should be performed by a person of the same ethnicity.
Subject	1. Subject determines whether ethnic diversity is already self-evidently present in the story. If not, it is the task of the makers to make it so.

Table 1: Factors playing a role in the portrayal of ethnic minorities with accompanying rationales

The interviewees all recognize that their own world and the production world in which they evolve is predominantly white, and they all see this reality as a serious impediment for ethnically diverse scenarios (as in "The Band", written from the personal experience of the writer and with obvious implications for the script):

[…] I was born in 1960, and this whole issue of multiculturalism or multi-ethnic diversity did not play a role in my youth. And because "The Band" is inspired by my own youth and my own band time, the series is white. This would be different should it be about rappers, I would have probably thought about Moroccans and Moroccan bands, but I'm simply too old for this.

A second factor of importance is the *broadcasting organization* airing the production. Usually one single contact person is playing the intermediary role between the production team and the broadcaster who commissioned the production. The contact varies between once and several times a week to discuss story lines and role attributions. The producers acknowledge that to maintain their creative freedom, and ethnic diversity rarely seems to be an issue in the discussions: when brought up, it is never a goal in itself. In two instances the broadcasting organizations have put their stamp on the subject of the series. For example, "On the Way to Tomorrow" moved from the commercial broadcaster Yorin to BNN, a public broadcasting organization aimed at youngsters. This move resulted in doing away with some older characters and introducing some younger ones. Moreover, instead of a hospital set-up in its former version, the emphasis is put on life in the big city, which automatically brings along more ethnic diversity. The second case is "Children No Objection": the broadcaster explicitly asked the producer to make a product that caters to an audience similar to that of the previous program. However, this request did not have an impact on the degree of ethnic diversity in the series. The difference between commercial and public broadcasters is also pointed at: The former will only look at the interest of the advertisers and therefore consider the opportunities offered by programs and series to attract an audience as large as possible. Since ethnic minority groups are not yet seen as an interesting group by commercial broadcasters, their interest in catering programs for this group is still relatively low. As the public broadcaster is publicly financed and every tax payer should find his or her taste in its supply, it seems to be gradually more aware of its public role in diversifying its programs.

According to the informants each of the four fiction *genres* under study offer possibilities of their own in terms of portraying ethnic diversity. Multiculturalism can offer a prolific soil for misunderstandings and hilarious situations. Nevertheless, opinions are diverging here: while one informant sees difficulties in connecting multiculturalism with humour, another believes humour offers an excellent platform to keep away from the heavily loaded stereotypical images and portrayals as experienced in the news and current affairs formats. Soaps are seen as an excellent genre to show diversity because it is storytelling about the real issues of life. Soaps rely furthermore on a large cast, almost organically allowing the introduction of actors from a different ethnic origin. The producer of "Good Times Bad Times" first and foremost considers the series as fictitious, in contrast with real life and a meticulous representation of it. The maker of "On the Way to Tomorrow" on the contrary stages characters in the series that viewers identify themselves with.

A fourth factor that may somewhat colour a television program is its *production team, the crew*. This statement was at first qualified as nonsense by all our informants. When thinking about it further, the informants could imagine the potential impact of a culturally mixed crew on the content, whether or not this is relevant for the series' subject. All informants agree on the fact that too few people from another ethnic background are part of the profession. This seems to be changing currently but in this very moment it is still felt as problematic. Moreover, as the funds are shrinking, this is a rather bad period for hiring. Hence, the media logic or, in other words, the amount of time and money spent on a production, does play a major role on the ways in which diversity is visualized or not.

The informants aim at catering to a large *audience*, which has its implications for the degree of prominence of ethnicity in the program. They all see a connection between the representation of a certain minority group and their viewing of the program. The maker of "Van Speijck" refers to reactions of Turkish viewers to the portrayal of Turks in the program. Also the Internet site of "On the Way to Tomorrow" makes it possible to maintain active contact with the BNN members and thus with the viewers of the series. This allows the producers to consult their audience and make (colour) adjustments in the series if needed, on the basis of appreciation given in relation to certain characters and issues dealt with.

In contrast with the problematic hiring of crew members of colour, the scouting of *actors* with an ethnic minority background is experienced as a lot easier. There are enough good actors with an ethnic minority background, so it seems. The answer to the question whether actors have a true impact on the way in which ethnic diversity is visualized in the series varies. The maker of "Children No Objection" believes that actors do not impact on the portrayal of ethnic diversity. "They play a role that is written in the script, and in principle nothing is changed to it." The other informants do believe the actors have an impact on their role as they serve as some sort of sounding board against which the makers can check their story lines. Actors also happen to co-decide about issues that are acceptable or not according to their culture. Of course each actor brings in a personal style, a personality, which determines the way the character looks.

Finally the *subject* of a series can exert some influence in that diversity is not always self-evident. In "I am Willem" a white little boy is being followed; in "Children No Objection" a white mother and father with white kids are presented, and the series "The band" is about five white band members. Only in the first series the makers have tried to bring in some secondary characters of colour. In the other two nothing of the like has happened. In the other series, the subject lent itself better to ethnic diversity: "On the Way to Tomorrow" is about youngsters in a big city and "Van Speijk" evolves in and around a multicultural area in Amsterdam. In "Good Times Bad Times" multiculturalism is brought up in the context of (extended) family lines.

> Because life in Amsterdam is like that. That is why we have introduced Hicham, a Moroccan boy who is very popular and cute but also behaving very badly... ("On the Way to Tomorrow")

> Amsterdam West, where the series evolves, is a Turkish bulwark, that is why we casted a Turk, but also in real life the police force has tried to hire a lot of allochtones in order to work well in these areas. ("Van Speijck")

Overall, the in-depth interviews made it clear that the program makers are at all times conscious about the impact multiculturalism and ethnic diversity may have when chosen as topics in TV content. In their daily work they tend to reflect a great deal about the social responsibility issue. They also pointed out that the societal climate plays a central role in their decision-making about visualizations of multiculturalism and ethnic diversity. But ideas are diverging: the producer of "Good Times Bad Times" thinks he is above all making a fiction program and therefore he believes it is up to the viewer to decide whether to go along with the story or not. The maker of "On the Way to Tomorrow" does find herself fulfilling a social responsibility. The danger of political correctness was brought up several times in the interviews, but it remained unclear what political correctness precisely is and consequently, what a realistic account of society is or should be. In fact, it is seen as the potential death of diversity. Visualizing ethnicity is considered clearly as a conflict variable in the production of fiction, given that it is socially loaded.

5. Conclusion

Overall, the in-depth interviews made it clear that the program makers are at all times conscious about the impact multiculturalism and ethnic diversity may have when chosen as topics in TV content. In their daily work they tend to reflect a great deal about the social responsibility issue. They also pointed out that the societal climate plays a central role in their decision-making about visualizations of multiculturalism and ethnic diversity. But ideas are diverging: the producer of "Good Times Bad Times" thinks he is above all making a fiction program and therefore he believes it is up to the viewer to decide whether to go along with the story or not. The maker of "On the Way to Tomorrow" does find herself fulfilling a social responsibility. The danger of political correctness was brought up several times in the interviews, but it remained unclear what political correctness precisely is and consequently, what a realistic account of society is or should be. In fact, it is seen as the potential death of diversity. Visualizing ethnicity is considered clearly as a conflict variable in the production of fiction given that it is socially loaded.

As a result of our diversity monitor 2005, the Dutch public broadcaster has recently decided (at the end of 2006) to prescribe guidelines for the amount of multicultural subjects that should be portrayed and quotas for the number of guests with an ethnic minority background who should be staged in which programs. Moreover, the public broadcaster also intends to spend 2 more million euros in order to continuously measure the viewing behaviour of ethnic minority groups. These measures clearly illustrate the firm intention to formulate clear-cut guidelines and to keep away from the former attitude characterized by a great extent of freedom from obligation. In addition to these important and perhaps temporary quantitative measures, an approach in which diversity is seen as an integral part of program quality management seems to be a fruitful way of looking at the matter. This entails taking into account staffing strategies, improving intercultural competences of the current staff, fostering ongoing communication with diverse audience groups, as well as polishing the overall image of the broadcasting organization. However, a smooth implementation of all this requires a bearing among the staff: in other words, the staff should share the same vision.

6.   References

Aarden, R. (2006): 'Hoe meer kleur hoe beter, maar het moet wel passen'. Een kwalitatief onderzoek naar de constructie van etnische diversiteit in Nederlandse fictieseries en de beoordeling hiervan door jongeren ['The more colour the better, provided it fits'. A qualitative research on the construction of ethnic diversity in Dutch fiction series and perceptions of it by youngsters]. Nijmegen: Radboud University Nijmegen, Department of Communication (Unpublished M.D. thesis)

Bardoel, J. (2001): "Open media, open society. Rise and fall of the Dutch broadcast model: A case study." In: Zassoursky, Y./Vartanova, E. eds.: Media for the Open Society. Moscow, pp. 98-121

Bardoel, J. (2003): "Back to the public. Assessing public broadcasting in the Netherlands", In: Javnost/The Public 10 (3), pp. 81-96

Bink, S. (2006): Nearly 25 years of media and minorities policy in the Netherlands. (Available online at http://www.equalisnotenough.org/followup/papers/SusanBink.pdf; accessed on December 28, 2006)

Castles, S./Miller, M. J. (1993): The Age of Migration. International Population Movements in the Modern World. Basingstoke

Hallin, D.C./Mancini, P. (2004): Comparing Media Systems. Three Models of Media and Politics. Cambridge

Koeman, J./Peeters, A./d'Haenens, L. (2007): "Diversity Monitor 2005. Diversity as a quality aspect of television in the Netherlands." In: Communications. The European Journal of Communication Research 32(1), pp. 97-121

RMO (Council for Social Development) (2006): "Niet langer met de ruggen naar elkaar. Een advies over binden." Advice 37 [No Longer with the Backs Towards Each Other. A Study About Binding]. The Hague. (Available online at http://www.adviesorgaan-rmo.nl/downloads/advies/RMO%20advies%2037%20compl.pdf; accessed on December 27, 2006

RMO (Council for Social Development) (2005): "Eenheid, verscheidenheid en binding. Over concentratie en integratie van minderheden in Nederland" [Unity, Diversity, and Ties. About Concentration and Integration of Minorities in the Netherlands]. Advice 35. The Hague (Available online at http://www.adviesorgaan-rmo.nl/?s=9; accessed on December 27, 2006)

Sterk, G. (2006): "Visible representation and the paradox of symbolic diversity." In: d'Haenens, L./Hooghe, M./Vanheule, D./Gezduci, H. eds.: 'New' Citizens, New Policies? Developments in Diversity Policy in Canada and Flanders. Gent, pp. 159-170

Sterk, G./Van Dijck, B. (2003): Monitor Diversiteit 2002 [Monitor Diversity 2002]. Utrecht

Van der Haak, K./Van Snippenburg, L. (2001): "The Netherlands." In: d'Haenens, L./Saeys, F. eds.: Western Broadcasting at the Dawn of the 21st Century. Berlin, pp. 209-235

Souley Hassane

Mainstream Media vs. Ethnic Minority Media: Integration in Crisis

1. Introduction

For all segments of French society, the media are at the center of political, economic and cultural concerns. They are cultivated by politicians in their quest for power, while companies pursue them as a means of making money. The force of such pursuit is hardly surprising and is readily apparent in the concentration of the media in the hands of manufacturers and arms dealers. The collusion between politics and business is a major characteristic of our era. In France, any control over the media exercised by politicians and businessmen has always been under scrutiny; however, the last presidential election (2007) did reveal a mutual corruption of sorts in the relations between the current president and some owners of French media. The Berlusconi media in Italy indicate a similar conflation. The business world is increasingly interested in the media because they provide opportunities to amass money and power, make and remake opinions with one sweep. Magnates enhance their existing economic power with the power to produce, diffuse or censor a program, an opinion or some information according to the principle of supply and demand.

Eighty-five percent of the Socpresse Group, with its concentration on the written press, belongs to Serge Dassault, the famous manufacturer of cannons. Socpresse includes *Le Figaro, L'Express, L'Expansion*, etc. Hachette Filipacchi Médias has belonged to Lagardère since 2004. Worth 2.1 billion euros, he is the owner of, for example, *Télé 7 jours, Paris Match, Elle, Nice-Matin, Choc, Public*, and *La Provence*. In sum, Lagardère owns 200 press groups all over the world. The group Ouest-France is worth 953 million euros. *Le Monde*, the fourth major press syndicate, was worth 639 million euros in 2004 and controls *Télérama, La Vie, Courier International, Le Monde des religions, Le Monde de l'Education, Midi Libre, Les cahiers du Cinéma*. The Amaury group, with 25% owned by Lagardère, consists of *Le Parisien* and *L'Equipe*. The Hersant family runs the France Antilles group, owner of the free *Paru Vendu*, published in 240 editions. France Antilles is estimated to be worth 618 million euros. Prisma Presse, held by the German Bertelsmann corporation, controls *Prima*, and *Femme Actuelle* at a total of 567 million euros. Finally, Emap France, which publishes 28 titles, controls *Télé-Poche, Téléstar, Biba, Max*, and *Science et Vie*, among others, at a total of 437 million euros. Bouygues, the king of concrete and employer of millions of workers of African descent, also controls Channel *TF1*. Vincent Bolloré exploits transportation networks in Africa and is a vendor of cocoa, coffee, rubber, palm oil and wood. The activities of his 70 companies in Africa are the source of his wealth. A friend of president Sarkozy, he has invested 10% of his assets in various mass media.[1] The mainstream media, then, are a sphere involving huge amounts of capital and occupy a central position in the world of business (Observatoire français des media 2005, p. 95-96).

In the face of such an audiovisual landscape controlled exclusively by large-scale corporations, the media of the minorities, more often referred to as "community media" (or as the media of ethnic minorities), have been active since 2000. These are media created by French people of foreign origin, not to be confused with foreign media in France. Today, there are hundreds of such magazines, FM radio stations, Internet radio stations, and Internet television stations in France. Compared to the mainstream media, their capital, which varies from 400 to 4000 euros, is practically negligible. The owners are individuals, groups, associations or small publishing houses. Even so, they are far from inefficient. They make information in reaction to the monologue or monopoly of the dominant forms of information and, in particular, to contest their own negative representation in the mainstream media. Minority media are the consequence of a rejection of information from a direction that makes French people of foreign origin the anti-heroes of the 'news-in-brief' columns, of violence, or of fundamentalism. Such mainstream media reports are often

---

1   Compare Daniel Sauveget: „Vincent Bolloré: l'ex-roi du papier à cigarettes, nouvel empereur des médias?", November 17, 2004. One can read here: „1. Audiovisual production and provisions since the privatization of SFP (2001), acquisition made with Euromédia: Bolloré holds 30% of the SFP, Euromédia 70% – but Bolloré possessses 24% of Euromédia. The group Euromédia Télévison (EMT) have the studios of Saint-Denis and of Arpajon, and run the previous studios of the Victorine in Nice. SFP has its studios Bry sur Marne, Saint Ouen, and Boulogne-Billancourt as well as its power of reporting and filming. 2. VCF (Video Communication de France), resold in 2003: technical provisions. 3. Streampower: video and Internet. 4. A movie theater in Paris, the Mac Mahon. 5. Direct 8, digital television station currently being created, approved by the CSA within the grouping of free digital channels (director: Philippe Labro), and specializing in direct broadcast, as its name implies. 6. RNT, (la Radio des Nouveaux Talents), AM radio and Internet created in 2004. 7. 10% of Gaumont, TV and cinema production, distribution and exploitation. 8. A small percentage of RCS Media, in Italy – but Bolloré also holds shares in the bank Mediobanca which plays an important role in the reorganization of the press section of Rizzoli-Corriere della Sera. 9. More than 22% (end of October) of Havas, an advertising group detached from Vivendi after the fusion of the no longer existing group Havas with Vivendi."

told with disregard for these people, their culture, and especially, for their status as full-fledged French citizens.

Internet media have encouraged thousands of people to engage in reading texts on the Web, and are a genuine democratic revolution in terms of letting French people of foreign origin speak their minds. Never before was there production on such a scale related to minority society and their connection with the media. The influx of factors related to ideological confrontation on the network is also without precedent with regards to their number, insistence and presence. Minorities use the Internet as an identity establishing network to be able to hold their position against the fortresses of the mainstream media. The more heated the debates are, the greater is the interactivity of the agents. This interactivity continues to be fed by the ever-increasing alternation of statements and actions on the parts of politicians and the dominant press. The events of 9/11 facilitated a renunciation of the French republic's former taboos involving a torrent of essentialist criticisms of Arabs and Muslims in the dominant press. Six years later, the left and right have met halfway on this point. The anti-religious tradition of the left has converged with the anti-Arab passion of the right. French society has not managed to put this behind itself; on the contrary, a competitiveness of sorts can be noticed in this domain. From 2001 to the present, there have constantly been confrontations between the dominant and minority media related to discrimination, racism and xenophobia, all revived by a "Le Pen-ization" of popular opinion.

A public, political and democratic move to the right has been a major part of Nicolas Sarkozy's agenda in his climb to power. The spirit of the right, now allegedly freed from its complexes, has revived traumas, anxieties and fears in the hearts of French people of foreign origin. Hence, an analysis of the minority press is the key to understanding the ever-widening schism not only between the two types of media, but between their respective target groups as well.

2. From the French audiovisual landscape to that of the minority media

The minority media landscape in France is dominated by two main components: African/Caribbean media and Arab/Muslim media. This corresponds to the two main groups of French people of foreign origin, who are, respectively, the principal target groups. These media include approximately a hundred magazines, journals and Internet sites of African origin, and thirty of Arabic origin. The specific feature of these media is their focus on a group for which they homogenize cultural references, harmonize a specific vision of the world, and in particular, facilitate the group's presence in the media. Ethnic media transform readers, listeners and spectators into components of the media, into active sources of information, and most importantly, into constant recipients. The work of constructing a community readership and audience in a minority situation depends on the ability of the initiators to combine various ideological components of interest to the group. As a consequence, community, culture, religion and politics all mix in editorial policy making. In other words, a single magazine allocates space to the religious, political and ideological sensibilities of the community. This defining principle is similar to a large net which captures the diverse interests of a maximum number of people. A minority medium which addressed itself only to the "Shiites of the community", or the "Tunisians of Marseille", to the "natives of Djerba in Ile-de-France", or the "Nigerians of Bordeaux", the "Guyanan people of Lille" etc. would take as its starting point only a very restricted perspective. Thus, the need to interest a number of people as large as possible leads the minority media to deal with subjects that the mainstream media do not cover, and to give voice to people boycotted by the major public media.

The Internet revolution has given a preponderant role to the media in the lives of its users. A site such as *Oumma.com* is a point of reference for the French and francophone 'Muslim community'. When Tariq Ramadan, the Swiss specialist on Islam, was banned from the mass media in France, *Oumma.com* gave him coverage. *Beur FM, Radio Orient de Paris* and *Radio Gazelle* did the same with others ignored by the mainstream media. At this point, the question arises as to how the mainstream media's opposition to the minority media is constructed. Which interests govern the mediatization of 'Arabs' and 'blacks' in France? In what way is this media coverage connected with the integration crisis involving these populations in France? How can the media landscape of minority media best be characterized? Can these media be automatically associated with communities residing in France? Is there a systematic oppositional relationship between these new media and the mainstream media? How far does the relationship between the two call integration (insofar as this means that the various parts of French society function better together) into question, especially for those whose familial origins lie beyond the borders?

The representations of social groups often correspond to existing social configurations and correlate exactly to structures of established forms of domination. These are aggravated in France by its colonial history with an ideology based on racial hierarchy. This heritage intensifies the power of stereotypes on French populations from the former colonies and their descendents.

3.   Contradictory paradigms and functions

A major problem related to the dominant media in France has to do not only with their method of producing information, but also with their culture of class and of complicity. These two aspects significantly attribute a fixed role in the media to each component of society. More precisely, there is a specific way of speaking of Arabs and blacks on the radio, on television and in the press. Any "normal" treatment is therefore practically impossible because of the petrified image of the "Other" and the underlying ideology.

The leader of a Parisian group in an impoverished neighborhood stated in front of journalists and researchers: "Whenever I watch television, I look to see in which distorting light we will be shown this time, to see how they will treat the information on the poor areas, our neighborhoods and the people that live in them." This statement demonstrates the discontent with how these populations and neighborhoods are treated as topics of information. Many people from these areas recall one or more broadcasts in which Arabs and blacks were shown in a negative light, confined to specific, predefined roles by the newsmaker journalists. Apparently, a class culture maintains in which the mainstream media produce information which is advantageous to the dominant group.

Information disseminated in *Le Figaro, l'Express* or *Le Point* typically depicts Arabs as "suspicious, violent, terrorist and macho", while blacks are often portrayed as "illegal aliens", as dancers, or as being athletic and corrupted by economic misery. Such reductionism leads to the stigmatization of individuals. The prevailing atmosphere associated with these people reveals a sense of anxiety. The media speak of "youth", of "the neighborhoods", the "susceptible areas", "the dwellers of troubled areas", of "bands", of "young Muslims" of "fanatics" and of "fundamentalists". In other words, the context is one of problems for the dominant society. There is even more cause for concern, as these people are spoken of as bodies foreign to the society at large.

Whenever the media relates negative news events, it is responsive to these paradigms of production and uses them for its aims. The wording and staging of news events is not only a technical procedure, but is also always ideologically and politically oriented. Composing information clearly consists in examining and disseminating locations, in attributing values and significance, and in sending messages. None of these operations is neutral; they are profoundly ideological and, indeed, prone to being ideologized. When Nicolas Sarkozy speaks of "scum" and of "karcher" (highly pressurized water pistols), such vocabulary promotes the sale of newspapers. The media's perpetual quest for show and sensation zeroes in on the political spectacle of the candidate. Media communication has become an irreplaceable political tool in a country in the midst of a permanent election campaign. The use of such words in the public sphere reveals a 'special' treatment for the populations of poor areas.

Since 2001, French society has undergone a systematic and progressive loosening of the limits of acceptable verbal expression. Essentialist and stigmatizing ways of thinking are manifested and relayed by the media. The words of media intellectuals converge with those of politicians, and, as a result, xenophobia and racism become the norm in their discourse. Which symptomatic themes of the confrontations between mainstream and minority media reflect socio-economic, political or cultural problems? How and why do these confrontations occur? What are the effects of this confrontation on integration *à la française*, or even on respect for human rights and living together?

In order to answer these questions, I will examine two important French Internet sites: *Afrikara.com* and *Oumma.com*. The first was created by a group of African/Caribbean journalists to defend the black community in France. *Oumma.com* is a communal Islamic site created in 1999 and dedicated to an "Islam of freedom". *Oumma.com* and *Afrikara.com* are both francophone encounter sites run by people who wish to make their mark towards a humanistic France. *Oumma.com* registers approximately 65 million visits per month. *Afrikara* is one of the best-regarded sites of the African community in France because of the direct, compelling language it employs when addressing subjects related to Africa and to the black diasporas of France, the Caribbean, and the Americas. Cases of discrimination are presented in full detail, the stakes and possible outcomes involved well explained. The same degree of commitment is present at *Oumma.com*, which answers to attacks against Islam and the Muslims of France. The events of 9/11 were a turning point for this community site, which responds daily to articles, reports and statements made by media intellectuals, politicians or journalists. Support for the Palestinian cause is one of its main focuses, just as support for Africa is one of the main focuses of *Afrikara*. These commitments influence the treatment and follow-up of information. Journalists who contribute to these sites are obliged to scrutinize as much information disseminated by the dominant media as possible – a fastidious task whose practical completion is supported by their long-term vision. Their reactions are sometimes immediate, almost instantaneous. This is a journalism charged by urgency, far removed from the comforts of mainstream media. Both sites insist on justice and equality in the treatment of information on French populations of foreign origin.

3.1 *Oumma.com* and the specter of 9/11

The events of September 11, 2001 constituted the framework of a new relationship between the media and Islam, and dealing with the topic of Islam in media production became increasingly questionable. Before this dramatic incident, French media coverage of Islam focused on Algeria, and its Islamists and military. The French media took part in an occidental trend of misinformation and over-information, setting a very questionable backdrop for ensuing debates. The media coverage was disastrous for the image of Muslims and Arabs in the world. Within a period of two years, the press wrongly established a link between Islam and violence, terrorism and war. The French press engaged in a form of symbolic warfare through reports, forums, articles, and interviews with specialists, etc. The question I will address here concerns how and why dealing with such topics generally proceeds in much the same way and with the use of the same terms.

This is the context in which *Oumma.com* was obliged to take a stand against attacks on Muslims; thus, the articles from this site should be read with this context in mind. After 9/11, certain journalists of the dominant media published articles employing especially violent language which ran contrary to the established notions of professional standards. *Oumma.com* had to then simultaneously condemn the attacks, and to unswervingly refute the link between Islam and terrorism and the allegation that Muslims are loyal to the cause and instigators of these attacks. Furthermore, it was necessary to answer to a French press which, on the one hand, sympathized with the suffering of the Americans, and on the other, allowed itself to oversimplify matters, confuse various issues, and disseminate stereotypes and even lies. Many important figures of French journalism, politics and media urged caution against these anti-Arab and anti-Muslim statements.

Yet, within two years, this atmosphere made a strange way of being racist and of affirming and proclaiming racism publicly acceptable. From this point on, populations of foreign origin began to feel that a lamentable era was on the rise, insofar as it progressively did away with the achievements of the French model of integration. The aims of certain politicians fell on fertile ground here. French Arabs, Muslims and Africans who were in no way linked to terrorism made the front pages of *Libération, Figaro, Le Point, L'Express* and *Le Monde*. Media workers engaged in making events out of non-events. This created and continues to create the impression that the media are focused on some sort of local, regional and national symbolic geopolitics.

The law passed on 15 March 2004 regulating women's use of the veil marks the culmination of this atmosphere, in which all political colors fuse into one. The media presentation of the veil issue is uniformly negative, and many title pages of magazines indicated profound ideological problems. The reaction of *Oumma.com* corresponded precisely to the avalanche of articles from the dominant press.[2] There was much direct confrontation on both sides. This is a continuous, direct and massive confrontation, in which the implication of politicians, media, intellectuals and experts has given rise to especially lengthy media coverage and deepened the schism between the identities of French people of the Muslim faith and those of the "others".

Apart from the question of the necessity of such a law, this political and media consensus should be examined in its own right. I find the apparent unanimity on this issue troubling because the motivations of the various groups are not one and the same. The convergence between racists and anti-Arabs of the extreme right and Republican secularists is alarming and shows that French society is taking a dangerous turn in terms of its views of minorities. The disastrous media coverage of 9/11 has made this all possible. Furthermore, sensationalism is becoming ever more salient in news reporting. Xenophobic phraseology is used to stage the news and make events "worthy" of media coverage.

3.2   Phraseology in the media

On October 24, 2004, the director of the magazine *Le Point* openly declared on Channel LCI: "I am slightly Islamophobic. I'm not embarrassed to admit it. [...] I have the right, I think (and I am not alone in this country), to say that Islam, (and I specify Islam, I'm not even speaking of Islamists) as a religion has about it a certain irrationality [...] which does in fact make me Islamophobic [...] There is no reason, under the pretext of tolerance, to lower oneself to the

---

2   Yahya Michot, "Le voile jaune", November 3, 2003; Eric Vandorpe, "Suspension d'un an sans salaire pour une fonctionnaire voile!", November 18, 2003; Felwine Sarr, "Le port du voile: un rapport à sa propre corporalité", December 18, 2003; Francis Moury, "La question du voile dans l'Islam et le monde moderne", December 29, 2003; Liliane Bénard, "Des valeurs universelles et du voile...", September 22, 2003; Noureddine Aoussat, "Affaire du voile: Le Cheikh Tantaoui d'Al-Azhar désavoué par les autres savants de cette institution", January 1, 2004; Eric Vandorpe, "Retour sur le rapport Stasi et ses dérives islamophobes", January 18, 2004; Zine El Abiddine Omar, "La symbolique du combat de la République contre le foulard", January 31, 2004; Asma Lamrabet, "Au-delà du voile...", February 2, 2004; Françoise Lorcerie, "L'affaire du voile sous le projecteur de la science politique: une analyse renouvelée de l'affaire en France et de son écho à l'étranger", July 5, 2005; Pierre Tévanian, "L'affaire du voile, deux ans après: un consensus lourd de conséquences", March 15, 2006 (All these articles come from Oumma.com).

point of denying one's own deep convictions." This statement provoked intense indignation on the part of the Muslim communities in France. *Oumma.com*, also target of this affront, responded in this way: "This injurious statement is unacceptable from the mouth of the founder and editor of an important French weekly, who displays, proclaims and justifies his visceral racism against Muslims. This is all the more unacceptable in that it is participating in a frightening and intolerable banalization of Islamophobia, whose backdrop is the hatred of Arab-Muslim populations." Claude Imbert was the next person to inaugurate a series of Islamophobic or Arabophobic phrases and expressions, engaging in behavior which, up to this point, had been exclusively reserved for the extreme right. Such phrases have been extremely successful in the media sphere, sparking audience interest while leaving the collective conscience cold. They are not uttered involuntarily; on the contrary, their authors are well aware of their media impact.

Fath Allah Mezianne says (Mezziane 2003), "Mr. Imbert is unconcerned with the possibility of sanctions, reprobation or condemnation. His Islamophobia is respectable, coming, as it does from on high. He is opposed to the vulgar and impolite racism of the French low-culture bistros."

The counterattacks of *Oumma.com* are, in every case, without concession. Its journalists read and re-read the editorials of Claude Imbert in which he congratulated the Italien pamphleteer Oriana Fallaci. *Le Point* published a dozen pages of these scathing articles. It was the thing of the moment. In a 10-page spread, *Le Point* represented her as "the woman who said no to Islam" (Le Point, May 24, 2002). *Oumma.com* published protests of the MRAP and of the Muslim Youth of France. The editors share the viewpoint of their readers and religious colleagues.

The same effect is produced when Alain Finkelkraut explains "the ethno-religious causes of the riots in the depressed suburbs" in the Israeli journal *Haaretz*, when Hélène Carrère D'Encausse identifies their cause in polygamy, and when Georges Frêche, president of the Regional Council of Languedoc-Roussillon speaks of the Harkis (Algerian soldiers who fought on the French side) as "subhuman". Of course, this train of thought is only reinforced when Sarkozy, in his quest for power, calls the youth of the poor neighborhoods "scum" to be best handled with "a pressurized water gun", etc.

This verbal abuse was a source of anxiety and disquiet for the targeted populations, for such words directly counteract the integration of the groups into French society. Moreover, these statements were not at all justified by any actions of Muslims in France. What would the media have written if France had been the victim of a terrorist act? Was there not perhaps an orchestrated need for scandals, provocations, discord and flagrant offences? Without *Oumma.com*, the reactions to these allegations and instances of defamation would have remained largely unknown. The Internet de-territorialized the outcry from *Oumma.com*, taking it into North and sub-Saharan francophone Africa. The image of a France which continuously hounds Muslims is becoming disseminated throughout the francophone Muslim world, one of the important segments of the "French-speaking world", with which the values of peace, equality and diversity have long been associated.

The interconnection between the intellectual and political scene and the media is noteworthy. The comments made by a politician with electoral aims are used to the greatest advantage by the media. The central significance accorded to communication in French politics can explain this phenomenon. The overlap between the world of the media and that of politics, between owners of media and political leaders, makes the dimensions and scope of the media impact of these populist phrases apparent. They are at the heart of a strategy for the conquest of political, media and economic power. The major effect detrimental to integration is that the authors attack from as many vantages as possible the most vulnerable populations, those who are incapable of deterring or penalizing them. Striving to increase popularity among audiences and the electorate by attacking one section of the French population can only lead to further resentment, hate, fear and reactionary behavior in that group. Sacrificing one part of the French population in the conquest for power is irresponsible. Society is taking a far-reaching ideological and political turn backwards. In this sense, this development is a serious hindrance to integration.

3.3 *Oumma.com* in the face of complacent reporting

A further matter to be examined here is the relationship of information to television. Television combines image and sound (Deltombe 2005, p. 382). The effect of documentary broadcasts is extremely complex, involving an interplay of elements on symbolic and physical levels. Yet, it is easy to cut an interview and manipulate the images, that is, to display something as reality which is, in fact, a fake. This practice has even been sanctioned by the charter of journalism signed in Munich in 1971, and implemented, for example, in the broadcast *"la marche du siècle"*, hosted by Jean-Marie Cavada in 1995. Images were retouched so that a supposed Islamist could appear with a beard to satisfy audience expectations of stereotyped representations.

In the context of these issues, Tariq Ramadan has been portrayed in a negative light in the major media of France. On 16 November 2003, Karl Zéro broadcasts on *Canal Plus* an 'interview' with this Swiss scholar, who is of Egyptian descent. It was manifestly clear that the host was searching for 'double meaning' and especially for anti-Semitism in the words of Tariq Ramadan. The broadcast, then, distorted the interview's content, according to *Oumma.com*, which immediately sprang to the defense of one of its own writers and mentors.

"The method", writes Yamin Makri (Makri 2003), "is very simple: interview Tariq Ramadan, then cut his statements into smaller sequences and re-arrange them to demonstrate the 'double meaning' of his responses, his duplicity and his eminently dangerous character." Tariq Ramadan remained in the headlines, even though no evidence was ever found to support his alleged ties to Islamic extremists. On *Oumma.com*, Mohsin Mouedin wrote (Mouedin 2003): "We are all Tariq Ramadan", in allusion to media headlines after 9/11 ("We are all Americans").

The controversial debate between Tariq Ramadan and Sarkozy of 20 November 2003, broadcast on the program "100 minutes pour convaincre" on *France 2*, stimulated a number of reactions in the press (Sarkozy 2003). It was the culminating point of the new ideological communion between the political and intellectual scenes on the one hand and the media on the other. Objectively, the debate between the Minister of the Interior and a Swiss citizen was of little interest. But a better cast was not to be had. Sarkozy gained an immense symbolic advantage from the debate as the person who 'unveiled the fundamentalist' in a France ready to abandon social taboos. This communion between spheres united in their aim to sensationalize information warrants further examination.

On December 2, 2004, *France 2* broadcasts a "special report" on Tariq Ramadan by Mohammed Sifaoui. The report was presented as an excursion into the center of the Islamist 'network' in France. The report shows Tariq Ramadan followed by a hidden camera. The author promises his audience an outstanding account. In reality, not only is nothing 'discovered', but also the splicing and taping of the filmed sequences is clearly visible. This provoked a general outcry among the Muslim population. The Algerian nationality of the "reporter" only stoked the fire over the fabrication which was evident in the story. Subsequently, the author refused to participate in a broadcast focused on demystifying the media "Arrêt sur l'image (Stop. Image check!)", planned for December 3, 2004. In an article published by *Oumma.com*, Tariq Ramadan went to his own defense by denouncing Sifaoui's work. Several other journalists and researchers also harshly criticized the widely disseminated broadcast and the public channel responsible, reflecting the general indignation among professional journalists.

It is the shame and repugnance of sharing the same profession with Mohammed Sifaoui that pushes me to react after the broadcast of the 'portrait' of Tariq Ramadan on *France 2*. […] There is a lack of new information, incorrect supposition, malicious interpretation, manipulated quotes of interviewees, and a litany of double, triple, and quadruple meaning which continue to pursue Tariq Ramadan. Nothing can justify the angle chosen by the reporter. […] It is true that Ramadan is a subject that sells. But the denunciation of Islamists and fundamentalists, of which there is a consensus, in no way justifies turning a blind eye to the absence of any sense of ethics in this case (Dolé 2004).

The Internet site received texts from writers sharing a certain ethical standpoint who directly attacked the stigmatizations and instances of discrimination proffered in the broadcast (ibid.). The open editorial policy allows those who are not Muslim, but who share the political commitments of *Oumma.com*, to air their views. This approach also crosses the borders of religion, community and identity and is a genuine indication of an integration which favors solidarity and good rapport.

In 2004, the media event of the year was, without a doubt, the affair of the fictional assault on Marie-Léonie. The young woman claimed to have been attacked by "6 blacks and 7 Arabs" on a suburban train. The uproar was all the greater since Marie-Léonie was carrying her baby and a swastika was drawn on her clothes. The signs of misogyny and anti-Semitism were concentrated into hyper-charged negative media coverage. In the end, the ostensible attack emerged as having been imagined by the young mother. But by that point, politicians, intellectuals and the editorial staff of the major media had already jumped on the bandwagon, indistinctly and invariably taking up and employing the same xenophobic categories and repertoires. Within only a few hours, one could no longer keep count of the ways to stigmatize the "youth of the poor neighborhoods". The writers seemed to be engaged in a competition of sorts, each one searching for the best way to formulate the stereotypical phrases.

> This pathetic episode casts a cold light on the Islamophobic and Arab- phobic climate in this country. […] The most remarkable observation is the strange unanimity of the media and the political parties, which put them all – in differing proportions of course – into the same pot, snubbing traditional ideological divergences. (Koues 2004)

The reactions indicate what could happen if a similar or worse situation actually occurred. The reluctance to run the risk of being left an outsider only amplifies such tensions. Hopefully, the media have learned their lesson from this incident.

3.4 Dominant media, minority media and the emergence of the black question in France

The 'black question' became a major media topic with the adoption of the Taubira law[3], which condemns slavery as a crime against humanity. The law officially documents the transatlantic slave trade in which France participated. This was the beginning of the media coverage of an issue that had up to that point been largely ignored. The Internet revolution has brought many aspects of such issues to light. The connections between peoples of African descent have furthered their interests in how other communities of African origin, in particular African Americans, establish their identity. The American model functions as a paradigm of better opportunity for blacks, while France is seen as a location of elementary struggle for recognition. *Afrikara* is one of the most assertive African/Caribbean sites. Created in 1997, it is establishing itself as a militant and alternative site with a major focus on Africa, France, and blacks in the world. Reporting on instances of discrimination is one of the major focuses of its articles. Analysis of the political and economic situation in Africa constitutes another. Articles focusing on blacks in the world also have a broader impact. Information is often staged in such a way as to highlight the contrast between the situation of blacks in France and their situation in the USA. In the context of the resurgence of post-9/11 xenophobic ideas, much the same scheme can be observed in the treatment of information: sensationalist and racist statements, individuals targeted and condemned by the media, and corresponding reactions.

Here, the year 2003 is an important point of reference. In a program on channel *France 3*, Marc-Olivier Fogiel sent an SMS to the Franco-Cameroonian comedian Dieudonné in these words: "Would it be funny if we did a sketch on the odors of blacks?" The scandal surrounding this SMS led to weekly demonstrations of groups of blacks in front of the headquarters of *France 3*. In 2005, the TV host was brought to trial.

Afrikara stresses that: "Marc-Olivier Fogiel acknowledges both the SMS which failed to shock a soul in the high-end of France nor in the French media, and his violent and gratuitous gesture to the person Dieudonné. At this point, references were made to an "American-Zionist theme" of the comedian where he was dressed in a costume "that recalled without ambiguity that of an orthodox Jew disguised as a terrorist" (Akamayong 2004). While Dieudonné was accused of anti-Semitism, Fogiel was accused of anti-black racism. Several groups demanded Fogiel's resignation. When there were protest actions in the middle of the program, this triggered open tension between the public

---

3   See http://www.christiane-taubira.net/cms/index.php?page=loi-taubira.

television service and groups of blacks. A demonstration on October 9, 2005 protested against what was seen as the perversion of the public broadcasting service's obligations. The Internet played a decisive role in the coordination and the dissemination of information on the subject. In the end, the TV host and the director of France Television were found guilty of promoting racism, but notwithstanding, the host retained his position. This, in turn, led to more demonstrations, which did, in fact, lead to Fogiel's resignation. With this media event, blacks made their mark on the French audiovisual landscape, so that, in contrast to earlier coverage, the opening story now regularly features blacks.

This affair was soon to be eclipsed by the question of slavery, of memory and of the 'competition among victims' in the French media. The question of slavery became a subject of debate following media reports on Pétré-Grenouilleau's book entitled *Les traites négrières* (Pétré-Grenouilleau 2002). The author speaks of an "African slave trade", and the media set the stage for public debate by giving preeminence to this theory. Afrikara documented the indignation of the black community. A communiqué by the "Collectif Dom" (a group of people of Caribbean and African descent) reads as follows (Le Collectif DOM 2005):

> Olivier Pétré-Grenouilleau suggests the subject of slavery should have remained mute, and not been declared a crime against humanity, in order not to be "compared with the Shoah". He also suggests that this law is responsible for further anti-Semitism. Where does this unjustified indictment come from? In what way can the recognition of the slave trade and slavery as crimes against humanity be seen as anti-Semitic? Should we now renounce the qualification of other crimes against humanity such as those against the Armenians, the Yugoslavians or the Rwandans? In intellectual perversity, Pétré-Grenouilleau considers the suffering of blacks at the hands of slavery to have been less than the suffering of the Jews of the Holocaust, rightly recognized for its atrocities. Is it because slaves were supposedly objects without souls? All the while proclaiming "there is no Richter scale of suffering", Olivier Pétré-Grenouilleau is author of a strange comparison which gives rise to a competition of victimization, and continues to unleash hatred between communities.

Afrikara added (Afrikara 2006b):

> The slavery question, whether referring to memory or to history, discharges an irrepressible release and eruption of racial hatred onto the French audiovisual landscape which is far from having been expunged of colonial nostalgia and of a particularly profound form of color phobia: the commemoration of crimes perpetuated against

blacks, Africans and their descendants, and other non-whites is perceived by many groups of intellectuals, journalists, politicians and the makers of opinion as a form of humiliation. An indignity to which, as though pushed on by a higher mission, they do not hesitate to respond, hardly hiding a hypersensitive racism, a hierarchy of suffering, and an unconscious attitude of individual and racial superiority. All this for the worse of the country, dissertating the length and breadth of their editorials.

History and its interpretation would remain one of the main issues for protest at *Afrikara*. A further text there reads (ibid.): "In France, some of the best-respected journalists advance insane and injurious theses regarding the history of blacks without any strong media or political reaction."

Many utterances in the media have specific ideological functions and promote a specific way of thinking. On 17 November 2005, the philosopher Alain Finkelkraut said the following about the French soccer team: "They say that the French team is admired because it is black, white and Arab [...]. In fact, today it is black, black, and black, and we are made fun of all over Europe." His words were to travel around the globe, and to start a compilation of racist statements made by media intellectuals. This was certainly a premeditated act. The philosopher alluded to the words of Georges Frêche, who thought there were too many blacks on the French team. Staging information constantly follows the same pattern, in which the media are used to pass along the message. Media such as *Afrikara* consider such utterances to be an expression of Negrophobia. Many African/Caribbean sites express similar views and also ask: Why now?

One is surprised to hear comments like that of Roger Hanin, who was invited to speak on *Europe 1* by Jean-Marc Morandini (Akamayong 2006):

Roger Hanin: What drives me nuts is to hear: 'There aren't enough blacks!' Enough already! Stop crying! When I look at TV, all I see are black singers! I don't give a damn. It's fine! But don't tell me that blacks are penalized.

Morandini: But there is a problem after all in terms of visible access to TV for minorities.

Roger Hanin: That's a load of bull: why not stutterers, homos or dwarfs. [...] When they say that blacks can't express themselves it's a bunch of bull! Look at soccer, they can express themselves. If you look at it that way, what about the whites, they can't express themselves. There are 8 blacks out of 11 and that's fine! You could say to a trainer: 'You couldn't find a white player?' But it would be stupid, he just takes the best.

Afrikara answers him in these terms (ibid.): "The presence of blacks and their representation in current French society? He reduces them to music and soccer. Another brilliant mind of our times!"

Eric Zemmour, a columnist, affirms in the broadcast "Ca se dispute (Leave no stone unturned)" of *I-Télé* on May 12, 2006: "It's colonization that put a stop to slavery! I'm tired of hearing of people talking about France being guilty of a crime against humanity because it used slaves. First of all, that's wrong – there were never any slaves on French territory." On the channel *Paris première*, March 26, 2006, on the broadcast "93 Faubourg Saint-Honoré", he had already said: "Black slavery was invented by blacks. In Africa, they were the ones selling other blacks, because there is no such thing as black brotherhood – it doesn't exist."

But the pinnacle of such racist media utterances was reached when Pascal Sevran, the television host, wrote in his book, *Le privilege des jonquilles* (Sevran 2007, p. 207): "The black prick is responsible for the famine in Africa." When asked to clarify his stance by *Nice Matin*, he insisted, "It's the truth! Africa is finishing itself off with all those children born with parents who have nothing to feed them. I'm not the only one to say it. We should sterilize half the planet." The journalist also had much to say in his book about the case of Niger, where authorities have commenced with prosecuting the crime of defamation of a people. *Afrikara's* response was as follows (Da Siva/Elinga 2007):

> France has recently become a textbook case in terms of the democratization of racist discourse and of concrete practices translating into the inferiorization of blacks in all acts of daily life. The political theater of anti-immigration or housing expulsions have, for about a decade now, displayed and socialized an image of a population who can take the most implacable violence from politics and police, without soliciting any kind of reprobation or ethic consideration. This is physical violence in the name of the fight against clandestine immigration, and verbal violence paired with public insult on prime time media in front of giant audiences.

The same tone is, however, not to be perceived in the principal mainstream media, which empathize with the TV host. "Is Pascal Sevran racist?" (*Le Figaro*. December 7, 2007), "The TV host Pascal Sevran accused of promoting racism and of praising eugenics" (*Le Monde*, December 6, 2006), "Pascal Sevran attacked for inciting racial hatred" (*Libération*, December 13, 2006). None of these headlines actually accuse the TV host. Instead, they either simply state a question or deliberate the accusations. The two types of media converge neither in their perception nor in their understanding of the issue.

Journalists at *Afrikara* attempt to respond to any wayward comments made towards Islam, Muslims and Arabs. The debates on the positive effects of colonization have reinforced the distinction between mainstream and minority media. Analysis of the responses reveals that the concepts employed are often taken from social criticism and from the American experience, its success and ideas. The French system is directly confronted with its ostensible long-term values of freedom, equality and brotherhood.

Reference is made to François Xavier Verschaves' work on *françafrique* (French Africa) to explain French neo-colonialism's methods of domination. But this work cannot explain why journalists, politicians and intellectuals suddenly abandon all pretense of respect for one another. The explanation for this is to be found in the ideological staging of information.

If, indeed, there are many articles and interviews in *Oumma.com* from researchers and friends of the 'Arab world', similar texts are not to be found on *Afrikara.com*. Solidarity with African/Caribbeans is much too complicated. African specialists are more or less absent from African sites, whereas specialists of Islam are numerous on *Oumma.com*. This is true despite the fact that studies of Islam and of Africa stem from the same colonial inspiration. 'Orientalism' and 'Africanism' function with the same basic paradigms, those of a study of populations demeaned by a fundamental disciplinary essentialism. Apparently, society is not yet prepared to deal with diverging collective memories. In this context, the question of the media's role in 'restructuring' or 'de-structuring' society is certainly a legitimate one.

What will become of integration if the confrontation between the two media persists, and how is the ideological turnaround formulated on a global scale? In order to understand the nature of this confrontation, its content and its objectives, the actors should not be isolated from their actions, but should be seen as part of a global, coherent and integrated symbolic system. Statements originating from the national press make sense within a specific vision and ideology of the world, just as everyday political and cultural actions do. The "abandonment of taboos" (Lindenberg 2002, p. 90) in French society proceeds from what Daniel Lindenberg has called the new reactionaries. The new era has firmly established the public vindication of racism, authoritarianism, a specific 'moral order', and security forces at the service of business.

Behind the statements against Islam, Arabs and Blacks, is the condemnation of equality, brotherhood, freedom and human rights through public statements of certain intellectuals. These people, who freely admit their own xenophobia, also warn against European decadence, the deterioration of the values of knowledge and authority at school, and the loss of excellence and competitiveness in society. They criminalize the poor and accuse them of willful dependency. The renaissance of the state is seen as a struggle against permissiveness and entails the reconstruction of political authoritarianism. These people praise an America at war with Iraq and are indignant at France's refusal to interfere in an unjustified war. To sum up, there is a coherence exhibited by these phrases and actions connecting these media-hyped statements to a specific worldview. In his *Rappel à l'ordre*, Daniel Lindenberg writes (Lindenberg 2002, p. 12):

> The impulse to counteraction is now expanding in broad daylight in different areas: that of May 1968, that of mass culture, that of the rights of mankind, that of anti-racism, and most recently that of Islam. So many untouchable totems are now being toppled one after the other by an iconoclastic verve which is progressively losing its sense of guilt. *Progressively*, because we are speaking of a mechanism; each procedure favors the freeing-up of the next, all the while making opinions acceptable which were formerly judged intolerable. Therefore, the assault on the events of May '68 makes all the easier the attacks against schools and the university, and make the expression of 'anti-youth' points of view banalities. In the same way, the trial of anti-racism allows xenophobic discourse to become everyday as well, going beyond its traditional limits, as the recent wave of Islamophobia shows. In total, the destruction is weighty: open reflection itself is suddenly paralyzed in the face of passions hereto considered inadmissible.

France, then, takes on the colors of American neo-conservatism without the elements of religious revival. Is this only due to the 'negative influence' of the neo-conservative United States? Can all of this be accounted for by American mercantile, ultra-religious, political neo-conservatism? It is necessary to consider the ideological heritage of France's colonial past in this context. Colonial archives on the Muslim policy of colonial France reveal that the current concepts are to be found at the center of the colonial machine. In colonial literature, the Muslim and the 'Negro' are associated with barbarism and non-civilization in caricatured, stereotyped and, in particular, racist terms. In re-reading colonial archives, one finds 'un-thinkables' which currently express the shift to the right in French thought. When Georges Frêche speaks of "sub-human", Pascal Sevran of the "black prick", and Fogiel of the "odors of blacks", there is a direct link to the colonial theories on the 'noble savage'. In much the same way, the link between Islam and fanaticism and violence has its ideological roots in the dark night of colonialism. The connection to American neo-conservatives complements an ideological conception nurtured in part by colonial literature. Yet, this return to colonial theory proves to be even more reactionary than American conservatism. Recourse to these colonial 'unthinkables' nurtures the ideological turnabout with its abandonment of social taboos. Hence, the individual statements appearing in widely scattered media settings can be interpreted on a global scale by resituating them in their historical context.

Although many observers of the media have perceived an almost 'bornagain' dimension in Sarkozy, there are other sources of his ideology. "I am a new man," he declared when he accepted the candidacy of the UMP on January 14, 2007. During his campaign, he strongly insisted on the Christian roots of France. Yet, the greater affinity to the reactionary ideology just mentioned is not to be seen in religion, but in values related to 'moral order', security forces, the ideal of excellence, authority at school and in society, and in the condemnation of May '68. Less than two years after 9/11, the intellectual, media and political groundwork for this ideological turnaround had already been laid. Writers, philosophers, journalists and politicians profited from a well-prepared situation.

Community media also look to the USA and attempt to emulate the gains made by African Americans in civil rights conflicts. At *Afrikara*, hundreds of pages deal with African American personalities and their progress in areas of equality, civil rights and everyday matters. Here, the American experience provides a counterexample to France, and the USA is seen as a model of integration. Still, this does not prevent community media from criticizing American hegemony in the world much as the mainstream media does. African/Caribbean media also adopt the American cult of excellence to promote business and see success as achieved through wealth and prosperity. The doctrine of prosperity transforms the rich into the mouthpiece of the black community in a world abandoned to the market. At this level, the principles of American Pentecostal thought are expressed through the ideology of prosperity. "African leadership", "ethnic management", "ethnic networking", and the "gospelization of the black identity" are concepts that mobilize African/Caribbean media in France. These activities are intimately linked to a certain form of Pentecostalism, which, once entrenched in the group's identity, inevitably leads to a struggle between good and evil, a war against the devil.

3.5 A black anchor on the 8 pm news: channel *TF1*, Harry Roselmarck and African/Caribbean media

On July 17, 2006, a 34-year-old black journalist replaced the star anchor Patrick Poivre d'Arvor for a month. This was met with great surprise in

France, and was a gesture contrasting with the discriminatory and racist phrases which had led to the opposition between mainstream and community media. France is a country of interesting paradoxes. Several elements converged at this juncture: business, common sense, and an emphasis on the sensational. Interestingly, this did not happen within the context of the public television network, but, as mentioned above, on the private channel *TF1*.

The overwhelming media coverage of this event reveals the cultural schisms in this country and, at the same time, a surprising voluntarism. Several black journalists from cable stations, Christine Kelly of channel *M6*, Karine Lemarchand, Sylvère Cissé, and Arsène Valère, expressed their satisfaction and high expectations regarding Harry's nomination. "I crossed my fingers and said: Let's hope that everything goes right, that he doesn't fall on his face, that he succeeds! Because I knew without a doubt that if he failed, they would have had no pity for him. Because the difficulties associated with our origins means we don't have any margin of error. He absolutely has to succeed", said Sylvère Cissé. This unexpected event provided a surface for projection and led to identification with the first French black anchor in the black communities of France – an emotional event involving a new sense of belonging. The excitement evoked by this event reflects how little headway had actually been made in terms of promoting equality and diversity in society. The African/Caribbean press warmly welcomed the news and did not fail to recall that the U.S.A. and Great Britain, in contrast to France, had been implementing corresponding policies for more than 30 years. Roselmarck himself commented (Roselmarck 2006):

> I unabashedly admit that my color had played a role. And I say all the better! It was time for a TV station to make this gesture. [...] TF1 did this voluntarily; they took the lead and said: We'll take him. We'll put him on at 8 o'clock. I find this simply fantastic. If being black was one of the factors involved in their choosing me – I mean, I don't have any problem at all with that in so far that I know that I have the capacity to fill the position. [...] And it's a positive signal. If it had been negative, I wouldn't have taken it [...].

Harry Roselmarck's 8 o'clock news hour was perceived as a collective effort of the black community of France. The community apparently now had to demonstrate whether a black presenter of the evening news was acceptable.

Afrikara organized a survey within the French black community that revealed that more than 85% of those interviewed supported the nomination. This figure reflects both the experience of minorities with negative representations and their fear that failure could mean another wave of destructive and racist comments. After ratings showed that viewer loyalty had remained constant, a wave of satisfaction traversed the French black community. The original uproar was easily forgotten, and Roselmarck became a media star with a new dimension. The situation inspired *Afrikara* to note (Afrikara 2006c):

> The pilot study was a stroke of genius because, in spite of the many professionals who spoke in its favor, many were those who anticipated, and still do, a turn-about of affairs. Harry certainly has no need for our advice in the managing of his career, nor even of his mission, which at times can certainly be just a little too close for comfort, but we wish in any case to wish him all the best in his endeavors - for that which he is, and for that which others see in him.

> There is probably no revolution at Bouygues[4], but the important thing lies elsewhere. In terms of the impact on the French sense of representation, whether of young blacks who finally witness the widening of their imagined horizon of possibilities, or of Whites brought up on the milk of prejudice and ignorance and shivering at the face of otherness, the discovery of a competent fellow-citizen will awaken a new reference in their hopes and dreams.

The establishment of the *Conseil representative des associations noires* (CRAN - Representative Council of Black Associations) in 2006 indicates a deleterious situation for minorities. CRAN's mission is to fight discrimination against blacks. Notwithstanding its critics, it remains an effective social framework and helps mobilize persons who are not black, but wish to join in the struggle against racism. One of CRAN's projects involves devising a 'barometer' of diversity. This is to display the level of integration of blacks into French society with reference to employment. In 2006, CRAN undertook a study on the status of blacks in France. This study shows that they represent 3.2% of the population and recognize themselves as a visible minority. Fifty-six percent report having experienced discrimination principally at work or in a public place. Those questioned recalled "disdainful, disrespectful, or demeaning attitudes", "verbal assaults", "insults", "difficulty in the purchase or leasing of housing", "police identity controls", "difficulties in relations with public services" and "the refusal of employment" (CRAN 2007, p. 16). "Sixty-one percent of 'blacks' report having experienced at least one situation of discrimination in the last 12 months" (ibid. p. 17) In their struggles against discrimination, the persons questioned appealed to the following for help:

---

4   The owner of TF1 Channel.

associative groups (81%), schools (72%), the HALDE[5] (68%), the law (59%), religious leaders (57%), the media (48%), the state (46%), the police (37%), businesses (35%), and politicians (29%) (op.cit., p. 21). These percentages reflect the way in which blacks are covered in the media and the derisive statements produced in the media and by politicians. For some time now, mainstream media have been staging xenophobic acts in order to enhance their own profits. The most marked acts of discrimination as revealed by the survey were insults and acts expressing disdain and hatred. Statements made by Pascal Sevran, Alain Finkelkraut, Hélène Carrère d'Encausse, Claude Imbert, Michel Houlebecq, Maurice Dantec, Marc-Olivier Fogiel, Georges Frêche, and Nicolas Sarkozy will not easily be forgotten. Civil rights groups and schools are seen in a more positive light than such celebrities and seem to function as forces promoting social integration in France.

4. Conclusion

The question of integration is recurrent in French political debate and has repeatedly appeared in political and media campaigns over the last 30 years. For certain parties of the right and the extreme right, the issue of integration guarantees their influence with their proposals against laws regarding discrimination, racism, and social cohesion and with their stance against the thousands of organizations that fight xenophobia. The last elections brought immigration to light once again through debates on a concept of 'national identity'. As a result, politicians were perceived as the sole generators of public discourse on integration and immigration. In fact, the major media participate in propagandizing and amplifying the issue, presenting the immigrant as more of a problem than as part of a solution. Since the very first contemporary immigrations, language expressing fear and suspicion has abounded in media reports (Hubsher 2005, p. 478). The French suburbs, residence of economically underprivileged groups, are described as lawless and violent, and as "the abandoned territories of the Republic". Those subjected to this media reporting are allocated no right to response. Until the dawning of the Internet, French people of foreign origin were without any substantial source of information. But the creation of Internet sites, of informative, feminist and general magazines, and of radio stations has transformed the relationship between society and the media.

---

5   Haute autorité de lutte contre les discriminations (HALDE – High Authority in the Fight Against Discrimination).

5. References

Afrikara (2006c): "Un Noir, Harry Roselmarck investit le 20 heures sacralisé de France avec brio", July 18, 2006

Afrikara (2006b): "La Négrophobie, un must journalistique français, l'exemple d'Eric Zemmour: La colonization a arête l'esclavage, les Noirs vendent les Noirs...", May 15, 2006

Afrikara (2006a): "Roger Hanin entre Négrophobie, Homophobie et Handiphobie chez Morandini? C'est la bêtise qui manque le moins...", February 22, 2006

Afrikara (2005): "Les insoutenables propos révisionnistes de Pétré-Grenouilleau", June 13, 2005, http://www.grioo.com/info4864.html

Afrikara (2004): "Les odeurs des Blacks: Fogiel, l'animateur de France 3 se défend sur afrikara.com", February 24, 2004

Akamayong, Akam (2004): "Les odeurs des Blacks: Fogiel, l'animateur de France 3 se défend sur afrikara.com", Afrikara.com, February 24, 2004

Aoussat, Noureddine (2004): "Affaire du voile: Le Cheikh Tantaoui d'Al-Azhar désavoué par les autres savants de cette institution", Oumma.com, January 1, 2004

Bénard, Liliane (2003): "Des valeurs universelles et du voile...", Oumma.com, September 22, 2003

Chami, Farah (2005): "Lorsque Le Monde "pleure" le départ des colons", Oumma.com, August 2, 2005

CRAN (2007): TNS Sofres survey, January 2007

Cypel, Sylvain (2006): Les emmurés, Paris: Èditions la Découverte

Da Siva, D.; Belinga, Z. (2007): "De la démence négrophobe et du devoir impérieux d'agir", Afrikara.com, January 17, 2007

Deltombe, Thomas (2005): L'islam imaginaire - La construction médiatique de l'islamophobie en France, 1975-2005, Paris: Éditions la Découverte

Dolé, Nathalie (2004): "Reportage d'Envoyé Spécial: honte et écœurement", Oumma.com, December 3, 2004

Draszen, Anaïs, Draszen, Paul (2003): "Taisez vous Tariq Ramadan!", Oumma.com, December 21, 2003

Hamel, Ian (2005): "Quand pourra-t-on critiquer honnêtement Tariq Ramadan?", Oumma.com, January 5, 2005

Hamel, Ian (2004): "Tirs croisés contre Tariq Ramadan", Oumma.com, October 27, 2004

Hubsher, Ronald (2005): L'immigration dans les campagnes françaises (19e-20e siècle), Paris

Koues, Fatiha (2004): "Critiques contre Tariq Ramadan, procès de l'islam" Oumma.com, July 21, 2004

Lamrabet, Asma (2004): "Au-delà du voile...", Oumma.com, February 2, 2004

Laribi, Meriem (2004): "Il a bon le dos le frère Tariq!", Oumma.com, November 2, 2004

Le Collectif DOM (2005): „Les insoutenables propos révisionnistes de Pétré-Grenouilleau", http://www.grioo.com/info4864.html, June 13, 2005

Le Figaro (2007): "Is Pascal Sevran racist?" December 7, 2007

Le Monde (2006): "The TV host Pascal Sevran accused of promoting racism and of praising eugenics" December 6, 2006

Le Point (2002): "Polémique: cette femme qui dit non à l'Islam: ‚Fallaci tente de regarder la réalité en face'", Le Point , May 24, 2002

Libération (2006): "Pascal Sevran attacked for inciting racial hatred", December 13, 2006

Lindenberg, Daniel (2002): Le rappel à l'ordre. Enquête sur les nouveaux réactionnaires, Paris

Lorcerie, Françoise (2005): "L'affaire du voile sous le projecteur de la science politique: une analyse renouvelée de l'affaire en France et de son écho à l'étranger", Oumma.com, July 5, 2005

Makri, Yamin (2003): "Karl Zero...Zero", Oumma.com, November 17, 2003

Mezziane, Fath Allah (2003): "Le ‚outing' de Claude Imbert ou l'islamophobie comme mode de pensée", Oumma.com, October 31, 2003

Michot, Yahya (2003): "Le voile jaune", Oumma.com, November 3, 2003

Mouedin, Mohsin (2003): "Nous sommes tous des Tariq Ramadans", Oumma.com, December 5, 2003

Moury, Francis (2003): "La question du voile dans l'Islam et le monde moderne", Oumma.com, December 29, 2003

Observatoire français des media – OFM (2005): Sur la concentration dans les médias, Paris

Omar, Zine El Abiddine (2004): "La symbolique du combat de la République contre le foulard", Oumma.com, January 31, 2004

Pétré-Grenouilleau, Olivier (2002): Les traites négrières. Essai d'histoire globale, Paris

Roselmarck, Harry (2006): "I unabashedly admit that my color had played a role", B-Connexion.com, December 28, 2006

Sarkozy, Ramadan (2003): „Les termes d'un débat", Oumma.com, November 26, 2003

Sarr, Felwine (2003): "Le port du voile: un rapport à sa propre corporalité", Oumma.com, December 18, 2003

Sauveget, Daniel (2004): „Vincent Bolloré: l'ex-roi du papier à cigarettes, nouvel empereur des médias?", http://www.acrimed.org/article1823.html, November 17, 2004

Sevran, Pascal (2007): Le privilège des jonquilles, Albin Michel

Tévanian, Pierre (2006): "L'affaire du voile, deux ans après: un consensus lourd de conséquences", Oumma.com, March 15, 2006

Vandorpe, Eric (2004): "Retour sur le rapport Stasi et ses dérives islamophobes", Oumma.com, January 18, 2004

Vandorpe, Eric (2003): "Suspension d'un an sans salaire pour une fonctionnaire voile!", Oumma.com, November 18, 2003

Weill-Raynal, Guillaule (2007): Les nouveaux désinformateurs, Paris

Augie Fleras

Ethnic and Aboriginal Media in Canada: Crossing Borders, Constructing Buffers, Creating Bonds, Building Bridges

1. Introduction: "Taking Aboriginal and Ethnic Media Seriously"

Canada constitutes a multicultural society whose 'multiculturality' reflects different layers of meaning. Four semantic levels can be discerned, including multiculturalism as demographic fact, as ideology, as government policy and programs, and as practice. Of these multiple meaning levels, references to multiculturalism as official policy prevail (Fleras and Elliott 2007). At the core of Canada's official multiculturalism is a commitment to institutional inclusiveness. According to the Multiculturalism Act of 1988, all institutions (but especially federal institutions) have a responsibility to proactively engage diversity through initiatives that are reflective of the community they serve, respectful of cultural identities, and responsive to minority needs and concerns (Annual Report 2004/05). Both public and private institutions have taken steps toward improving levels of responsiveness, in part by eliminating the most egregious forms of racial discrimination in service delivery, in part by modifying institutional structures to ensure equitable treatment, in part by creating positive programs to improve access and representation.

However well intentioned, a commitment to inclusiveness is not always do-able. So structured are mainstream institutions around racialized discourses of whiteness that minorities are systemically denied access or equity (Henry and Tator 2006). Nowhere is this institutionalized exclusion more evident than in mainstream newsmedia coverage of minority women and men. Despite modest moves toward improving diversity depictions, the newsnorms of a conventional news paradigm continue to frame minorities as troublesome constituents, that is problem people who are problems who have problems and who create problems (Fleras 2004/2006). This framing of diversity around a conflict/problem/negativity nexus is neither intentional nor personal. To the contrary, the unintended yet logical consequences of largely one-sided misrepresentation are systemic in logic: that is, newsmedia coverage of migrants and minorities is systemically biasing than a systematic bias. In that the cumulative effect of such monocultural coverage imposes a controlling effect − after all, what is not said may be more important than what is − newsmedia may well constitute an exercise in systemic propaganda (Fleras 2007).

To say that minority women and men are mistreated by mainstream newsmedia is true enough (Mahtani 2002; Henry and Tator 2006; Jiwani 2006). Multicultural minorities and aboriginal peoples remain overrepresented in areas that don't count ('crime'or 'entertainment'), underrepresented in areas that do ('political or economic success'), and misrepresented along all points in between because of a pro-white (Eurocentric) bias (Fleras and Kunz 2001). They continue to be rendered invisible except in contexts of crisis, negativity, or conflict, in the process reinforcing their status as troublesome constituents for removal or control. To circumvent or neutralize the effects of this systemically biasing coverage, ethnic (or 'racialized') minorities and aboriginal peoples have turned to alternative media institutions. In privileging minority experiences, identities, and priorities, ethnic and aboriginal media have proliferated accordingly, including: (1) ethnic and aboriginal print (2) ethnic and aboriginal broadcasting, and the (3) inclusion within mainstream newsmedia. Reaction has varied as well: For some, their expansion is commensurate with Canada's multicultural commitments; for others, aboriginal and ethnic media are essentially manipulative advocates for special interest groups; for yet others, they are regressive for disrupting immigrant integration; and for still others, ethnic and aboriginal media are more complex and nuanced than simplistic bifurcation into either good or bad.

Integration or separatist? Insular or isolationist? Inclusive or exclusive? Bonding or divisive? Buffer or barrier? Bridges or roadblocks? Inreach or outreach? Progressive or regressive? Society-building or society-bashing? Debates over aboriginal and ethnic media clearly resonate with overtones of ambiguity, with few signs of subsiding, and these controversies are part of a broader project around the contested role of media institutions in advancing the integration of migrants and minorities (Geißler 2005; Geißler/Pöttker 2005). In keeping with the conference theme, namely, the role of media in integrating migrants with respect to what can be done, what should be avoided, and what we can learn from each other, this paper explores the promises and perils of Canada's ethnic and aboriginal media as well as their politics and paradoxes. The paper argues that aboriginal and ethnic media constitute an integrative component of an inclusive Canada-building project: First, by advancing Canada's democratic discourses beyond what is normally conveyed by mainstream newsmedia. Second, by improving the sectoral interests of multicultural minorities and aboriginal peoples via alternative media discourses (Williamson and DeSouza 2006). Third, by securing crossover points for promoting intercultural awareness and exchanges. As social capital, ethnic media not only foster community bonding, but also constitute a bridging device for enhancing a two way process of integration ("you adjust, we adapt/we adjust, you adapt"). To the extent that aboriginal and ethnic media are multidimensional in logic, process, and outcomes, no single assessment is possible or desirable (Riggins 1992; Ojo 2006). Content is organized thematically as follows:

1. to conceptualize the contrasts between mainstream media (namely private and public) and populist media (including ethnic and aboriginal media) in terms of underlying logic, operating principles and process, and anticipated outcomes;

2. to theorize aboriginal and ethnic media as both insular and integrative, that is, inward- and outward-looking as well as active and proactive;

3. to focus on the nature of news coverage in ethnic media. What topics are covered – local stories or homeland stories for diasporic community members (Lin and Song 2006)?

4. to look into the popularity and success of ethnic and aboriginal media in Canada;

5. to discuss their implications for facilitating migrant integration (ie. to settle down, fit in, and move up) while helping established minorities to construct community & culture.

6. to demonstrate how ethnic media are critical in constructing a multilocal sense of belonging by linking contemporary migrants with Canada and their homeland.

7. to entertain the possibility that, for purposes of analysis, mainstream newsmedia constitute a type of ethnic media (but with power)

8. to acknowledge the role of ethnic and aboriginal media in contributing to a robust public sphere (Husband 2005), in part by asking those awkward questions beyond mainstream expertise (Color-Line 2002)

9. to demonstrate how the logic underlying Aboriginal media differ from that of ethnic media, given the distinctive constitutional status of Canada's Aboriginal peoples.

10. to explore the possibility of framing ethnic and aboriginal media as social capital because of their bonding and bridging 'functions'.

11. to determine the status, role and responsibility of both mainstream and aboriginal/ethnic media within the context of an inclusive multiculturalism.

2. Conceptualizing Media Institutions

Media scholars have long acknowledged the existence of three major media institutions – private, public, and populist. Although the differences are not nearly as distinct as often assumed, the underlying logic of each differs with respect to what is being communicated, why, how, and with what purpose (Fleras 2003)

- *Private media* represent commercial enterprises. They are privately owned, concerned primarily with making money or profit (usually through advertising or subscriptions), focused on providing consumers with safe and formulaic content, of appeal to the lowest common denominator, and generally reject any social responsibility for actions and outputs unless involving the bottom line. According to the underlying logic, private commercial media do not exist to inform, entertain, or enlighten per se; their goal is to make money by providing a commodity (or programming) that connects the right demographic with advertisers.

- *Public media* constitute a public service for advancing public interest. Public media are government or tax payer owned, focused largely on the enlightenment of citizens across a broad range of programming, and are geared to maximizing public good or advancing national interests. They also are viewed as elitist because of their mandate to provide audiences with programs they need for citizenship, belonging, and participation. To be sure, references to public media embrace a wide range of arrangements, from the publicly funded but arm's length system in Great Britain to the mixed funding model of the CBC in Canada and PBS in the United States to state-owned and government controlled system in China (Lincoln et al 2005). Such a range of public media process makes it difficult to define or characterize.

- *Populist (or alternative) media.* Populist media differ from mainstream (public (state) and private (market) because of content, structure, distri-bution, and consumption (Skinner 2006). In occupying mediaspace abandoned by increasingly homogenous mainstream media, populist media provide an alternative service for those without demographic clout and political power. These media tend to be independently owned and service-oriented, reflect localized interests by providing news and infor-mation of direct relevance to the communities they serve, embrace news values that differ from the mainstream newsmedia, communicate along horizontal lines rather than top-down hierarchies, encourage community wide participation in the production process (Lalley and Hawkins 2005;

Rennie 2006), and are highly partisan in empowering the disempowered Not surprisingly, populist news values differ from those of the mainstream. Whereas the latter emphasize the centrality of conflict or abnormality as newsworthy, especially when involving minority women and men, populist news values focus on minority success stories and positive role models.

The concept of populist media can be further subdivided into *alternative, community, ethnic* and *aboriginal* media. Although classification of these media into a single category may conceal more than it reveals, they share much in common, including closer relations with audiences, less preoccupation with the bottom line, more attention to areas of local interest, including city politics, offer an alternative to mainstream indifference to homeland issues, provides useful information for settling down and fitting in, promote public dialogue and exchange of ideas for the mobilization of audiences into social action, and challenge the status quo with its prevailing distribution of power and privilege (Journalism.org 2004; Rennie 2006; Downing 2000; Skinner 2006). The exponential growth of ethnic or minority media not only reflects global migration patterns, but also an internet-inspired emergence of various participatory, collaborative, oppositional, alternative, and community media practices that embrace the changing ways in which people 'use' and 'make' their media (Deuze 2006). In challenging the concentration of corporate media power by way of a participatory global media culture, Skinner (2006:217) says:

> Rather than tailor content, organizational structure, and production practices to maximize return on investment, alternative media foreground special social issues and values. In terms of organizational structure, they often purposefully shun traditional hierarchical models of organization to facilitate as much input as possible into the production. And in terms of production, in order to countermand the tendency to have professional values dictate the subjects, structures and sources of content, they often seek participation and contributions from the communities they serve rather than rely on professional journalists.

But while relatively easy to glamourize the populist case, populist media are not nearly as unsullied by crass business concerns as many believe. Despite a niche based orientation, their commercial dynamics may not altogether differ from mainstream media. Publishers and producers are known to follow a time proven trajectory: track what is profitable, repackage it as authentic in bolstering the bottom line, and link the package with a preferred demographic (Jeff Yang in Hsu 2002). Even issues of cooperation and consensus are problematic. Their potential as sites of conflict cannot be dismissed, particularly when homeland strife is played out in the ethnic press, with publishers suffering serious consequences when siding with the wrong faction (Nallainathan 2007).

	private	public	populist a)alternative b) ethnic c) aboriginal d) community
logic	escapist (Give consumers what they want)	elitist (Give citizen what they need)	Empower (give the community the power/ voices denied to them)
Goal	profit (market driven)	public good and national interests	Partisan: for the people, by the people, about the people
function	Entertain	Enlighten	Embolden – Adapt, Challenge, Transform
scope	Market niche via mass commercial casting	universality (broadcasting)	Narrowcasting - Untapped 'minority' Group
perception of audience	Consumer	Citizen	Community/minority
ownership	corporate owned	general public taxpayer funded	Locally owned/controlled/ produced
programming content	Safe/ routine/ familiar	broad range with emphasis on high brow/ high culture	Different news values (Give the people what the mainstream media ignore)

Table 1: Media Institutions: A Comparison of Models

The table above compares media institutions models - private, public and populist (Fleras 2003). On the left hand column are the criteria that provide a basis for comparison - albeit in highly idealistic terms and categorically rather than contextually. The three columns to the right provide the comparison. It should be noted that the establishment of the user-generated internet content suggests the possibility of a new personal media model, one based on the ability of ordinary citizens to create, distribute, and consume media products beyond conventional channels of creation, distribution, and consumption (Rennie 2006; Ojo 2006).

To be sure, the distinction between mainstream and ethnic media may be overstated. Mainstream media consist of those private or public outlets that cater to the general public; by contrast, ethnic media are thought to specifically target a specific ethnic minority. However intuitive such a divide, difficulties abound. Where exactly do mainstream media end and ethnic media begin? To the extent that aboriginal and ethnic media are more mainstream than many think, whereas mainstream media are more 'ethnic' than often thought, the distinction dissolves. Consider the seemingly counterintuitive possibility that mainstream media may be *interpreted* as ethnic media in servicing the interests of a white constituency:

> All mass media content could be analyzed from the experience of what is revealed about ethnicity. The New York Times, for example, could be read as an ethnic newspaper, although it is not explicitly or consciously so. (Riggins 1992:2)

The consequences of this 'inversion' are revelatory. In reminding us that all newsmedia are ethnically located whether conscious of this placement or not, media institutions and texts are neither neutral nor value-free but encoded in a fundamentally racialized (or ethnicized) way. Inasmuch as mainstream media are owned and controlled by corporate interests, they are organized by, for, and around 'white' experiences, realities, and priorities (Jiwani 2006). However unintended or incidental, content is designed to promote and normalize Eurocentric norms, while alternative discourses are discredited as inferior or irrelevant. This Eurocentric whiteness not only serves as the normative standard by which others are judged, evaluated, and criticized. The Eurocentrism that is embedded within institutional structures, processes, and outcomes also generates a 'palemale' gaze that tends to project fantasies or fears upon racialized others. Admittedly, media decision-makers and gatekeepers may not be consciously biased toward non whites. Nevertheless, they unconsciously frame their narratives in a way that selects, highlights, and imposes a preferred way of seeing and thinking. The end result? Whites and non whites stand in a different relationship to mainstream media: Whites see themselves painted into the picture as normal or superior, whereas minorities find themselves racialized by Eurocentric discourses that demean, deny, and diminish. Under the circumstances who can be surprised by the success and popularity of ethnic and aboriginal media?

Parallels between ethnic and mainstream newsmedia are unmistakable: Both serve the information needs of their primary consumers and advertising demographic (serve the people). Each is tribal in orientation, must target a specific audience, rely on advertising and subscription base for survival, and must adjust their content accordingly. But even if mainstream media can be conceptualized as ethnic media, the parallel breaks down because of a major difference - power. But unlike ethnic media which are relatively powerless outside their sphere of influence, mainstream newsmedia possess the power, resources, and resourcefulness to make a difference, from agenda setting and defining public discourses to advancing national interests. That fact alone makes it doubly important to theorize aboriginal and ethnic media as dynamics in their own right as well as players coping with the challenges of a global and participatory media culture.

3. Theorizing Ethnic and Aboriginal Media: Putting Social Capital to Work

They respond to the needs of ethnic and racialized minorities; they provide a voice in advancing the welfare of the community; they challenge social injustices; they foster a sense of cultural pride; and they articulate the essence of their communities (Gonzales 2001). The 'they' refers to ethnic and aboriginal media whose collective objectives address the informational, integrative, and advocacy needs of those historically disadvantaged or diasporically situated. This multi-dimensionality is crucial in clarifying the origins and rationale behind ethnic and aboriginal media; the role they play in society at large, minority communities in particular; the challenges in navigating mediaspace; and their growing popularity because of increased participatory dynamics (Deuze 2006).

3.1 Framing Ethnic and Aboriginal Media

Ethnic and aboriginal media consist of mostly small broadcasters, cable channels, newspapers, and magazines that target racial and ethnic minority audiences, including aboriginal peoples, racialized women and men, and immigrants and refugees (also Lieberman 2006). Many are 'mom and pop' startups, published on a weekly or intermittent basis in languages other than English (or French), and distributed free of charge. Other ethnic media tend to resemble mainstream media, that is, sophisticated in operation, content, and distribution, employing sufficient resources to publish on a daily basis for profit (Lin and Song 2006). As well, ethnic media can be classified according to origins: To one side are homegrown ethnic media that are conveyed in either the native tongue or host country language or combination of both. To the other side are ethnic media produced abroad but circulated in the host country (Weber-Menges 2005). And while some ethnic media are meant to be intercultural in the sense of generating intergroup dialogue, many cater to a single target. Even here internal variations prevail, with some ethnic media directed at the distinctive needs and concerns of immigrants, while others target native-born minorities, and still others address different demographics within each category.

This plethora of ethnic media suggests the need for a comparative structural framework along the lines proposed by Donald R Browne (2005), albeit intended for analysis of ethnic electronic media:

1. types of outlets and levels of service (licensed, unlicensed, radio, TV, presses, internet),

2. policy (by government or advertisers or community members),

3. financing (advertising, licensing fee, government grants donations, subscriptions),

4. primary audience (accessible to everyone or minority audiences; target group within the community)

5. programming type (information, education, entertainment

6. links with community (language used, staffing)

7. operational goals (links with ancestral homelands, preservation of language and culture, pride in community, information source, combating negative stereotypes)

Few would dispute the relevance of these dimensions in theorizing ethnic and aboriginal media. However valid such an assessment, this paper focuses primarily on the role of ethnic media in facilitating the integration of new Canadians. These media are shown to represent an exercise in social capital that bonds as it bridges by *connecting the 'here' with the 'there' by way of the 'in between'*. No one should be surprised by the bridging role of ethnic media in crossing borders. Nor should there be surprise by the bonding and buffering dynamic of ethnic media, thanks to information flows that are community-based, culturally-sensitive, communication-responsive and locally-relevant.

Ethnic media provide social capital in paradoxical ways. As Robert Putnam pointed in his landmark book, *Bowling Alone*, the quality of peoples lives and the life of society/community depends on establishing reserves of social capital. And yet the more ethnically diverse a community, Putnam (2007) more recently concedes, the less likely are people to connect or to display trustworthiness. The potential loss of social capital puts the onus on ethnic media to neutralize this disconnect and distrust, in part by providing both the bridging capital between different groups (ties to people unlike you), in part by way of bonding capital within one's own group (ties to people like you). To one side, ethnic media play an intermediary role by connecting community with society; to the other side, ethnic media provide a strong migrant identity for making the transition from there to here by fostering a more multilocal sense of belonging (Cheng 2005). Or as Madeleine Bunting (2007) writes in linking the bonding with the bridging: "A strong community identity gives them the confidence and the self-respect to establish themselves and get on." (also Riggins 1992; Lam 1996).

Of particular note is the provision of relevant information that minority women and men want but cannot readily access. Ethnic and aboriginal media offer an alternative to those mainstream newsmedia that many perceive as increasingly centralized, standardized, and preoccupied with the trivial or sensational. Myopic and distorted coverage of global issues because of mainstream newsvalues creates a pent-up demand for more accurate information that speaks to diasporic communities (Tan 2006; Karim 2006). As a clearinghouse of information, ethnic and aboriginal media not only draw attention to those stories that the mainstream glosses over. Issues are also framed in ways that impart a fresh perspective in a language that resonates with community members (Hsu 2002). In their role as bulletin boards for announcements of upcoming events governments often use ethnic and aboriginal media to convey information or change attitudes, while commercial interests rely on them to expand their market penetration (Wu 2005). The advocacy role played by populist media is no less critical. Aboriginal and ethnic media not only crusade for justice and equality, but also pose those awkward questions that mainstream media avoid for fear of censure or reprisals.

In light of such a (dis)array of functions, reactions to ethnic and aboriginal media vary. For some, there is much to commend in processes that reflect the community, act as a political mouthpiece, foster a collective purpose, enhance group consciousness and sense of place, and create a sense of community consensus.[1] For others, this advocacy commitment inspires a softer journalism

---

1   Consider, a proposed European Manifesto to support, recognize, and underline the importance of minority community (ethnic) media (Online/More Colour in the Media 2004 cited by Pat Cox). Below are select passages from the Manifesto.

In the Manfesto, minority community media call upon the European Parliament, the European Commission and the Governments of member states:

-    to recognize the important role that minority community media play in Europe as actors to implement social inclusion policies

-    to see the minority media being recognized as a public community service that, as such, they will be contained in all European and national media legislation and will obtain a "must see" status on all relevant broadcast platforms

-    to ensure that freedom of speech, the right to receive information and the right to communicate for all, including the right for minorities to receive

that ultimately privileges ideology over balanced coverage (Hsu 2002). To be sure, evidence suggests that not all ethnic minorities are gung-ho over ethnic media as sources of help or information (Lam 1996; Mahtani 2007; but see Gillespie 2005). Outlets that pander exclusively to ethnic minorities may be criticized for ghettoizing minority experiences or for excessively 'soft' news

media in their own language, are recognized as basic human rights for all citizens. These rights should be included as part of the concept of civic citizenship and they should be enshrined in all media policies, legislation, and all social inclusion policies of the European Union and national member states.

- Being aware that sensitizing the majority populations to the benefits and challenges of immigration are core elements in a proactive social inclusion policy and that the mass media have a major responsibility in their role as educators of public opinion.

- Being aware that mainstream media have great difficulties in attracting ethnic minority audiences and to make their mainstream products a real reflection of the multicultural society.

- Being aware that unlike mainstream media, minority community media are able to link into networks of spokespeople and community leaders, and thus can act as a mediator.

- Being aware that minority community media, as part of the public ser vice…can play a major role in encouraging equal and full participation of immigrants and ethnic minority groups, by addressing issues of impor tance…and by offering them a platform for discussion within their own communities on important national and local issues, as well as providing them with a platform to share these views with the rest of the national population.

- Convinced that minority community media can contribute to the participation and emancipation process of immigrants and ethnic minority groups within the concept of civic citizenship, the improvement of intercultural communication, common understanding and dialogue.

- Convinced that by using the language of their audience, minority community media are able to effectively reach out to immigrants and ethnic minority audiences, which cannot normally be reached by other national and local media.

- Convinced that minority community media can have an important supporting role to mainstream media, as mediator between minority communities and mainstream society, in providing access to minority networks, and to alternative sources of information.

- Convinced that minority community media is a basic public service and that, as such, they should be a structural part of the national and European media environment.

- Convinced that minority community media need meaningful and relevant support in order to fulfil their important role.

coverage. No surprises here, argues Lawrence Lam (1996:255) since people are selective vis-à-vis their interests in what they see or read – especially in a media rich country like Canada. For others still, the inward looking nature of ethnic and aboriginal media not only postpones migrant integration into their adopted homeland, but also sabotages the integrationist logic behind a living together. This, of course, raises the question of what is meant by integration, how to bring it about, what it hopes to achieve, and what must be done to prevent mistakes from the past (Neill and Schweder 2007, but see EC Commission of the European Communities (Com (2005) 389/1-9-2005)[2] For yet others, the persistence and popularity of ethnic and aboriginal media attests to the multiculturality that informs and defines democratic governance.

---

2   There is much talk of (civic) integration as a social contract to replace multi-culturalism. Yet there is little consensus regarding what integration means and how to bring it about (Neill and Schwedler 2007). To overcome this lacunae, the European Council adopted a commitment to integration in 2004 whose principles are paraphrased below (For critique, see Joppke 2007).

-   Integration is a dynamic two way process of mutual accommodation by immigrants and host country.
-   Integration implies respect for the basic values of the European Union.
-   Employment is a key part of the integration process for immigrants and host country.
-   Basic knowledge of the host country's language, history, and institutions is indispensable to integration.
-   Access to education is critical to the integration of immigrants.
-   Immigrant integration requires full and non-discriminatory access to institutions, public and private goods and services.
-   Frequent encounters and creative interaction between immigrants and member state citizens secures to successful integration.
-   Integration is predicated on guaranteeing the practice of diverse cultures and religions, provided these practices do not conflict with rights or laws.
-   Immigrant participation in the democratic process is critical especially in the formulation of programs and policies that impact on their lives.
-   Integration is contingent on mainstreaming integration polices and measures in all relevant portfolios and levels of government and public services.
-   Clear goals, indicators, and evaluation mechanism must be in place to adjust immigration policies and evaluate progress.

3.2 Accounting for Ethnic and Aboriginal Media: Reactive/Proactive; Outward/Inward

Ethnic media originated for a variety of reasons, both *reactive and proactive* as well as *outward and inward*. On the reactive side, ethnic and racialized minorities resent their exclusion from the mainstream newsmedia (Husband 2005; deSouza and Williamson 2006). Historically, newsmedia (mis)treatment of aboriginal peoples, immigrants, and racialized ethnic minorities left everything to be desired, given their placement into one of five negative frames, namely as invisible, problems, stereotypes, adornments, or whitewashed (Fleras and Kunz 2001). In an industry driven by the logic that only bad news is good news, the framing of minorities as troublemakers resulted in one sided coverage that demonized and denied (Butterwege 2005). Teun A. van Dijk (1993) writes:

> The strategies, structures, and procedures of reporting, the choice of themes, the perspective, the transfer of opinions, style and rhetoric, are directed at presenting "us" positively and "them" negatively...Their cause is only worth reporting when they cause problems, are caught in criminality or violence or can be represented as a threat to white hegemony.

Despite modest improvements in the quality and quantity of coverage, mainstream newsmedia remains a problem in two ways: first in a systemically biasing way that frames minorities as troublesome constituents; second, in their failure to frame 'deep' diversities except as conflict or problem (Fleras 2004/06). This problematic should come as no surprise: Newsmedia are fundamentally racialized because of how rules, values, practices, discourses and rewards are dispersed (both deliberately or inadvertently) thereby reinforcing white interests and eurocentric agendas. The end result? By framing diversity around conflict or problems as catalysts for newsworthiness to the exclusion of alternative frameworks – ie. by normalizing invisibility while problematizing visibility – newsmedia coverage of minorities has proven systemically biasing rather than systematically biased (Everitt 2005).

Newsmedia mistreatment of minorities and aboriginal peoples continues unabated (ERCOMER 2002; Jiwani 2006; Miller 2005; also Kelley 2006). But while news media may have once openly vilified minorities as aliens in a whiteman's country, it is no longer socially acceptable to do. A growing reluctance to say anything negative about minorities for fear of being branded racists or reactionary (McGowan 2001) encourages thinly veiled criticism that are subliminally pro white. First, minorities are criticized for not fitting into the framework of society as they should (minorities are ok if they are useful or know their place); second, minorities are associated with negative contexts related to crime or terrorism; third, their cultural values and practices are dismissed as incommensurate with contemporary secular society; and fourth, minority realities and concerns are refracted through a pro white gaze (perspective) that invariably diminishes or distorts. However subtle and understated, such a negativity framework not only reduces minorities to the status of problem people, but, by essentializing minorities as little more than ethnics, also feeds into a national discourse over who is acceptable and what is normal (see also McLeod 2007/2006).

Nowhere is this negativity more evident than with media coverage of Muslims or those of Arabian appearance (Canadian Islamic Conference 2005). Positive and normalizing images of ordinary Muslims or Arabs are almost non existent in the mainstream media (Alliance of Civilizations 2006; Starck 2007). Coverage of Muslims as violent and irrational is heavily skewed towards international conflicts without providing a historical context (Manning 2006). For newsmedia, the debate over the so-called clash of civilizations – Islamic vs Western – tends to frame their coverage accordingly, that is, protagonists ensnared in global geopolitics (in the same way the Cold War once served as a framing function for geo-political developments) (Seib 2004/05). Newsframes routinely portray Muslim/Arab males as tyrants or terrorists, while Muslim/Arab women are reduced to the level of burqa-bearing submissives at odds with modern realities. Visual images about Islam immediately triggers a subliminal negativity:

> A bearded Middle Eastern looking man wearing a black cloak and turban can trigger an entire series of images of a fanatical religious movement, of airplane hijackings, of western hostages held helpless in dungeons, of truck bombs killing hundreds of innocent people, of cruel punishment sanctioned by Islamic law, and of suppression of human rights – in sum of intellectual and moral regression (Karim 2006:118).

Clearly, then, mainstream media stand accused of being racist, including the use of loaded terminology (Islam as extremist, fundamentalist, terrorists, or primitive) and simplistic and negative stereotypes (deSouza and Williamson 2006). The combination of insult and injury, together with diminished self-esteem, fosters resentment and rage over what many see as white propaganda. Such racialized one-sidedness also intensifies the risk of racial tensions and increased discrimination. Not surprisingly, perhaps, when a Gallup poll asked 10,000 respondents in predominantly Muslim countries what the West could do to improve relations with the Muslim world, 47 percent (the single largest response) said the western media must stop disrespecting Islam by portraying Muslims as inferior or threatening (Alliance of Civilization 2006).

In short, mainstream newsmedia are criticized for reneging on their commitment to integrate minorities (Whyte 2006). Criticism revolves around the media's refusal to treat minorities as individuals and active agents, but as faceless, homogenous, and unruly mob; their reluctance to go beyond the tokenistic; and a refusal to depict minorities within a holistic context of normalcy or acceptability (Weber-Menges 2005). The proliferation of these biases and blindspots creates resistance and reaction: What option is there except to adopt alternative media as sources of information that reflects minority realities in a language that relates to their experiences (Ahmad 2006). An alternative discourse offers a different menu of newsvalues from mainstream communication agendas. Instead of framing minorities as potentially troublesome constituents, profiles of success promote a positive self image that helps foster a collective community confidence. Even coverage of negative news is framed differently. With ethnic media, intergroup conflict and community problems may be situated within a historical context that apportions blame to the system rather than minorities (Ojo 2006; Lin and Song 2006).

Against this backdrop of negativity and the problematic, ethnic media *proactively* strive to celebrate minority successes, accomplishments, and aspirations. They are positioned to operate in a counter-hegemonic manner by providing the missing social and cultural context for understanding the complex social realities that minorities must endure. By amplifying a sense of culture and community, ethnic media secure a haven from the stereotyping and distortions that abound in mainstream media. Ethnic media also constitute an information system about the homeland that is crucial for adaptation; after all, news from or about home taps into an immigrants longing for content about the 'there' as basis for fitting in 'here' (Lin and Song 2006). No less critical is their role in supplying specific information needs, including information about settling down, fitting in, and moving up (Whyte 2006). Consider the potential benefits: An ethnic media may prove more accessible than mainstream outlets when publicizing free services or fund raising events; a range of information about upcoming events and visits from overseas dignitaries; in depth stories about their communities; advice on how to book a vacation or find legal representation; or a window to catch up on the latest cricket matches or rugby scores. Of particular importance are information tip sheets for manoeuvering one's way through government bureaucracies and service agencies (Silverstone and Georgiou 2005). In that people pay attention to media that pay attention to them, it is this dedication to community service that anchors the credibility of ethnic media (Husband 2005).

Ethnic media also play both an *outward-* and *inward-looking* role. *Outwardly*, by supplying information of relevance and immediacy to the intended demographic, including how to navigate the labyrinth of a strange new world. Ethnic media provide communities with a voice to articulate their concerns with the wider public, while providing a counterweight to an increasingly corporate mainstream newsmedia (Hsu 2002). This building of bridges with the outside world reinforces and advances the social capital of minorities both as individuals and community members. *Inwardly*, as a marker of identity by reporting news of relevance to the community through a perspective and tone that resonates meaningfully with these audiences. Focusing on homeland news or events in the immigrants native language strengthens identities, heritage and culture, especially since mainstream media tend to ignore minority issues or unnecessarily problematize them. In offering an alternative view to mainstream media, ethnic media focus on issues related to social justice, institutional inclusion, and the removal of discriminatory barriers. By providing local news of direct and immediate relevance, ethnic media acquire the potential to mobilize residents to act upon injustices and problems within the community (Lin and Song 2006).

Clearly, then, ethnic media can be aligned along a reactive-proactive and outward-inward dimension. With the globalized flows of migrants, ideas, information, capital, and technology around the world, traditional notions of belonging between people and place are changing. Immigrants now have the option of being firmly rooted in their adopted countries, without losing multiple links to their homeland, thereby exerting pressure on ethnic (and immigrant) media to construct a multilocality and transnational sense of belonging (Cheng 2005). In acknowledging the possibility of community as imagined or locality as narrated across national borders, the concept of multiple homelands and attachments challenges conventional notions that reduce the relationship between host country and home country as either-or dichotomies for winning immigrant attention and affection. Even questions regarding the role of ethnic media in helping or hindering the integration process may have to be rethought, according to Cheng. Rather than boxing them into one of these dimensional categories, most ethnic media are multidimensional. If these dimensions (inward-outward; reactive-proactive) are aligned along two continua and then bisected at right angles, a four cell table is created that acknowledges the dynamics and complexity of ethnic media:

	Reactive (defensive)	**Proactive** (affirmative)
Inward (insular)	Reaction to media negativity/ invisibility by offering a minority perspective including access to local and homeland information. "constructing buffers"	Focus on celebrating both personal and community accomplishments to foster community cohesion and culture pride. "creating bonds"
Outward (integrative)	Counteract social injustice by advocating positive changes for leveling an unlevel playing field. "crossing borders"	Utilize positive images of minority success for bolstering minority civic participation in inclusive society. "building bridges"

Table 2: Dimensions of Ethnic Media

Of course, not every agrees with ethnic and aboriginal media as integrative in intent or outcome. Critics argue that ethnic and aboriginal media may dampen integration, especially with the inception of satellite TV and the internet, both of which allow disaporic migrants to easily retain their homeland roots by tapping into the latest news, fashions, and trends. The concern is understandable: In their commitment to transcend the limitations of mainstream media, members of ethnic communities tend to be the most enthusiastic and technology aware consumers of communication services (Online 2007). And once engrossed in their own media world, critics contend, immigrants no longer need to communicate or interact with others, resulting in the fragmentation of society into self-contained enclaves (Husband 2005; Weber-Menges 2005). For example some third language broadcasters in Canada, including Cantonese, Mandarin, and Punjabi offer modest amounts of local and current affairs news but most ethnic broadcasts include little Canadian editorial content – in effect, depriving minority audience of Canadian news, views, and cultural content. Admittedly, migrants neither live in media ghettos nor rely exclusively on a diet of ethnic media (Lam 1996; Mahtani 2007), but rather selectively rely on a rich media menu for closing the multilocality gap (Weber-Menges/Geißler 2007).

To summarize: In refusing to either canonize or demonize ethnic media, a rethinking is in order. Rather than typecasting ethnic media as divisive or integrative, a dialectical dynamic is in play. The interplay of the reactive-proactive with the inward-outward generates an insular and integrative process that pushes as it pulls – bonding and buffering as well as bridging and border crossing. A preoccupation with homeland and ethnic news may delay societal incorporation by virtue of reinforcing cultural identities and community networks (Lin and Song 2006). Neverthless, in a world where the global is the local, and vice versa, such a focus does not necessarily preclude integration. By creating a comfort zone in a strange new land, ethnic media insulate migrants and minorities from the harshness of readjustment, thereby providing a buffer between the 'here' and the 'there' by way of the 'inbetween'. Ethnic media also serve as a bridging device for facilitating integration into society at large while securing a reassuring bond of community, identity, and culture (Open Society Institute 2005). In that, ethnic media represent instruments of cultural preservation as well as agents of incorporation, their status as pockets of insularity as pathways to integration cannot be underestimated. No more so than in Canada where the popularity of ethnic and aboriginal media may well constitute the quintessential expression of Canada's inclusive multiculturalism.

4. Aboriginal and Ethnic Media in Canada: Pockets of Insularity as Pathways to Integration

Canada has long campaigned to promote and preserve its cultural diversity in the face of globalization, trade liberalization, and border-busting technology. Support for the principle of cultural diversity is formulated in three ways: first through the promotion of ethnic or third language broadcasting within the framework of Canadian broadcasting system (Lincoln et al. 2005); second, through the mainstreaming of private and public media; and third, by acknowledging the legitimacy of ethnic and aboriginal newspapers/presses. Yet success secures neither clarity nor consensus. Although ethnic and aboriginal have enjoyed a long history in Canada, there is no agreement over magnitude and impact. Numbers fluctuate as new publications arise as quickly as they disappear because of costs, competition, and intimidation. Even the expression ethnic and aboriginal media is problematic because of internal diversity. Does ethnic refer to new Canadians or Canadian-born? To visibilized minorities or white European ethnics? To aboriginal people with status or without status? Despite these uncertainties and confusion, aboriginal and ethnic media can be divided into three main categories: Aboriginal and ethnic print, aboriginal and ethnic broadcasting, and mainstreaming of public and private media. First, however, a brief overview of Canada's mediascape.

4.1   Canada's Mediascape

Canada is widely regarded as a media rich society whose impressive achievements are particularly striking despite a daunting geographic, demographic, diversity, and historical obstacles (Attalah and Shade 2006). In articulating the objectives of the broadcast system, the Broadcasting Act establishes several priorities for Canadian broadcasting, including an emphasis on Canadian-owned and controlled media, responsiveness to the needs of all Canadians, and a commitment to engage language diversity without losing sight of Canada's official French-English bilingualism. While operating primarily in English and French to ensure the integration of immigrants into Canadian society, broadcasting in Canada is expected:

> [...] through its programming and the employment opportunities arising out of its operations, [to] serve the needs and interests, and reflect the circumstances and aspirations, of Canadian men, women, and children, including equal rights, the linguistic duality and multicultural and multiracial nature of Canadian society and the special place of aboriginal peoples within that society.

This diversity agenda has culminated in the development of a sophisticated and complex broadcasting system that serves both English and French as well as aboriginal peoples, in addition to a range of third language services that now constitute an important tile in Canada's media-mosaic (Lincoln et al 2005). Ethnic radio programming is present in most Canadian cities, ranging in scope from time slots at mainstream stations to ethnic radio stations in third languages. Television is particularly important, including an aboriginal television network. Multicultural channels (OMNI 1 and 2 in Toronto) are found in major Canadian cities, in addition to time slots on community cable, commercial stations and a national network (Vision TV). In total, Canada's system of mixed private-public-populist arrangement comprises nearly 700 private and public television services (511 English, 115 French, and 53 third language) together with 1, 158 radio services (867 English, 253 French, and 38 third language) (CRTC 2006).

Canada also possesses a lively if increasingly beleaguered publishing sector. Currently, there are 105 daily papers across Canada, down from a peak of 138 in 1938, but up from 87 in 1945. Ownership of newspapers has devolved as well to several major chains including CanWest Global, Hollinger International, Torstar, Quebecor, Osprey Media Group (recently purchased by Quebecor), and Power (Canadian Newspaper Association 2006). Although 5.2 million Canadians receive a daily paper (down from 5,7 million in 1989), readership continues to remain steady with a total of 11,8 million weekly readers in the major 17 markets – a figure that remained steady between 2001 and 2005 despite immigration driven population increases. Readership of online papers continues to grow; in 2005, 15 percent of adults 18 years and over read an online edition of a newspaper. Equally impressive is the growth of free daily papers; for example, up to 27 percent of Toronto adults and 23 percent of Montreal adults read a free daily each week. In short, despite holding their own in these trying times, according to the Canadian Newspaper Association, the outlook for newspapers appears bleak:

> Canadian newspapers continue to face challenges and competition in their role as bearers of news in the information age. While information itself proliferates at an astonishing rate in a variety of forms, methods of storing and distributing it have grown more encompassing and complex.

Compounding media woes is a seeming inability or disinterest in cracking the ethnic market. Despite Canada's Multiculturalism Act, its Broadcasting Act and Ethnic Broadcasting policies, newsmedia remain divided along a colour line between the normalized white and the racialized "other" – in the process forfeiting an opportunity to connect with a largely untapped demographic.

Finally, ethnic media have expanded significantly over the last decade, playing a much larger role in the lives of the fastest growing ethnic groups (Chinese and South Asian Canadians) than traditional media measurements would indicate (Karim 2006). These media range in size from small newspapers printed in home basements to well established and professionally run broadcast stations. Hundreds of ethnic newspapers publish on a daily, weekly, or monthly cycle, including some that are increasingly sophisticated in operation and quite capable of competing with non ethnic papers. There are those that speak to specific groups (Share – Caribbean and African), while others are directed at immigrants in general (New Canada). Some are printed in English, many in native languages, others in both. Foreign based services are available as well, either through specialty cable channels or satellite television, thus reinforcing how ethnic media quickly adapt to new communication technologies to secure access to often small and frequently scattered audiences (Karim 2003). Of particular note is the emergence of the internet as a vital media option and communication tool for ethnic groups, possibly contributing to a diminished reliance on traditional media for major ethnic groups in Canada's MTV cities (Solutions Research Group 2006).

Of course, Canada is not alone in the ethnic newsmedia sweepstakes. The United States has also seen a major spike in the number of ethnic radio stations both local and national, newspapers, magazines, web portals, and public and cable television stations (Hsu 2002). (Scholarly interest in ethnic media as an instrument of assimilation by shaping immigrant worldviews and sense of belonging goes back to 1922 and the publication of Robert Parks *The Immigrant Press and its Control*). In contrast to mainstream newsmedia which are experiencing a decline in readership, revenues, and stock prices, ethnic media continue to expand (Annual Report 2006). Admittedly no concrete figures are available for ethnic media nationwide, nevertheless, a study in the state of California estimated that 84 percent of Asian Americans, Blacks, and Latinos were exposed to ethnic media, more than half indicated a preference for ethnic broadcasts or publications over English language sources, and 40 percent said they paid more attention to ads in ethnic publications than to those in mainstream media (Briggs 2005). With ethnic minority audiences now accounting for nearly a third of the purchasing power in America, advertisers no longer dismiss this demographic as too small or too poor, but are pitching to these niches as vigorously as they do to the mainstream (Lieberman 2006).

4.2   Aboriginal and Ethnic Publications

The centrality of ethnic newsmedia in Canada cannot be denied. Ethnic newspapers are no stranger to Canada's mediascape - from the first ethnic papers written in German in Halifax at the end of the 18th century (Die Neuschottlaendishe Kalendar 1787) to the publication in 1835 of Waterloo Region's Das Museum Canada, followed by the emergence of the black papers of the 1850s (including the Provincial Freeman and The Voice of the Fugitive). Estimates at present suggest up to 350 ethnic papers (including about 200 third language publications) that cater to their audiences on a daily, weekly, monthly, quarterly, or bi-annual basis. Most of these paper are local or regional in scope, but a few are national including the Chinese language version of Canada's national newsmagazine (Macleans). In British Columbia the Indo-Canadian *Punjabi Times* competes with three English-language weeklies and four Punjabi weeklies that address Indo-Canadian issues, while in Southern Ontario there are seven Punjabi weeklies and a twice-monthly English newspaper targeted to the same audience.Their collective impact is immeasurable argues Ben Viccari (2007), President of the Canadian Ethnic Journalists and Writers Club: "These media keep their readers and audiences informed about Canada as well as providing a vehicle for expression of freedom of thought that many editors and broadcasters never found in their country of origins".

4.3   Aboriginal and Ethnic Broadcasting

No less significant are ethnic and aboriginal broadcasting – both radio and television. In contrast to the ethnic print media that are relatively free to come and go as they please, ethnic and aboriginal broadcasting is tightly micromanaged. On the assumption that airwaves belong to the public and must serve public interests, Canadians Broadcasting Acts (1991) not only asserts the importance of diversity within the broadcast system, but the goals for ethnic and aboriginal broadcasting are established as well. The Canadian Radio-Television and Telecommunications Commission (CRTC) stipulates how to put these principles into practice by specifying the conditions for the dissemination of ethnic and multilingual programming (Karim 2006).

For the CRTC, ethnic programming is defined as any radio or television programming aimed at any ethnically or racially distinct group other than aboriginal peoples, and those descendents of French and English settlers. The programming may be in any language, including English or French, or combination of languages. Depending on size of the target group and resources available, stations that feature ethnic programming must incorporate several ethnic groups within their service catchment area. As the CRTC (1999) puts it:

> Ethnic stations are required to serve a range of ethnic groups in a variety of languages. This is because the scarcity of broadcast frequencies may not permit the licensing of an over-the-air single-language service for each ethnic in a given market. This approach also allows for the provision of service to groups that would not otherwise be able to afford their own single-language service.

Other restrictions apply as part of the mandatory licensing arrangement. According to CRTC regulations, ethnic radio and television stations must devote at least 60 percent of their schedule to ethnic programming. The other 40 percent of the schedule allows stations to establish a business model for generating revenues in support of ethnic programming. To reflect Canada's linguistic diversity, 50 percent of their programming schedule must be in third languages, i.e. languages other than French, English, or the many Aboriginal languages. Ethnic radio stations must fulfill this requirement each broadcast week; compliance with this requirement for ethnic television stations are measured monthly. It should be noted that non ethnic radio and television stations may air unlimited amounts of ethnic programming in French or English, but only 15 percent of their schedules can be in third languages, unless they obtain CRTC approval for up to 40 percent.

Such a high level of micro-management may appear excessively bureaucratic. But there is a rationale, namely, the need to protect ethnic broadcasting from undue competition while providing non ethnic stations with the flexibility to reflect local diversity. As is the case with mainstream broadcasting, Canadian content requirements apply to ethnic radio and television stations (generally speaking, radio programming must reflect 35 percent Canadian content – at least for category 2 general music, but only 7 percent for category 1 ethnic music). Television programming must reflect 60 percent Canadian content, including 50 percent during the evening ('prime time') broadcast slot.

4.3.1   Ethnic Broadcasting

The CRTC drafted its first ethnic broadcasting policy in 1985. The policy was predicated on the multicultural premise that new Canadians would have a stronger sense of belonging if provided with programming from within their community and in their own language (Whyte 2006). Since the CRTC issued Canada's first license for ethnic broadcasting to CHIN radio in 1966, the number of licensed ethnic radio and television services has grown dramatically. At present, licensed ethnic and third language services consist of five over the air TV stations in the MTV cities (Montreal, Toronto, Vancouver), 18 ethnic radio stations that offer nearly 2000 hours of third language programming each week), 10 specialty audio services that require special receivers, 5 analog specialty services, 11 launched category 2 digital specialty services and 50 approved but not yet launched (cited in Lincoln et al 2005; also Cardozo 2005). (category 2 services are digital, pay, and specialty services that are not obligated to be carried by cable or satellite distributor) (Kular 2006). OMNI 1 and OMNI 2 are world leaders in this field in producing in excess of 20 hours of original programming per week, including 60 percent that is non-French or non-English (Quill 1996). Vision TV, a national broadcaster, also hosts about 30 programs about different religious faiths and practices. Inroads are also evident in the private sector, where multicultural issues since 1984 have been addressed by Toronto's CITY-TV station through two large blocks of non-English, non-French programming.

4.3.2   Aboriginal Media and Broadcasting

Like ethnic minorities, Aboriginal peoples too have indigenized media institutions as a tool of empowerment for linking the past with pathways into a globally integrated future (Meadows and Molnar 2001; Roth 2006). But aboriginal and ethnic media operate on different wavelengths: While ethnic media provide an alternative service to that offered by mainstream newsmedia, aboriginal media strive to provide a first level of service since the mainstream does not service aboriginal audiences (Avison and Meadows 2000). Not surprisingly, because of differences in sociological and constitutional status aboriginal media reflect a different logic compared to ethnic media (Fleras and

Elliott 2007). Ethnic media are directed at immigrants/refugees and descendents of immigrants/refugees – those who sociologists define as voluntary minorities because of their decision to come to Canada. Generally speaking, their primary concern upon 'getting in' is to settle down, fit in, and move up – without necessarily sacrificing their homeland identity in the process. Rather than challenging Canada or separating themselves from society, the goal is improve the terms of integration, in part through removal of those discriminatory barriers that preclude inclusiveness, in part by capitalizing on special measures when necessary to facilitate the integration. Towards that end, Canada's ethnic media play a major role in the integration process by providing a set of inward and outward looking functions that facilitate the transition from 'there' to 'here' by way of the 'inbetween' – that is, linking immigrants with home country while bolstering a commitment to Canada.

By contrast, aboriginal peoples are defined sociologically as involuntary minorities. As descendents of the original occupants, aboriginal peoples were forcibly incorporated against their will into a colonial constitutional framework. Instead of looking to 'fit in' into a society not of their making, their primary goal is to 'get out' of this colonial predicament by restructuring their constitutional relationship along the status of a "nations within" status. Nothing less politicized will do for those who claim status as fundamentally autonomous political communities sovereign in their own right yet sharing sovereignty with society at large (Maaka and Fleras 2005). In rejecting a view of aboriginal peoples as ethnic minorities in need of assistance or information, aboriginal media tend to resonate with information that advances aboriginal peoples' claims as "first nations" for reasserting a right to self-determining autonomy, instead of a dominated people who are subject to dominant values and labels (Retzlaff 2007).

Admittedly, not all aboriginal media are politicized. Many incorporate an informational and community agendas that provide Aboriginal peoples with one of the few places where they can find a reflection of their lived experiences (Raudsepp 1996). For example, consider the mission statement by Anishnabek News, an aboriginal paper in Ontario, whole goal is: "…to foster pride and share knowledge about Anishnabek current affairs, culture, goals, and successes". Objectives include "…Sharing: Provide opportunities for people from the four corners of the Anishnabek Nation to tell stories and record achievements , and to keep our citizens informed about the activities of the Union of Ontario Indians. Strength: To give voice to the vision of the Anishnabek Nation that celebrates our history, language, and culture, promotes our land, treaty, and aboriginal rights, and supports the development of health and prosperous communities." To counteract and resist the dominant Euro-Canadian discourse, combat stereotypes, and ensure that histories and contemporary issues reflect Aboriginal perspectives, aboriginal media emphasize different newsnorms to challenge and change (Retzlaff 2007). In brief, another slogan may capture the distinction between ethnic and aboriginal media. If ethnic media are about improving the prospects of *living together with differences,* then it may be more accurate to describe aboriginal media as advancing the challenge of *living apart together.*

Canada's Aboriginal Peoples may possibly possess one of the most advanced broadcasting systems in the world (Roth 2006). Nowhere is this more evident than in Northern Canada, where aboriginal communities have exercised control over the local media, largely by appropriating satellite technology to meet social and cultural needs (Meadows 1995; Molnar and Meadows 2001). The Broadcasting Act in 1991 proved pivotal as well. It not only enshrined an aboriginal right to control over their own communications, but also instructed mainstream broadcasting to ensure 'the special place of aboriginal peoples' in its programming and employment. In keeping with the spirit of the Broadcasting Act, the CRTC approved the creation of a national Aboriginal network (APTN) in 1999 with an availability to 8 million Canadian homes (all cable companies are required to carry APTN as part of their basic consumer package, costing each subscribers about 15 cents a month, which is then allocated to APTN). As a national network by, for, and about aboriginality, APTN provides a platform to produce culturally and linguistically relevant programming for aboriginal men, women, and children, while providing Canadians with a window into the aboriginal world. Creation of national mediaspace that is enshrined in federal legislation also promises to counteract mainstream miscasting by promoting a positive and realistic portrayal of Canada's First Peoples across a broad range of topics (Molnar and Meadows 2001 Baltrushchat 2004; Retzlaff 2007). As Lorna Roth (2006:327) puts it when describing APTN as a symbolic meeting place for aboriginal peoples and non aboriginals to communicate their common interests:

> APTN has enabled indigenous messages to be heard by constituency groups that might have never had access to a live person of Aboriginal descent; it provides an opportunity to share national imageries and histories, to build bridges of understanding, and to bridge cultural borders.

To what extent have Aboriginal Peoples (and indigenous peoples in general) and diasporic populations embraced the information superhighway to bridge and to bond? In response to the question of what can the electronic frontier deliver to a peoples on the fringes of power and far from the centres of influence, the answer is increasingly clear: Greater empowerment for the historically disenfranchised by changing the subjectivities and practices (both online and offline) of the marginalized and disempowered (Landzelius 2006). This transformation goes beyond a simple asking of 'use' or 'effects' of the new media. Emphasis instead is on how members of a community are making themselves a(t) home in a global communicative environment.

Four patterns can be discerned according to Kyra Landzelius: (1) aboriginal/indigenous peoples are appropriating and moulding ICTs to reflect, reinforce, and advance their needs, interests, and identities - including the use of cyberactivism to promote their ends; (2) ICTs as forum for making claims in the name of ethnicity (or indigeneity or aboriginality); (3) for naming ethnicity or claiming ethnicity (or aboriginality); and (4) shifting the boundaries by which the politics of ethnicity/aboriginality is rethought, reworked, and revitalized.

To date, aboriginal peoples engagement with ICTs stretches along two directional pulls, namely, inreach (bonding) and outreach (bridging) (Landzelius 2006). Inreach orientations range from promoting localized interests and community services, including the dissemination of ingroup information to the importation of expert knowledge for community use. For example, aboriginal leaders are turning to ICTs to deliver high quality health care to remote Canadian communities (Gideon 2006). Telemedicine enables medical specialists to observe patients via real time links, thus providing an affordable way to defeat the tyranny of distance across Canada's vast expanses, while balancing Western medical knowledge with aboriginal health beliefs and practices. Outreach orientations tend to focus on bridging with the outside world, ranging in scope from simple tourist information to full blown indigenous revolutionary movements. The uprising of the indigenous and metizo peasants of the Chiapas in their resistance against the Mexican government constitutes one of the more spectacular examples of an indigenous cybercampaign against the new geopolitical order - thus reinforcing the web's potential for local empowerment (Belausteguigoitia 2006). In short, far from being at odds with each other or canceling each other out, inreach and outreach functions are mutually reinforcing by embedding the local with the global and their implications for the articulation of identities, experiences, and outcomes (Landzelius 2006).

4.4   Mainstreaming Ethnicity

References to ethnic and aboriginal media in Canada include an additional stream. Mainstream media in Canada are under pressure (both formal and informal) to respect, reflect, and be more responsive to ethnic and aboriginal differences (i.e. "mainstreaming" – to bring into the centre what once was at the margins). The government Task Force on Broadcasting Policy, co-chaired by Gerald Caplan and Florian Sauvagneau in 1986, addressed the need to include aboriginal peoples and racial minorities (Raboy 1988). The Broadcasting Act of 1991 made provisions for Canadian broadcasting, both in terms of programming and employment opportunities, 'to serve the needs of a diverse society and reflect the multicultural and multiracial character of Canada.' The Act not only reinforced the case for "cultural expression" by expanding air time for racialized ethnic minorities; it also insisted on sensitivity training for program and production staff, language guidelines to reduce race– role stereotypes, and monitoring of on-air representation of racial minorities. The institutionalization of the Ethnic Broadcasting Policy established guidelines for portrayal of minorities; in turn a regulatory body was charged with developing broadcasting services that reflected Canada's diversity. The CRTC requires all television broadcasters (and increasingly radio applicants) to file seven year plans on how they will reflect diversity in their programming and operations, and report annually on their progress (Cardozo 2005) (for comparable developments in the Netherlands, see d'Haenens 2007).

Mainstreaming diversity can prove a win/win situation. According to Madeline Ziniak, chair of the Task Force for Cultural Diversity on Television and Vice President at Omni Television, advertisers are waking up to the advantages of multicultural advertising to minorities (cited in Prashad 2006). Demographics are propelling the changes: When people of colour compose nearly 40 percent of the populations in Vancouver and Toronto, the media have little choice but to acknowledge that diversity sells. Despite a more accepting social climate and a powerful business model, institutional inclusiveness does not come easily to commercial mainstream media. Put bluntly commercial media do not see themselves as reform agencies to promote progressive change or to accommodate, even if they may have social responsibilities because of the power they wield. They are a business whose raison d'être is simple: to make money by connecting audience to advertisers through ratings. Institutional practices that generate revenues (for example, stereotyping) will be retained; those that don't will be discarded. Such a bottom-line mentality will invariably clash with minority demands for balanced and contexted coverage, given media preference for morselization over context, conflict over co-operation, the episodic over the contextual, personalities over issues (see Atkinson 1994).

That competing agendas are at play is no less detrimental to mainstreaming diversity. Whereas mainstream media provide a key cross over point for intercultural understanding and exchanges (deSouza and Williamson

2006), the very changes that minorities want of the newsmedia (responsible coverage of minority interests, less sensationalism, more context, toned-down language, and less stereotyping) are precisely the newsnorms that media rely on to sell copy or capture eyeballs.

Challenging the conventional news paradigm will prove a difficult sell. To the extent that changes happen, it will arise only when the issue of power (-sharing) is addressed by transformation to the structural constraints that inform newsmedia production and the ideological mindsets of media workers (Mahtani 2007).

5. Ethnic and Aboriginal Media in Canada: A Blueprint for Living Together Differently

How then do ethnic and aboriginal media reflect and reinforce Canada's commitment to an inclusive Multiculturalism? Consider how multiculturalism originated and continues to exist as a response to the realities of new and racialized Canadians. Canada is a destination of choice for immigrants around the world. Just under half of Canada's population at present (47%) can claim some non French, non English, and non aboriginal ancestry. Visible (or racialized) minorities constitute 13.4 percent of the population in 2001, a sharp increase from the 6 percent that existed in 1981. This figure is expected to expand to about 20 percent by 2017 (Canada's 150th birthday), in large part because of Canada's robust immigration program including approximately 250 000 new Canadians each year, with about 60 percent arriving from Asia and the Middle East. Neither immigrants nor racialized minorities are distributed evenly across Canada. Racialized minorities account for nearly 40 percent of the population in Toronto and Vancouver, while about one half of the population is foreign born ('immigrant'). Not surprisingly, perhaps, about 70 percent of Canada's population growth is immigrant driven (reflecting a low replacement rate of Canadian births). By 2017, the entirety of Canada's population (and labour market) growth will reflect immigration intake.

Of those initiatives at the forefront of 'managing' this demographic revolution, the most notable is official multiculturalism (Kymlicka 2001, 2008; Fleras 2002; Stein et al 2007; Banting et al 2007). In contrast to the colonial paradigm that equated Canadian culture with the unquestioned mainstream while ethnic cultures and minorities were marginalized as subcultures, a commitment to multiculturalism signified a major paradigm shift (Canada Heritage 2003). Canada is now widely recognized as a multicultural society whose engagement with the inclusiveness principles of multiculturalism is unmatched. But notwithstanding over 35 years of official multiculturalism and widespread acceptance, confusion continues. Both critics and supporter are prone to interpret multiculturalism in the literal sense of many cultures coexisting in harmony side by side. For some the idea of celebrating differences and promoting ethnic diverse communities is doable and worthwhile; for others, however, such diversity poses problems of cohesiveness. Having outlived its usefulness in an era of politicized diversity, multiculturalism is perceived as a recipe for divisiveness and danger, and counterproductive to the safety and success of society.

In reality, the rationale behind Canada's Multiculturalism model is inclusive in logic and intent. According to an inclusive multiculturalism, a Canada of many cultures is possible as long as peoples cultural differences don't get in the way of equal citizenship or full participation. A social climate is fostered that tolerates cultural differences as long as this commitment does not preclude belonging, equality, and involvement. To the extent that cultural differences are tolerated under Canada's multiculturalism, these differences cannot break the law, violate individual rights, or contravene core constitutional values (Fleras 2003). Canada's official multiculturalism reflects its modernist roots in promoting liberal universalism. That is, people should be treated the same as a matter of course regardless of their differences because everyone is equal before the law. Our commonalities as freewheeling and morally autonomous individuals are more important - at least for purposes of recognition or reward - than that which divides us as members of racially distinct groups. Insofar as cultural differences exist, they are largely superficial, tend to get in the way, and should rarely be deployed as a basis for reward or recognition even for progressive reasons.

The conclusion seems inescapable: Canada's multiculturalism model is not about celebrating diversity but removing disadvantage, not about separation and isolation but about interaction and integration, not about exclusion but about inclusion, not about differences but about tolerance, not about a one way process of absorption but a two way process of integration (you adjust, we adapt/you adapt, we adjust). Admittedly, differences are not entirely dismissed. They may have to be taken into account under extenuating circumstances; after all, a commitment to formal equality does not necessarily guarantee against exclusion or exploitation. However valid or valuable at times, these differences must conform with what is permissible in Canada with respect to laws, values, and rights. Yet another multicultural inversion is inescapable: If its goal is on removing disadvantage, promoting tolerance, and fostering integration and inclusion, Multiculturalism is more about the 'we' rather than the 'them'. The focus is not about changing the 'other' but about ensuring 'reasonable accommodation' at the level of structures/institutions and individuals/mindsets.

The paradoxes implicit in an official multiculturalism may well parallel those of ethnic and aboriginal media. To one side, ethnic media in general conform to a modernist notion for living together with differences, in part by acknowledging the need for new and racialized Canadians to be treated equally regardless of their differences. To the other side, ethnic media by definition constitute a postmodern reflection of an official multiculturalism. Cultural differences are important and may have to be incorporated in some circumstances into the existing institutional framework. That is, equal treatment as a matter of routine; differential treatment when the situation arises. In other words, ethnic media confirm the need for respecting cultural diversity and ethnic community while pursuing the goals of institutional inclusiveness and social justice, while facilitating dialogue where the two principles intersect (Alliance of Civilizations 2006).

By contrast, aboriginal media are unlikely to endorse the principle of multiculturalism. For those at the political forefront in politicizing the concept of a new postcolonial social contract, a multicultural governance cannot possibly cope with the politics of deep diversity, especially when addressing aboriginal demands for self-determining autonomy over land, identity, and political (Maaka and Fleras 2005). Aboriginal difference is key to survival, and aboriginal media play a key role in securing a special relationship with central authorities, with its corresponding flow of powers and entitlements. And yet aboriginal media also acknowledge that aboriginal peoples require the same kind of information and community as new Canadians, especially for those aboriginal peoples who live in cities (over one half of aboriginal peoples are urban although this urbanity may be fluid and imprecise). Aboriginal media content must be customized to address these concerns for integration through pathways of information and connection. To the extent that aboriginal media are expected to convey this complex dynamic of difference yet commonality, the challenges are striking.

Notwithstanding these limitations and insecurities, both aboriginal and ethnic media remain in the forefront of Canada building. In reflecting, reinforcing, and advancing the inclusiveness principles of Canada's multicultural model, ethnic and aboriginal media play an integrative role for advancing a cooperative coexistence. Aboriginal and ethnic media are simultaneously inclusive and insular: Insofar as aboriginal and ethnic media concurrently promote social integration and cultural insularity without sacrificing a commitment to community or to Canada they are both inward and outward looking. Aboriginal and ethnic media also reflect a reactive and proactive dynamic: reactive, in buffering minorities from the negativity of mainstream media; proactive, in building bridges by capitalizing on alternative media discourses. In doing so, they serve as a reminder: Before mainstream media can assist in the integration migrants and minorities into society, they have yet to institutionally integrate diversity. And because people pay attention to media that pay attention to them, namely, ethnic and aboriginal media, therein lies their success and popularity: In securing a normative blueprint that buffers as it bonds, that bridges as it crosses borders, that insulates as it integrates, aboriginal and ethnic media are proving pivotal as social capital in advancing a living together without drifting apart.

6.   References

Ahmad, Fauzia. (2006): "British Muslim Perceptions and Opinions on News Coverage of September 11." In: Journal of Ethnic and Migration Studies 32(6), pp. 961-982

Alliance of Civilizations (2006): Research Base for the High Level Group Report. Analysis on Media. United Nations, New York

Attalah, Paul and Leslie Shade, eds. (2006): Mediascapes. 2/e Toronto

Baltrushchat, Doris (2004): Television and Canada's Aboriginal Communities. Canadian Journal of Communication 29, pp.47-59

Belausteguigoitia, Marisa (2006): "On line, Off Line and In Line. The Zapatista Rebellion and the Uses of Technology by Indian Women." In: K Landzelius, ed.: Native on the Net. New York, pp. 97-111

Briggs, J. E. (2005): "Press Guide Shows Ethnic Diversity" In: Chicago Tribune. November 3

Browne, Donald R. (2005): Ethnic Minorities, Electronic Media, and the Public Sphere. A Comparative Approach. New Jersey

Bunting Madeleine (2007): "Don't hunker but embrace instead." In: Guardian Weekly. July 6

Burgess, Diane. (2000): "Kanehsatake on Witness: The Evolution of CBC Balance Policy." In: Canadian Journal of Communication, 25, pp. 231-249

Butterwege, A. (2005): "Migrants and the Mass Media" (Available online at http://www.mbtranslations.com/articles.php?filenum=1; accessed October 26, 2008)

Canadian Ethnic Media Association (2006): "Constitution and Bylaws" (Available online at: http://canadianethnicmedia.com/wp-content/CEMA_constitution.pdf, accessed October 26, 2008)

Canadian Ethnocultural Council (2003): "Cultural Policy Initiatives for a Multicultural Canada" Ministers Forum on Diversity and Culture, Ottawa, April 22-23. (Available online at http://www.pch.gc.ca/special/dcforum/info-bg/02_e.cfm; accessed October 26, 2008)

Canadian Heritage (2006): "A Convention on the Protection and Promotion of the Diversity of Cultural Expressions" (Available online at: http://www.canadianheritage.gc.ca/progs/ai-ia/rir-iro/global/convention/index_e.cfm; accessed October 26, 2008)

Canadian Islam Congress (2005): "Anti Islam in the Media". Summary of the 6th Annual Report for the year 2003. January 31. (Available online at http://www.canadianislamiccongress.com/rr/rr_2003.pdf; accessed October 26, 2008)

Canadian Newspaper Association (2006): "The Ultimate Online Guide to Canadian Newspapers" (Available at http://www.can-acj.ca)

Cardozo, Andrew (2005): Cultural Diversity in Canadian Broadcasting. Ethnicity and Media Symposium. Toronto: March 21

Cheng, Hau Ling (2005): "Constructing a Transnational, Multilocal Sense of Belonging. An Analysis of Ming Pao (West Canadian Edition)" In: Journal of Communication Inquiry 29(2), pp. 141-159

Cox, Pat (2004): "A European Manifesto" Produced by Online/More Colour in the Media. (Available online at http://www.olmcm.org/section.php?SectionID=3; accessed October 26, 2008)

Canadian Radio-Television and Telecommunications Commission – CRTC (2006): Report. The Government of Canada Asks the CRTC to Report on the Impact of New Technologies. (Available online at: http://www.pch.gc.ca/newsroom/index_e.cfm?fuseaction=displayDocument&DocIDCd=CBO060337; accessed October 26, 2008)

DeSouza, Ruth/Williamson, Andy (2006): "Representing Ethnic Communities in the Media" In: AEN Journal 1(1), June (Available online at http://www.aen.org.nz/journal/1/1/AENJ.1.1.Williamson-DeSouza.pdf; accessed October 26, 2008)

Deuze, Mark (2006): "Ethnic media, community media, and participatory culture." In: Journalism 7(3), pp. 262-280

d'Haenens, Leen (2007): "Whither Cultural Diversity on the Dutch TV Screen?" Paper Presented to the Media – Migration – Integration Conference at the University of Dortmund, Germany. June 21

ERCOMER (European Research Centre on Migration and Ethnic Relations) (2002): Racism and Cultural Diversity in the Mass Media: An Overview of Research and Examples of Good Practices in the EU Member States 1995 - 2000. Vienna: European Monitoring Centre on Racism and Xenophobia

Everitt, Joanna (2005): "Uncovering the Coverage. Gender Biases in Canadian Political Reporting" Breakfast on the Hill Seminar Series sponsored by SSHRC. November 17

Explore North (2006): "Milestones in Television Broadcasting in Northern Canada" (Available online at: http://explorenorth.com/library/weekly/more/bl-milestones.htm; accessed October 26, 2008)

Fleras, Augie (2002): Multiculturalism in Canada. Toronto

Fleras, Augie (2003): Mass Media Communication in Canada. Toronto

Fleras, Augie (2004/2006): "The Conventional News Paradigm as Systemic Bias: Rethinking the (Mis)Representational Basis of Newsmedia-Minority Relations". Paper presented the Media and Integration Conference at Siegen University, June 2004. Subsequently published in a proceedings from the Conference

Fleras, Augie (2007): "Misreading Minorities: Newscasting as Systemic Propaganda". Paper presented to the '20 Years of Propaganda Conference' University of Windsor. May 15-16

Fleras, Augie/Lock Kunz, Jean (2001): Media and Minorities in Canada. Toronto

Fleras, Augie/Elliott, Jean Leonard (2007): Unequal Relations. 5/e. Toronto

Gideon, Valerie (2006): "Canadian Aboriginal peoples Tackle E-Health: Seeking Ownership Versus Integration" In: Landzelius, K. ed.: Native on the Net. New York, pp. 61-79

Geißler, Rainer (2005): "Media Integration of Migrants. Reflections on a Key Concept." Paper presented to the ICA Conference. New York, May 2005

Gonzales, Juan. (2001): "Passion and Purpose for the Ethnic Press" Quill 89(3), pp. 42-44

Hassane, Souley (2007): "Mainstream Media vs. Ethnic Minority Media. The Integration in Question". Paper presented to the Media-Migration-Integration conference at the University of Dortmund, Germany, June 21

Henry, Frances/Tator, Carole (2006): The Colour of Democracy. 3/e Toronto

Hsu, Hua. (2002): "Ethnic Media Grow Up". ColorLines, Fall. (Available online at: http://www.colorlines.com/article.php?ID=372; accessed October 26, 2008)

Husband, Charles (2005): "Minority Ethnic Media As Communities of Practice: Professionalism and Identity Politics in Interaction." In: Journal of Ethnic and Migration Studies 31(3), pp. 461-479

Jiwani, Yasmin (2006): Discourses of Denial. Mediations on Race, Gender, and Violence. Vancouver

Karim, Karim (2006): "American Media's Coverage of Muslims: the Historical Roots of Contemporary Portrayals." In: Poole, E. and J.E. Richardson, eds.: Muslims and the News Media. I B Taurus: NY, pp.116-127

Karim, Karim (2003): The Media of Disapora. New York

Kular, Kulvinder (2006): "Making the case for more third-language television". In: Toronto Star, July 22

Lalley, J./Hawkins, K. (2005): Vital Sources: A Guide To Chicago's Ethnic, Community, and Independent Press. Chicago

Lam, Lawrence (1996): "The Role of Ethnic Media for Immigrants: A Case Study for Chinese Immigrants and their Media in Toronto." In: Nancoo, S./Nancoo, R., eds.: The Mass Media and Canadian Diversity. Toronto

Landzelius, Kyra (2006): "Introduction. Native on the Net." In: Landzelius, K., ed.: Native on the Net. New York, pp. 1-42

Lieberman, David (2006): "Media tune into ethnic audiences" In: USA Today. June 6

Lin, Wan-Ying and Hayeon Song (2006): "Geo-ethnic Storytelling" In: Journalism 7(3), pp. 362-388

Lincoln, Clifford/Tasse, Roger/Cianciotta, Anthony (2005): Integration and Cultural Diversity. Report of the Panel on Access to Third Language Public Television Services. Department of Canadian Heritage

Mahtani, Minelle (2007): Exploring the "Ethnic Audience". Racialized Group Perceptions of Canadian English Language News Coverage. RIIM Working Paper (draft)

Mahtani, Minelle (2002): "Representing Minorities: Canadian Media and Minority Identities." In: Canadian Ethnic Studies xxxiii (3), pp.99-131

Maaka, Roger/Fleras, Augie (2005): The Politics of Indigeneity. Dunedin NZ

Manning, Peter (2006): "Australians Imagining Islam." In: Poole, E./ Richardson, J. E. eds.: Muslims and the News Media. New York, pp. 128-141

McLeod, Sean (2007/2006): "From Exotics to Brainwashers: Portraying New Religions in the Mass Media" In: Religion Compass 1(1) (2007), pp. 214-228. Published online: October 27, 2006

Meadows, M./Molnar, H. (2001): Songlines to Satellites. Sydney

Media Awareness Network (2006): "The Development of Aboriginal Broadcasting in Canada". (Available at http://www.media-awareness.ca/english/issues/stereotyping/aboriginal_people/aboriginal_broadcasting.cfm; accessed October 26, 2008)

Miller, John (2005): "Ipperwash and the Media. A Critical Analysis of how the Story was Covered" Prepared for the Aborinal Legal Foundation, Toronto (Available online at http://www.attorneygeneral.jus.gov.on.ca/inquiries/ipperwash/policy_part/projects/pdf/ALST_Ipperwash_and_media.pdf; accessed October 26, 2008)

The National Ethnic Press and Media Council of Canada: Constitution and By-laws. (Available at http://www.nepmcc.ca; accessed October 26, 2008)

Nagda, Biren A. (2006): "Breaking Barriers, Crossing Borders, Building Bridges: Communication Processes in Intergroup Dialogues" In: Journal of Social Issues 62(3), pp. 553-571

Nallainathan, Meena (2007): "Staring Down the Tigers" In: Ryerson Review of Journalism. Spring, pp. 40-47

Neill, W. J. V./Schwedler, H. U. (2007): Migration and Cultural Identity in European Cities. New York

Ojo, Tokunbo (2006): "Ethnic Print Media in the Multicultural Nation of Canada." In: Journalism 7(3), pp. 343-361

Online/More Colour in the Media (2007): "UK's ethnic minority groups watch less TV" (Online at http://www.olmcm.org/show_news.php?SectionID=5&NewsID=328; accessed October 26, 2008)

Open Society Institute (2005): OSI Forum: Ethnic Media. Communicating with Ethnic America. (Available at http://www.soros.org)

Prashad, Sharda (2005): "CRTC pushes diversity strategies". Toronto Star March 22

Project for Excellence in Journalism (2006): "The State of the News Media 2006. An Annual Report on American Journalism." (Available online at http://www.stateofthenewsmedia.org/2006/narrative_overview_intro.asp accessed October 26, 2008)

Project for Excellence in Journalism (2004): "The State of the News Media 2004. An Annual Report on American Journalism." Available at: http://www.stateofthenewsmedia.org/2006/narrative_overview_intro.asp accessed October 26, 2008)

Raudsepp, L. (1996): "Emergent Media the Native Press in Canada." In: Nancoo, S./Nancoo, R., eds.: Mass Media and Canadian Diversity. Toronto

Rennie, Ellie (2006): Community Media. A global Introduction. Toronto

Retzlaff, Steffi (2006): "Power over Discourse: Linguistic Choices in Aboriginal Media Representations." In: Canadian Journal of Native Studies xxvi, pp. 25-52

Roth, Lorna (2006): "First Peoples Television Broadcasting in Canada" (Available online at http://www.museum.tv/archives/etv/F/htmlF/firstpeople/firstpeople.htm; accessed October 26, 2008)

Roth, Lorna (1998): "The delicate acts of colour balancing: Multiculturalism and Canadian Television Broadcasting Policies and Practices." In: Canadian Journal of Communication 23(4), pp. 487-506

Seib, Philip (2004/2005): "The Newsmedia and the 'Clash of Civilizations'". Parameters: Winter (Available online at http://www.carlisle.army.mil/usawc/parameters/04winter/seib.pdf; accessed October 26, 2008)

Solutions Research Group (2006): Diversity in Canada. Available online

Srinivasan Ramesh (2006): "Indigenous, ethnic and cultural articulations of new media." In: International Journal of Cultural Studies 9(4), pp.497-518

Starck, Kenneth (2007): "Perpetuating Prejudice or Merely Telling a Story? Media Portrayal of Arabs in the United States". Paper presented to the Media – Migration – Integration Conference at the University of Dortmund, Germany. June 22

Tan, Lincoln (2006): "There's scope for more Asian involvement in mainstream media." Available from the New Zealand Journalist Training Organisation: http://www.journalismtraining.co.nz/diversity.html

Viccari, Ben (2007): Daily News. Mediacaster Magazine. Available online

Weber-Menges, Sonja (2005): The Development of Ethnic Media in Germany. Paper presented to the ICA Conference, New York, May

Weber-Menges, Sonja/Rainer Geißler (2007): Media Integration – Ideas on this Concept among Turkish, Italian, and Russian Migrants in Germany. Paper presented to the Media-Migration-Integration Conference at the University of Dortmund, Germany. June 21

Whyte, Murray (2006): "Forgotten in media's culture gap." In: Toronto Star, June 24

Wu, Esther (2005): "Study Details Rising Tide of ethnic media." In: Dallas Morning News. June 15

Kenneth Starck

Perpetuating Prejudice: Media Portrayal of Arabs and Arab Americans

> Let me tell you 'bout A-hab The A-rab
> The Sheik of the burning sand
> He had emeralds and rubies just dripping off 'a him
> And a ring on every finger of his hands
> He wore a big ol' turban wrapped around his head
> And a scimitar by his side
> And every evening about midnight
> He'd jump on his camel named Clyde...and ride
> *by Composer Ray Stevens (see Appendix A)*

1.   Introduction

Arabs today arguably are one of the world's largest groups of people that have been marginalized by the rest of the world. Insofar as the United States is concerned, Arabs are "people who have lived outside of history" (Suleiman 1999a, p. 36).

What is it about Arabs that over the centuries has evoked images that others perceive as negative? Or is it less about Arabs and more about others? And if the perceptions are negative, what is their origin? Or are the images more Islamic than Arabic? And if so, why the confusion? What is the role of the media in presenting information that leads to perceptions regarded as negative?

Those are a few questions driving this paper. The focus is on the United States – the settling of Arab immigrants in the United States and the portrayal by US media of Arabs and Arab-American communities in the United States. In many ways, the coverage of Arabs and Arab-American communities is inseparable. The overall objective here is threefold: (1) to review from a historical perspective the nature and extent of Arab immigration to the United States, (2) to identify and analyze media research portraying Arab immigrants in the United States, and (3) to offer suggestions for improved performance. More specifically, the paper will:

-    Place the U.S. Arabic immigrant in context by reviewing historically the story of peoples from Arab lands migrating to the United States.

- Present a conceptual basis centering on framing and "othering" in an attempt to explain media coverage of the Arabic immigrant communities.

- Review studies of how U.S. media have depicted peoples of Arabic heritage who live in the U.S.

- Show how the Arabic community has tried to refute negative stereotyping through the establishment of organizations and media promoting Arabic interests.

- Finally, identify means by which media might achieve a fairer, more accurate portrayal of an entire ethnic group.

Appearing regularly in the news media are items such as these:

- An Arab immigrant, Mohamed Ben Abdallah, filed a lawsuit saying he had been subjected to such ethnic slurs as "Bin Laden" and "Terrorist" as well as other indignities in his work as a plumber for a contractor (Bulkeley 2006).

- Northwest Airline apologized to 40 American Muslims barred from a recent flight returning to Detroit from a Hajj pilgrimage (Northwest 2007).

- A U.S. Congressman objected publicly to a newly elected Congressman (from Minnesota) who wanted to (and eventually did) use the Koran for his ceremonial swearing in (Zeller 2006).

There's more. USA Today reported on several promotional messages that Arab organizations objected to – and which ultimately were withdrawn (Koch 2006):

- An advertising billboard promoting ethanol, a corn-based product used in a blend with gasoline, showed a farmer in a cornfield and King Fahd of Saudi Arabia with this question between them: "Who would you rather buy your gas from?"

- Another billboard, this one planned for North Carolina and New Mexico, was designed to make driver's licenses more secure and showed a man in a traditional Arab head scarf holding a grenade and a driver's license with this message: "Don't License Terrorists, North Carolina."

- Boeing and Bell Helicopter apologized for a magazine advertisement that showed U.S. armed forces in one of their helicopters descending by rope from a plane onto a mosque surrounded by smoke and fire.

\- A nutritional health company targeted a U.S. Congressman for opposing its interests by sending out flyers with a picture of U.S. Senator Dick Durbin in a turban with the messages: "Get a Turban for Durbin!" and "Keep Congressional Terrorists At Bay!"

At the outset we should fully understand that not all Muslims are Arabs. Nor are all Arabs Muslims. This is a confusion that persists widely, contributing to careless generalizations about groups of individuals. An effort will be made here to avoid such confusion, though the terms have become so intertwined that some ambiguity may still intrude. A few statistics concerning religion and ethnicity may lift some of the fog.

Though it is difficult if not impossible to classify with any precision immigrant populations over time, estimates are that of the roughly 3.5 million people of Arabic heritage living in the U.S. about 63 percent are Christian, 24 percent are Muslim and the remaining 13 percent are other or no religion (Kayyali 2006, whose data are based on several sources, including the Arab American Institute Foundation and Zogby International). For further context, it is worth noting that: there are 1.7 billion Muslims in the world; 44 countries have majority Muslim populations; Arabs make up about 16 percent of Muslims worldwide; and 90 percent of Arabs are Muslim.

Research for this paper is based on an extensive review of the literature pertaining to Arabs in the United States. It draws heavily on two bodies of literature. One is historical, tapping into the rich body of work sketching Arab immigration patterns. The other and predominant body of work for this project comes from the literature on media. This includes theoretical formulations concerning the role and impact of media in society as well as specific studies of Arab representation in media ranging from textbooks to films, from newspapers to television. The works have been analyzed and results synthesized from a critical perspective. While many studies deal with media portrayal of the Middle East, this paper's primary focus will be on Arab Americans, that is, those who have immigrated and settled in the U.S.[1] This paper does not purport to encompass the substantial body of literature pertaining specifically to Muslim immigrants in the United States (e.g., Haddad, Smith & Moore 2006; Haddad 2004; Haddad 2002; Waugh, Abu-Laban & Qureshi 1983), including their portrayal by media (e.g., Noakes 1998).

---

1   A note concerning the hyphen: In general, the practice among scholars has been to omit the hyphen between "Arab" and "America" but to insert it when the two words are used in conjunction as an adjectival phrase, such as "Arab-American" community. That is the style employed in this paper and should not be construed to imply any particular significance.

2. Arabs in the United States: An Overview

The Arab connection with the United States goes back even before there was a United States. Though historians differ in the facts they uncover and the conclusions they draw, general agreement exists that Arabs came early to the new land and in subsequent years came in several waves. And despite post-9/11, which has subjected Arabs to rigorous scrutiny, they continue to migrate to the United States.

Who was the first Arab to arrive in the United States? In the overall scheme of events, it probably doesn't matter. But it is interesting to note that the first Arab may have accompanied Christopher Columbus on his voyage of discovery. In *The American Arabic Speaking Community 1975 Almanac*, Editor-Publisher Haiek cites a source claiming, somewhat curiously, that Columbus, believing his journey across the sea would take him to India, decided to take with him an Arab interpreter, Louis de Torre. De Torre had converted to Christianity, and hence the name, following the fall of Granada, the last Arab stronghold in Spain (Haiek 1975). Two Moroccans may have been the next pioneering Arabs to set foot in what was to become the United States. A former slave by the name of Zammouri is said to have led a Spanish expedition into Florida in 1528. A few years later, in 1539, the Viceroy of New Spain sent Estephan the Arab to assist as a guide in the exploration of the southwestern part of North America. The Moroccan connection was foretelling. In 1787 Morocco became the first nation to officially recognize the independence of the United States in a treaty signed by Mohammad III and George Washington (Orfalea 2006).

Scholars have identified several subsequent waves of Arabic immigration with economic considerations often serving as the motivating force. But other factors, namely family as well as turmoil in the Arabic world and changes in U.S. immigration laws, also have come into play.

Those who entered the U.S. with the first wave – roughly 1878-1924 – were among more than 20 million immigrants from all over the world who came to the United States during that period called The Great Migration. It is difficult to determine precisely where they came from. Many came from Syria and Lebanon. And many new arrivals were simply placed in broad categories such as "Turkey in Asia" or "Syria", according to Kayyali (2006).[2] By 1924 it is estimated that some 200,000 Arabs were living in the United States. They were predominantly Christians, in part because of the work of missionaries

---

2   Several excellent studies have been carried out on Arab immigration to the United States. Two relatively recent works primarily relied upon for this paper are Kayyali (2006) and Orfalea (2006).

who during this period established several universities in the region including what was to become the American Universities of Beirut and Cairo, both highly respected institutions to this day. The immigrants were mainly farmers and merchants. Males made up well over half of the early arrivals. Women were to come later. The experiences of these immigrants paralleled those of immigrants from other parts of the world. Finding funds and arranging travel, usually at the lowest level of accommodation called "steerage", were challenges not without danger. More than 100 Syrians were aboard the Titanic when it sank.

Arabs in the United States prior to World War I thought of themselves as "sojourners, as people who were in, but not part of, American society" (Suleiman 1999b, p. 4). Still, for many of these immigrants, their Arab ethnicity gave way relatively easily to Americanization. They gradually assimilated into the fabric of American society.

The second wave of Arab immigrants took place roughly 1925 to 1965. Much of the activity during this period was driven by world events. After World War II political and economic unrest made life untenable for many of those in the Arab world. Some Arab elites, especially from Iraq, Egypt, and Palestine, were permitted entry into the United States as political exiles. Others, such as the late Columbia University Professor Edward W. Said, came to the United States to study. During the 1950s and 1960s nearly 6,000 Palestinians came to the United States as political refugees. Their entry was facilitated by the U.S. Congress' passage of the Refugee Relief Act.

Immigrants during this period were markedly different from their earlier counterparts. Many were educated and had good English language skills as well as resources to draw on. They melded smoothly into mainstream American society.

During the third wave of immigration – roughly 1965 to 2006 – more than 400,000 Arab immigrants came to the United States. They were encouraged by changes in U.S. immigration law and quotas as well as continuing turmoil in the Middle East. The number of immigrants was significantly larger than those in the second wave and three times as large as those in the first wave, according to Kayyali (2006). Many of the immigrants fled their homelands following the humiliating defeat of the Arabs in the 1967 Six-Day War. Other conflicts, including the war in Lebanon and the 1991 Gulf War, resulted in the dislocation of many people in the region. Disenchanted with prospects for the future, people were attracted to the United States for its educational possibilities and its general attitude of tolerance. Kayyali (2006) notes that most of the immigrants after 1965 were Muslims who valued the freedom to worship and to build mosques.[3]

Immigrants normally do not fit into their new environment easily, especially if they are perceived as minorities and appear visibly different from others. Such was the case with Arab immigrants. Arabs come in varying shades of white and black, and until 1909 Arabs generally were regarded as white and were granted citizenship. But then the U.S. government changed its census and immigration categories, and after 1911 the Bureau of Immigration and Naturalization denied citizenship to Arab Americans. A number of court cases ensued, and it wasn't until late in the 1940s that Arabs could feel comfortable that they had established that they were to be classified as "white".[4] This was important due to struggles involving civil rights. Kayyali (2006) points to an interesting phenomenon among Arabs during this period of racial unease in the United States. In an effort to prove their worthiness to mainstream society, many Arabs gave up their cultural identity in favor of assimilating. Later, during the 1970-80s, the United States civil rights movement, along with revulsion over media coverage of the Six-Day War which depicted Arabs as evil, rekindled ethnic consciousness. Arabs also established a number of political and social organizations to assert their ethnicity and particular concerns.

Stereotypical images and offensive labels accompanied the establishment of Arab-American communities. One stereotype of early Arab immigrants was that of peddlers. This door-to-door selling became a popular way for immigrants to support themselves. The image quickly stamped itself into the mainstream mind. Because of their color, Arabs came to be called "wetbacks", "dago", and "sheeny" (Kayyali 2006, p. 53). Later the slurs turned ethnic with such terms as "camel jockey", "dirty Syrian", and "Turk.". Such labels were to multiply and become even more derogatory over time. Attitudes toward the later groups of immigrants were affected by events beyond their control, namely, the creation of Israel and subsequent disorder in the Middle East. As a result, some Arabic immigrants never completely became part of the American "melting pot" and have been searching for their American identity. Exacerbating the situation for Arabs in the U.S. were the attacks on 9/11 and events that followed.

---

3   There is some debate over where the first mosque was built in the United States. Orfalea (2006) suggests that the first mosque likely was built in Ross, North Dakota, in 1929. Both Orfalea and Kayyali (2006), however, indicate that the oldest surviving mosque in America was built in Cedar Rapids, Iowa, and that the dedication took place June 16, 1934 (Judge 2006).

4   For an interesting discussion of the Arab-American experience in relation to race, including possible implications in terms of social diversity, see Samhan (1999).

As to the number of Arabs in the United States, confusion abounds. The reason centers in large part on the definition of race, a volatile social issue for most of the history of the United States. U.S. Census Bureau efforts to compile accurate ethnic data have not been very successful when it comes to Arabs. For example, in one set of data collection, given a limited choice of racial categories, many Arabs marked "white" or "other." While the U.S. Census lists the total Arab-American population as 1.2 million, or 0.42 percent of the U.S. population, the Arab American Institute Foundation estimates the number to be 3.5 million, or 1.2 percent of the population. Problems associated with the data collection methodology aside, a U.S. Census Special Report helps provide a demographic profile of the Arab-American population in the United States (Brittingham and de la Cruz 2005). Based on 2000 data, the report shows that Arab families had a higher median income than all families ($52,300 compared to $50,000) while at the same time a higher proportion of Arabs than the general population was in poverty (17 percent compared to 12 percent). Arabs also were shown to be more highly educated than the general population with more than 40 percent holding at least a bachelor's degree. Also, more Arab Americans than the general population held management, professional, and related occupations (42 percent compared to 34 percent). Nearly half of U.S. residents of Arab ancestry were born in the United States (46 percent). The data also shed some light on the national origin of the Arab-American population according to ancestry:

National origin	Percentage of Arab-American population
Lebanese	28.8 %
Egyptian	14.5 %
Syrian	8.9 %
Palestinian	7.3 %
Jordanian	4.2 %
Moroccan	3.6 %
Iraqi	3.5 %
"Arab" or "Arabic"	19.7 %
Other Arab[5]	9.6 %

Table 1: National origin of the Arab-American population according to ancestry

---

5   "Other Arab" includes Yemeni, Kurdish, Algerian, Saudi, Tunisian, Kuwaiti, Libyan, Berber, Emirati (United Arab Emirates), Omani, Qatari, Bahraini, Alhuceman, Bedouin, Rio de Oro, and the general terms Middle Eastern and North African. Source: Brittingham and de la Cruz 2005, p. 3.

Arabs today live throughout the United States. About a third are in the states of California, New York, and Michigan. Cities with the largest Arab American populations are Los Angeles, Detroit, New York, Chicago, and Washington, D.C. (Haddad 2004).

With this as the backdrop, we now begin turning our attention to the media. The next section presents several useful concepts in carrying out this inquiry.

3. Toward a Conceptual Approach: Framing, Othering

Two primary concepts have been utilized in guiding the preparation of this paper. One has emerged in the area of media studies as a useful idea in the formulation, transmission, and interpretation of messages. That is the notion of framing. The other is just that – the "other," a concept which in its application attempts to define the self in relation to others, especially those who are different in some significant aspect, such as appearance, behavior, or belief. Both concepts have enjoyed wide popularity and, as a result, have generated a wide variety of applications and interpretations. The concepts of framing and othering, as used in this paper, will be assumed to have both serious political and social ramifications.

First, let us turn to framing. This is a relatively recent approach in media research. It simply, yet powerfully, tries to illuminate the ways in which information is selected from a larger context – say, an event or an issue – and then is organized and, ultimately, communicated to others and, in the process, takes on new or different meanings. Or, as Reese (2001) writes,

> Framing is concerned with the way interests, communicators, sources, and culture combine to yield coherent ways of understanding the world, which are developed using all of the available verbal and visual symbolic resources (p. 11).

Further, in a thoughtful review of media research utilizing framing, Reese offers his own working definition which, though oriented toward the social, has obvious implications in the political realm:

> Frames are *organizing principles* that are socially *shared* and *persistent* over time, that work *symbolically* to meaningfully *structure* the social world (p. 11; italics in original).

Organizing refers to comprehensiveness, while principle refers to something abstract and not necessarily conveyed explicitly in a message. Shared refers to communication that is mutually relevant. Persistence refers to durability that over time becomes routine. Symbolically points to various forms of expression, and structure is the organizing of the material into identifiable patterns, or frames.

What is the significance of framing? Framing is fundamental to what takes place in communication. It helps us identify and define the world around us and to find our place – or be placed – in it. As for the part that news media play, Reese states, "...the media are powerful, economic concerns, often distant from the audiences they serve, producing news as a commodity, generating frames that may distort as much as they illuminate..." (p. 29)

As for othering, this is a similarly ambiguous term. The concept traces its origin back several centuries to the works of a number of philosophers and scholars. Combined with the notion of symbolic interactionism, which holds that people actively and creatively participate in the construction of their social being, othering presents a potent tool in understanding oneself or groups of people in relation to others. Here is a visualization of what is meant: Two mirrors face one another; one individual or group (the self) looks toward the other person or group (the other) and vice versa.

Scholars have adapted the notion of othering to probe relationships among a variety of groups – professional, nationality, regional, sexual, among others. Our interest here involves minority groups. Othering, at least in one sense as used by Riggins (1997), is seen as the application of communication processes "that contribute to the marginalization of minority groups" (p. 1). Such analysis, Riggins asserts, can be useful in "advancing the study of prejudice and social inequality in modern multicultural societies" (p. 1).

An example of the application of the approach is Schneider's (2001) examination of the German debate on immigration and the search for national identity. In the study, Schneider referred to the self as the "internal Other," that is, German self-definition, while Others – he capitalized the first letter – referred to foreigners ("Ausländer"). Further, he stressed the role of the media "as the main transmitter of all sorts of public discourse" (p. 356) as well as access to and use of media by those in the other category.

This othering model of self-definition is also the conceptual basis of the approach used by Ibish (2001) in his examination of anti-Arab discourse in the U.S. To support his charge of negative stereotyping of Arabs, Ibis developed the thesis that building the "illusion of the unity of the collective self" requires creation of "an illusion of superiority" (p. 120).

The idea carries over into more extreme sentiments toward another group. In reviewing a variety of analytical approaches, Fiebig-von Hase (1997) wrote that extreme images – "enemy images" is the term used – seem to exist in all modern societies. He noted that such images are complex and imprecise. He continued:

> In its widest and colloquial form, an enemy image is a culturally influenced, very negative, and stereotyped evaluation of the "other" – be it individuals, groups, nations, or ideologies. (p. 2).

Feelings of one group toward another theoretically could range all the way from tolerance to violence. There's no problem tolerating a small, non-threatening group. But violence could come into play if one group threatened another's security. Sentiments toward others exist at several levels and especially come into play when immigrants – "foreigners", if you will – are involved. When immigrants begin organizing and ultimately form a nation, do they reach a point that they must negate others in order to discover and retain their own national or ethnic identity? This is an intriguing question raised by Fiebig-von Hase (1997) and harkens back to Schneider's (2001) probing of German identity, or "Germanness". Unfortunately, the examination of that question must remain for another time and another place.

To sum up, we've kept our conceptualization of this paper relatively simple. The goal was to devise an approach that offered possibilities of explanation and organization. So, to help us understand the way in which U.S. media have portrayed the indigenous Arab community, we have combined the notions of framing – media professionals conceptualizing and developing stories – with othering – the propensity for individuals and groups to define themselves by excluding or marginalizing others.

4. What Research Tells Us about U.S. Media Portrayal of Arabs and Arab Americans

This section will review studies that have centered on the ways in which Arabs have been portrayed in the U.S. media. Hundreds of such studies have been carried out, though few focus exclusively on Arab Americans. Most deal with Arabs and other people of the Middle East, but the impact of such coverage inevitably affects perceptions of those Arabs who have chosen to make their homes in the U.S. The intention here is not to present a complete or even exhaustive accounting of all the studies. Instead, we will identify what appear to be some of the more significant studies with the intention of attaining a relatively representative sample over time. Many of the studies contain extensive literature reviews up to the time of publication and thus would represent a rich pool of resources for anyone wishing to carry out a more extensive review of the literature. Let us begin with a few general observations.

In his seminal work exploring the relationship between culture and imperialism, the late Edward W. Said (1993) noted that media mold and manipulate perceptions and political attitudes. Since 1967 (year of the Six-Day War, also known as the 1967 Arab-Israeli War), he wrote that the Western press representation of the Arab world was "crude, reductionist, coarsely racialist", all of which, he noted, had been well documented earlier (p. 36). Despite this earlier documentation, film and television continued to portray Arabs as "sleazy, 'camel-jockeys,' terrorists, and offensively wealthy 'sheikhs'" (p. 36). Not much changed up to or during the first Gulf War. Media rallied behind the first President George Bush and devoted little attention to dealing with the political, social, and cultural developments in the Arab world. The same thing appears to have occurred with the second President George W. Bush's incursion into Iraq.

Said, who died in 2003 and is still recognized as one of the most profound scholars of East-West thought, was a severe and early critic of the media. Though focusing primarily on Islam, his ideas concerning Western attitudes toward the Middle East resonate in any discussion of Arab communities in general. In an introduction to a later edition of what has become at least a minor classic, Covering Islam, Said accused journalists of "making extravagant statements, which are instantly picked up and further dramatized by the media" (1981, p. xvi). Further, he argued journalists were only part of an inter-related apparatus that included the academy and government, all of which were driven mainly by politics rather than by truth or accuracy.

That media and government reciprocate in depicting the Middle East is perhaps nowhere more evident than in several addresses delivered by President Bush immediately following the events of September 11, 2001. Merskin found that the speeches turned popular cultural depictions of people of Arab and Middle East descent into a rhetoric that then drew upon the "collective consciousness to revivify, reinforce, and ratify the Arab as terrorist stereotype" (2004, p. 172). In constructing the enemy's image, President Bush used such terms as "them", "evil", "those people", "demons", and "wanted: dead or alive" in references to people of Arab and Middle Eastern descent. Merskin found stereotypical characterizations of Arabs and Middle Easterners in a wide array of media, from news to magazine stories, from cartoons to movies. While President Bush appeared to be speaking mainly about non-U.S. citizens, as Merskin notes, the remarks could not help but register with the millions of Arab Americans.

What is the danger of ethnic stereotyping? Shaheen, whose work on Arab American portrayals in films, put it well in one of his early works: "Ethnic stereotypes and caricatures corrupt the imagination, narrow our vision and blur reality" (1984, p. 3).

Several fundamental problems in U.S. media coverage of the Middle East were identified by Edmund Ghareeb (1983), a former journalist in the Middle East with a Ph.D. in history from Georgetown University. His study encompassed two time periods, 1975-77 and 1979-82. The research was supported by the American-Arab Affairs Council, a nonprofit group whose goal is to promote understanding between the U.S. and Arab countries. His approach was to interview nearly two dozen prominent journalists and review content analysis studies of U.S. newspapers and magazines by several scholars. He was interested to see if the media over time adopted a more balanced approach to covering the Middle East. He identified a number of reasons for media's failure to be fair, including cultural bias, the Arab-Israel conflict, media ignorance of the history and origins of the conflict, and a sophisticated Israeli lobby. Other factors were Arab failure to understand the U.S. media and apathy by the Arab-American community. During the second period, Ghareeb detected only a "perceptible change" of less distortion and bias in U.S. media performance. This resulted in part from the efforts of Arab-American organizations combating stereotyping. This 1983 examination of U.S. media treatment of Arabs included essays by scholars who were among the first to analyze other media – cartoons, contemporary fiction, television and textbooks – for bias and distortion. Their findings were similar to those found in the newspapers and magazines.

A scholar who has studied broadly and published widely on the topic of America and Arabs is Michael W. Suleiman. He has severely criticized media – films, the entertainment industry, television, literature, textbooks – for their general and repeated portrayal of Arabs in negative terms (1989 and 1999a). Further, he argues that Arab Americans tend to be visible and invisible at the same time – visible when there is turmoil in the Middle East and invisible when they experience bias and discrimination (1999a). Arabs in the U.S., he noted, are "white but not quite" (p. 44). Arabs and Muslims in the U.S. represent not only the "other," but their counterparts in other parts of the world are seen as even worse, leading Suleiman to assert that "...for Americans, the non-western Muslims/Arabs have become the other of the other of the other..." (p. 44).

In an extensive content analysis of the representation of Arabs in U.S. television and radio stations, Lind and Danowski (1998) found that stereotypes of previous research were being repeated and reinforced. They examined three years of transcripts of news and public affairs programming for three U.S. networks, ABC (American Broadcasting Company), CNN (Cable News Network), PBS (Public Broadcasting Service), and a non-profit radio station,

NPR (National Public Radio). They sifted through nearly 136 million words. They discovered the invisible Arab – references were made to Arabs only about one hundredth of one percent. Further, they found an "overwhelming association in the media between Arabs and violence, threats, and war, which serves to foster the stereotypes of 'Arab as barbarian/aggressor/terrorist'" (p. 165).

Books, including novels and textbooks, also have been scrutinized in efforts to identify inaccuracies, bias, and distortion. Seldom have the investigators come away empty handed. In an informal analysis of contemporary writing (e.g., biographies, histories, novels with Leon Uris' Exodus [published in 1958] serving as a prototype of popular literature), Terry concluded that the works demonstrated "the pervasive negative character of the portrayal of Islam and Arabs throughout a wide variety of popular writing" (1985, p. 107).

In her study of children's books, both fiction and nonfiction and over an extended period of time, Little (1998) identified five patterns of representation of Arabs, all associated with neocolonialism – Arabs are: (1) dirty and lazy; (2) ignorant, superstitious, and silly; (3) irrational, cruel, and violent; (4) guilty of mistreating women; and (5) hateful of Christians and engage in slave trade. From an historical perspective, she concluded that prevailing Arab stereotypes "are as deeply ingrained in Western teachings as mistrust of the West is a part of the typical Arab worldview", that the images simply "have been updated, dressed in the fashion of the time, directed at children, yet deliver the same negative message" (p. 267).

Other scholars also have pointed out how stereotypes somehow maintain their stereotypical tendencies yet change with events and the fashion of the time. Crime fiction centering on the Middle East provides another example. Simon found that writers had slightly altered the stereotyping of Arabs but basically perpetuated those stereotypes. The stereotypes had morphed, as Simon in her study of *The Middle East in Crime Fiction*, wrote, from an era of "camels to Cadillacs" and "nomad to petrosheikh" (1989, pp. 34-35).

A study of the first 100 years (1888 to 1989) of the popular U.S. magazine *National Geographic* also added to the notion that old stereotypes do not die; at best, they become clothed in new attire. Analyzing articles and photographs, Steet provides numerous examples of racist, colonialist, and sexist bias (2000). After her exhaustive analysis, Steet wrote that she found so little change "disturbing if for no other reason than that one would have liked to think that certain stereotypes and assumptions eventually die of old age" (p. 154).

To be sure, changing contexts and circumstances can figure prominently in how different groups, including Arab Americans, are portrayed over time. In a study of news media coverage of Arab American reactions to the 1991

Gulf War, Gavrilos (2002) found that sympathetic coverage of Arab American reactions to the war revealed a heightened loyalty of this group of people toward America. The author concluded that Arab Americans "were ultimately represented as part of the nation's imagined community," reinforcing the media's "hegemonic construction" of the United States (p. 443). The result was an image of patriotic Americans – an image distinctly different from the usual, negative stereotypical depictions. What Gavrilos found appears similar to Fiebig-von Hase's notion of "enemy images", wherein groups behave toward one another on the basis of self-interest, such as security.

A study that looked directly at a newspaper's coverage of the Arab American community in Detroit was carried out just before September 11, 2001 (Weston and Dunsky 2002). The study, which also looked at media coverage of Arabs abroad, found that the Detroit Free Press presented a multifaceted view of Arab Americans though not entirely absent of what the authors call the "strange and exotic". Themes emerging depicted Arabs as becoming a growing political force, as struggling immigrants, and as striving against discrimination and stereotyping. Significantly, the articles during the period under study were written by two reporters who spoke Arabic and aggressively covered the community. An important observation by the authors:

> [...] the local press tends to treat such (ethnic) groups as multifaceted members of the community and the stereotyping and over-generalizations increase as distance from the community increases. (p. 142).

Ibrahim (2003) prepared an extensive compilation of studies of U.S. media coverage of Arabs and the Middle East focusing on three main communication areas: production, content, and effects. The object was to point to possible gaps in the research, such as insufficient attention given to the journalistic producers and media websites. Many of the observations in this literature review which encompassed more than half a century underscore common themes that have emerged in the research. U.S. media depended heavily on American (as opposed to Arab) sources for coverage. Stereotyping in the 1950s regarded Arabs as dishonest, undemocratic, and unreliable with low standards of education and living. Stereotyping in the 1980s moved to association with oil, wealth, and extravagance. Coverage itself tended to lack historical and cultural context. In terms of media effects, the author rightfully points out that the research shows that the predominant negative portrayals of Arabs and the Middle East produce palpable effects on the lives of Arab Americans. The result for Arabs living in the U.S.: hate crimes, job discrimination, bomb threats, verbal and physical harassment, threats, and so on. The research cited included film and the work of Jack Shaheen, to whom we now turn our attention.

No one has studied more thoroughly or written with more passion about the negative depiction of Arabs in film than Jack Shaheen (2001). Of Arab descent, Shaheen is an American scholar who over a period of 20 years analyzed Arab portraits and themes in more than 900 films. These have been compiled in a 574-page book from A (*Abbott and Costello in the Foreign Legion*) to Z (actually Y, *Your Ticket Is No Longer Valid*, also known as *A Slow Descent Into Hell* and *Finishing Tough*). There is pertinent data about each film, plus a summary and the author's observations.

What emerges is not a pretty picture. Over the years Arabs appear in a wide range of settings, nearly always disparagingly and seldom as normal human beings. Shaheen wrote:

> I am not saying an Arab should never be portrayed as the villain. What I am saying is that almost *all* Hollywood depictions of Arabs are *bad* ones. This is a grave injustice. Repetitive and negative images of the reel Arab literally sustain adverse portraits across generations. The fact is that for more than a century producers have tarred an entire group of people with the same sinister brush (p. 11).

His evidence speaks volumes. There are the slurs – "rag-head", "devil-worshiper", "camel-dick", "dune dumper", "desert bandit", and more. There are the characters – billionaires, bombers, and belly dancers, as he writes. In sum, the "reel" Arabs are not, after all, real Arabs. According to his analysis, five Arab character types emerged from the films he reviewed:

- Villains – "Beginning with *Imar the Servitor* (1914), up to and including *The Mummy Returns* (2001), a synergy of images equates Arabs from Syria to the Sudan with quintessential evil" (p. 14).

- Sheikhs – "The word 'sheikh' means, literally, a wise elderly person, the head of the family, but you would not know that from watching any of Hollywood's `sheikh` features, more than 160 scenarios, including the Kinetoscope short *Sheik Hadj Tahar Hadj Cherif* (1894) and the Selig Company's *The Power of the Sultan* (1907) – the first movie to be filmed in Los Angeles" (p. 19).

- Maidens – "They (Arab women) appear as bosomy bellydancers leering out from diaphanous veils, or as disposable 'knick-knacks,' scantily-clad harem maidens with bare midriffs, closeted in the palace's women's quarters" (p. 22).

- Egyptians – "Reel Egyptians routinely descend upon Westerners, Israelis, and fellow Egyptians. Interspersed throughout the movies are souk swindlers as well as begging children scratching for baksheesh" (p. 24).

- Palestinians – "Absent from Hollywood's Israeli-Palestinian movies are human dramas revealing Palestinians as normal folk – computer specialists, domestic engineers, farmers, teachers, and artists. Never do movies present Palestinians as innocent victims and Israelis as brutal oppressors" (p. 26).

The author's own biases may creep through the excerpts cited here. The study, though exhaustive in its own way, lacks a clear scientific methodology. Yet the work deserves careful attention because of the author's observations, often simple descriptions, and insights. The study reveals what happens when framing turns into stereotyping which, in turn, leads to an unconscious – and even perhaps conscious – distancing of oneself from others, that is, engaging in "othering"[6].

Images in particular command authority in affecting viewers. In an aptly titled chapter ("Images That Injure: Pictorial Stereotypes in the Media"), Lester noted, "Because pictures affect a viewer emotionally more than words alone do, pictorial stereotypes often become misinformed perceptions that have the weight of established facts" (2000, p. 78). He is concerned primarily with different cultures and ethnic groups. Since people mostly encounter those of other cultures through mass media, he concluded, people aren't normally challenged to examine their prejudices. One might go further and argue that not only do prejudices go unexamined, prejudices are reinforced.

What impact did the events of September 11, 2001, have on the way media have dealt with Arabs and Arab Americans? Several studies suggest that after September 11 daily newspapers took a more sympathetic or positive view of Arab Americans (Weston 2003, Nacos and Torres-Reyna 2007).

Utilizing the Lexis-Nexis data base, Weston examined nearly 200 newspaper articles for the three months before September 11 and for the month following September 11. The pre-September 11 coverage centered on Arab Americans resisting stereotypes and discrimination. An example was the Los Angeles Times article headlined "Negative Stereotyping Distorts Arabs' Image" (Rosenberg 2001). Afterwards newspaper coverage presented Arabs as, in the words of the author, "double victims", having suffered from the attacks themselves, including the loss of loved ones, but also being subjected after-

---

6   See also Semmerling's examination of six films (e.g., The Exorcist, Three Kings, Rules of Engagement) in which he analyzes portraits of Arabs as imagined by America to exist in relation to American ideologies and myths (2006).

wards to harassment and intimidation. Headlines from two major newspapers reflect the framing of the stories: "St. Louis Muslims Lead Diverse Lives that Defy Stereotypes" (Aisha Sultan 2001) and "Overcoming the Stereotypes" (Saeed Ahmed 2001). Again, it is worth noting the Arabic names of the reporters. Weston concluded that portrayal of Arab Americans following September 11 contrasted "vividly with the historic stereotype of the Arab terrorist" (2003, p. 103).

Nacos and Torres-Reyna (2007), in their extensive content analysis of newspapers, magazines and broadcast media over a number of years, found "significantly more positive and less negative media coverage of American Muslims and Arabs" (p. 19) in the months following the September 11 attacks. Among changes cited were increased use of Muslim/Arab sources and more coverage that was thematic (in-depth) rather than episodic (short, snappy). But this change did not last long. Extending their analysis beyond the immediate aftermath of September 11, the investigators found coverage of the American Muslim and Arab communities reverted to pre-September 11 coverage, namely, stereotypical and negative.

Six years after 2001 the view from the Middle East reflects a similarly somber tone. In an article about Arab-American artists, a reporter for the Gulf News published in the United Arab Emirates, wrote that while millions of Arabs call America home many are searching for identity. They ponder such questions as whether they are Arabs or Arab Americans or U.S. citizens. While many Arabs still dream of a bright future in America, the events of September 11 "changed everything". The article goes on:

> Arab Americans became the target of hate crimes, illegal detention and unexplained deportations. Some suffered from civil rights violations... Suddenly, stereotypes against them multiplied and their lives became governed by the ever-changing laws and regulations (Patriot Act) [...] (Alafrangi 2007).

The reporter wrote that while Arab-American artists understood the problems, e.g., the generalization of all Arabs being Muslims, they also remained relatively optimistic. One artist, a comedian, commented that the U.S. was "the only place in the entire world where one can create something from nothing." Another artist, an actor, pointed to a basic problem in the portrayal of ethnic groups, namely, that so very few of them – in this case Arabs – work in the American media.

The point about being heard, that is, having a voice in the discourse on matters directly pertinent to one's own well-being, is terribly important if not essential to being able to correct inaccurate information and to dispel mis-perceptions. In the mid-1960s Arab Americans began finding that voice.

5.   Giving Voice to the Arab-American Perspective

Though it is not the focus of this paper, some mention must be made of efforts by Arab Americans to correct the inaccurate stereotypes and negative portrayals of themselves and their communities. Until the 1967 Six-Day War, Arab-American organizational activity centered on social and religious activities. The war signaled the need for Arab-American voices to be heard in political and foreign affairs. Samhan underscored this line of reasoning. While blaming Israeli propaganda for discrediting Arab-American activity, Samhan pointed to "a clear relationship between the pervasiveness of negative images and stereotypes in the media and anti-Arab prejudice" (1987, p. 18). During the late 1960s to the mid-1980s, Arab Americans formed a number of influential organizations (Kayyali 2006). Four are introduced here. Additional details about each appear in Appendix B.

The first national organization to promote Arab-American interests was the Association of Arab-American University Graduates (AAUG). It was founded in 1968. Besides trying to assure the dissemination of accurate infor-mation about the Arab world and the Arab-American community, it serves as a network for Arab academics and professionals. Its publications include the Arab Studies Quarterly. Among its founders was Edward Said. (More infor-mation about AAUG and other Arab organizations appears in Appendix B.)

A local organization with national influence is the Arab Community Cen-ter for Economic and Social Services (ACCESS) based in Dearborn, Michigan, which is among the largest and most prominent Arab-American communities in the United States. It was founded in 1972 to assist immigrants in coping with language, cultural, and social barriers.

Another organization established in 1972 was the National Association of Arab Americans (NAAA). Formed by businessmen and professionals with Arab backgrounds, the NAAA served as a lobbying organization, which, according to its Website (see Appendix B), is "dedicated to the formulation and implementation of an objective and nonpartisan U.S. foreign policy agenda in the Middle East". In January 2002 officials of the NAAA and the American-Arab Anti-Discrimination Committee (ADC) announced the merger of the two organizations, bringing together two of the oldest and most prominent Arab-American organizations.

The ADC, mentioned in the preceding paragraph, was founded in 1980 by former U.S. Senator James Abourezk of South Dakota and has chapters throughout the U.S. Abourezk was the first Arab American to be elected to the U.S. Senate. His parents of Lebanese descent were homesteaders and peddlers. The ADC is a civil rights organization committed to defending the rights of people of Arab descent and promoting their cultural heritage. The ADC Website (See Appendix B) states that it "is at the forefront in combating defamation and negative stereotyping of Arab Americans in the media and wherever else it is practiced." Members of the ADC Advisory Committee include Muhammad Ali, Her Majesty Queen Noor of Jordan, U.S. Congressmen John Conyers of Michigan, and radio personality Casey Kasem.

Arab language media also have been instrumental in helping build a sense of community among the diverse groups of Arab Americans. The first Arabic language publication in the United States was *Kawkab Amirka* (Star of America). A weekly, it was founded in New York in 1892 by two brothers, Ibrahim and Najib, of a prominent Syrian family, Arbeely. By 1919 some 70,000 immigrants supported nine Arabic language newspapers, many of them dailies. The most important publication of the time was a journal, Syrian World, whose distinguished writers included Gibran Khalil Gibran (1883-1931) of Lebanese descent (Al-Issa, 2003).

By the end of 2002, according to Kayyali (2006), there were some 45 Arabic print publications with a combined circulation of half a million. Electronically, Arabic media also have amplified the voice of Arab Americans. The Arab Network of America was the first Arabic-language cable television network to broadcast in North America and parts of Central and South America. The Internet also has seen the rise of sites focusing on political and social issues. One study showed Arab Americans boasting the highest level of connectivity of any group with three-fourths of all Arab American adults having access to the Internet and a majority regularly visiting Arabic websites (Stapp 2005).

Organization and influence, however, do not necessarily go hand in hand. This was evident during the Lebanese conflict of the summer of 2006. Both Jewish and Arab organizations sprang into action in the U.S. Arab-American efforts to get the White House or legislators to call for an immediate ceasefire were mostly rebuffed, as noted by James Zogby. Zogby has been a leader in the Arab-American community and a staunch advocate of Arabs telling their own story. He is founder and president of the Arab American Institute, which was established in 1985 to take on an activist role in terms of political and civic engagement. Concerning the negligible impact the Arab voice had on efforts to achieve a ceasefire, he commented, "I'm devastated. I thought we'd come further" (Goodstein 2006).

6. Analysis and Commentary: Toward Tolerance and Respect

The evidence of negative portrayal of Arabs is compelling. Arabs, both those who have settled in the United States and others, have been portrayed in a generally negative light by the media ever since research has focused on the topic. The early stereotype of, say, a struggling immigrant peddler, keeps re-emerging to be reincarnated constantly and variously from a camel-riding, nomadic Bedouin to a wealthy oil tycoon, from a profligate "petrosheikh" to a threatening, bearded terrorist.

The reasons for such treatment are not altogether clear, though it should be pointed out that media do not operate in a vacuum. Media are influenced heavily by the environment in which they operate. They are influenced by other circumstances including most especially government policies. This is a point underscored by Said (1981) in his discussion of the coverage of Islam. A full analysis of why this is the case with regard to Arab Americans is beyond the scope of this paper. Still, it is worth informed speculation. One reason certainly is simply the nature of the immigrant, that is, a person who not only comes to visit but to stay. Such people can represent a threat, economically, socially, culturally. In this regard, the Arab immigrant may be little different from other immigrants to the United States, say, Germans or Japanese. But there are other factors involved in the case of Arabs. These would seem to be largely political which in turn are related to economic and foreign interests. The Arab-American voice came late to the U.S. political process. It was only in the 1960s that Arab Americans caught on to the notion of organizing themselves in a way to care for one another and to have a voice in the political process. As noted earlier, it took the Six-Day War of 1967 to provoke Arab Americans to political and social action.

It is a shame that, as the research affirms, so little seems to have changed over time in the media portrayal of the Arab-American community. Could the research be suspect? Perhaps in some instances, say, where Arab organizations have sponsored the research. Or perhaps some investigators let their judgments be guided by the emotional and ideological nature of the topic. Even taking such factors into account, the evidence is overwhelming.

An unmistakable and easily recognizable example of how media can portray the same facts in decidedly different ways occurred in reporting results of a nationwide Pew Research Center poll of Muslim Americans. The report found that Muslim Americans were "largely assimilated, happy with their lives, and moderate with respect to many of the issues that have divided Muslims and Westerners around the world" ("Muslim Americans" 2007). Yet some media reports, including the Associated Press, focused on the finding that Muslims younger than 30 were more likely than older Muslim Americans to say that suicide bombing in the defense of Islam might be justifiable. While 78 percent of respondents said suicide bombings against civilian targets could never be justified, 13 percent disagreed – and the margin of error for this subgroup was plus or minus 10 percentage points. As the ombudsman pointed out, such decisions often come down to what is news and what is sensationalism (Parry 2007). Too often, sensationalism prevails.

Assuming U.S. media could do better, the question is how? Both media and their audiences have roles to play.

One of the basic roles of media, most especially in a society supportive of free speech, is to provide a means for individuals and groups in the community to carry on a dialogue. That is, media can serve as a conversational conduit for diverse communities. For example, a study of opinion discourse (editorials, letters to the editor, op-ed articles) in U.S. newspapers during the Iraq war suggested the "conversation" helped Arab Americans to "negotiate" their national identity during a time of crisis (Youssef 2005). She identified three main themes in the discourse. Though the author suggested findings should be considered preliminary, each theme throws a little light on the matter of ethnicity and media in the U.S. The first suggested what may be obvious, namely, that the term "American" stands for a multi-layered identity. The second theme was that in discussions of current issues references to past experiences (e.g., internment of Japanese Americans during World War II) were seen as relevant. Third, belief in "American" values defined what it was to be "American."

Lester (2000) pointed out that members of a multicultural society often become stigmatized because they are unable to understand and communicate in the symbols of the dominant culture. The effect is compounded when media professionals do not represent the diverse cultural groups. In the United States, according to Lester, only 5.8 percent of all media personnel identify themselves as members of another culture (e.g., Irish, German, Latino, etc.). No such data appear to exist for Arab media personnel in the U.S. Yet it is generally agreed that a communicator's background, including cultural, cannot help but influence perceptions of events and affect interpretation of those events.

Though Russell and Kelly (2003) were not studying culture in the sense we are using the concept here (they were studying homosexuality as a cultural phenomenon), their examination of what they call "subtle stereotyping" by media is instructive. Their research provides insights into media treatment of any group, cultural or otherwise. They studied the Boston Globe's 2002 coverage of the priests caught up in a sexual abuse scandal and how the newspaper sometimes erroneously linked gay sexual orientation to child sexual abuse. In the interests of fairer and more accurate reporting, they offered a number of recommendations worthy of consideration by all media professionals covering the activities of any ethnic group let alone any identifiable segment of society (pp. 21-22):

- Adherence to the journalistic goals of truth and fairness requires that journalists avoid activating false stereotypes that will result in the transmission of information that is both inaccurate and unfair to particular groups of people.

- Journalists need to cultivate an ongoing awareness of the false stereotypes that may be associated with particular stories.

- Editors should be aware that false stereotypes can be activated not only through the content of stories but also through their placement. They should be especially alert to the potential for stereotypes contained in and or implied by supporting documents accompanying news stories.

    When stereotypes and other false information are included within a story, journalists need to make clear-cut statements that correct the misinformation. Rebuttals are most effective when they a) explicitly acknowledge that false information is conveyed by the stereotype and b) offer accurate information to counteract the stereotype's false content. When rebuttals are cautious and unclear, they leave room for the stereotype to persist.

- In an ongoing story that involves the persistent presence of a particular stereotype, journalists and editors might focus specific articles on the stereotype itself: the nature of the stereotype, its origins, how it is expressed socially, and what is actually true.

- Because journalists stand in the midst of the culture they describe, they cannot be expected to achieve a perfect ability to rise above stereotypes. They should seek consultation from communication specialists to help avoid coverage that activates stereotypes, particularly when covering stories that are closely linked to strong cultural stereotypes that might easily be imbedded in the story over time.

From the standpoint of the audience, the best safeguard against being duped is *caveat emptor* ("buyer beware"). This is the advice from Steet (2000) who examined a century's worth of the magazine *National Geographic*. Readers must read critically and challenge assumptions. Each person, after all, is judge and jury in choosing what to read and assessing what is read. This, in turn, suggests the need to create a society that is not only media literate but also culturally literate.

Lester's concluding words on images that injure are appropriate as a conclusion here:

> When the media regularly show images of members of all cultural groups as normal, everyday people that are just like everyone else, the goal of ending prejudice and discrimination will come a little closer. (2000, p. 92)

7.   References

Aisha Sultan (2001): "St. Louis Muslims Lead Diverse Lives that Defy Stereotypes." In: St. Louis Post-Dispatch (Five Star Lift Edition), September 30

Alafrangi, Manal (2007): "The saga of the broken American dream." In: Gulf News, United Arab Emirates, February 9

Al-Issa, Fadi Ahmad (2003): Living on the Hyphen: The Literature of the Early Arab-Americans between 1870-1940. Unpublished MA Thesis, Florida State University

Brittingham, Angela/de la Cruz, G. Patricia (2005): We the People of Arab Ancestry in the United States: Census 2000 Special Report. U.S. Census Bureau

Bulkeley, Deborah (2006): "Immigrant claims workplace bias." In: Deseret Morning News, Salt Lake City, November 29

Fiebig-von Hase, Ragnhild (1997): "Introduction." In: Fiebig-von Hase, Ragnhild/Lehmkuhl, Ursula, eds.: Enemy Images in American History. Providence, RI/Oxford, pp. 1-40

Gavrilos, Dina (2002): "Arab Americans in a Nation's Imagined Community: How News Constructed Arab-American Reactions to the Gulf War." In: Journal of Communication Inquiry, Vol. 26, No. 4, pp. 426-445

Ghareeb, Edmund (1983): Split Vision: The Portrayal of Arabs in the American Media. Washington, DC: American-Arab Affairs Council

Goodstein, Laurie (2006): "As Mideast Churns, U.S. Jews and Arabs Alike Swing Into Action." In: New York Times, July 28

Haddad, Yvonne Yazbeck, ed. (2002): Muslims in the West: From Sojourners to Citizens. Oxford/New York

Haddad, Yvonne Yazbeck (2004): Not Quite American? The Shaping of Arab and Muslim Identity in the United States. Waco, TX

Haddad, Yvonne Yazbeck/Smith, Jane I./Moore, Kathleen M. (2006): Muslim Women in America: The Challenge of Islamic Identity Today. Oxford/New York

Haiek, Joseph R., editor-publisher (1975): The American Arabic Speaking Community 1975 Almanac. Los Angeles, CA: The News Circle

Ibish, Hussein (2001): "'They are Absolutely Obsessed with Us': Anti-Arab Bias in American Discourse and Policy." In: Stokes, Curtis, Meléndez, Theresa and Rhodes-Reed, Genice, eds.: Race in 21st Century America. East Lansing, MI, pp. 119-141

Ibrahim, Dina (2003): "The Middle East in America's News: A 20th Century Overview." Paper presented at annual meeting of the International Communication Association, San Diego

Judge, Michael (2006): "Mother Mosque: We're Americans with dreams and aspirations." In: Wall Street Journal, December 21

Kayyali, Randa A. (2006): The Arab Americans. Westport, CT

Koch, Wendy (2006): "Ads are yanked as offensive to Arabs, Muslims." In: USA Today, September 26 (article available at http://www.usatoday.com/news/nation/2006-09-26-offensive-ads_x.htm/; accessed June 8, 2007)

Lester, Paul Martin (2000): Visual Communication: Images with Messages. Belmont, CA (2nd ed.)

Lind, Rebecca Ann and Danowski, James A. (1998): "The Representation of Arabs in U.S. Electronic Media." In: Kamalipour, Yahya R. and Carilli, Theresa, eds.: Cultural Diversity and the U.S. Media. Albany, NY, pp. 157-167

Little, Greta D. (1998): "Representing Arabs: Reliance on the Past." In: Kamalipour, Yahya R. and Carilli, Theresa, eds.: Cultural Diversity and the U.S. Media. Albany, NY, pp. 261-272

Merskin, Debra (2004): "The Construction of Arabs as Enemies: Post-September 11 Discourse of George W. Bush." In: Mass Communication & Society, Vol.. 7, No. 2, pp. 157-175

"Muslim Americans: Middle Class and Mostly Mainstream" (2007): Pew Research Center, May 22 (report available at http://pewresearch.org/pubs/483/muslim-americans/; accessed June 4, 2007)

Nacos, Brigitte L. and Torres-Reyna, Oscar (2007): Fueling Our Fears: Stereotyping, Media Coverage, and Public Opinion of Muslim Americans. Lanham, MD

Noakes, Greg (1998): "Muslims and the American Press." In: Haddad, Yvonne Yazbeck/Esposito, John L., eds.: Muslims on the Americanization Path? Atlanta, GA, pp. 361-378

"Northwest Airlines apologizes to Hajj pilgrims" (2007): Reuters, January 17

Orfalea, Gregory (2006): The Arab Americans: A History. Northampton, MA

Parry, Kate (2007): "Poll of Muslims Presents a Conundrum." In: Star Tribune, Minneapolis-St. Paul, MN, May 26

Reese, Stephen D. (2001): "Prologue – Framing Public Life: A Bridging Model for Media Research." In: Reese, Stephen D./Gandy Jr., Oscar H./Grant, August E., eds.: Framing Public Life: Perspectives on Media and Our Understanding of the Social World. Mahwah, NJ/London, pp. 7-31

Riggins, Stephen H. (1997): "The Rhetoric of Othering." In: Riggins, Stephen H., ed.: The Language and Politics of Exclusion: Others in Discourse. Thousand Oaks, CA, pp. 1-30

Rosenberg, Howard (2001): "Negative Stereotyping Distorts Arabs' Image." In: Los Angeles Times (Home Edition), July 30

Russell, Glenda M. and Kelly, Nancy H. (2003): Subtle Stereotyping: The Media, Homosexuality, and the Priest Sexual Abuse Scandal. Amherst, MA: Institute for Gay and Lesbian Strategic Studies

Saeed Ahmed (2001): "Overcoming the Stereotypes." In: Atlanta Journal-Constitution. (Home Edition, p. 12A), October 4

Saïd, Edward W. (1993): Culture and Imperialism. New York (1994 edition)

Saïd, Edward W. (1981): Covering Islam: How the Media and the Experts Determine How We See the Rest of the World. New York (rev. ed., 1997)

Samhan, Helen Hatab (1987): "Politics and Exclusion: The Arab American Experience." In: Journal of Palestine Studies, Vol. 16, No. 2, pp. 11-28

Samhan, Helen Hatab (1999): "Not Quite White: Race Classification and the Arab-American Experience." In: Suleiman, Michael W., ed.: Arabs in America: Building a New Future. Philadelphia, PA, pp. 211-226

Schneider, Jens (2001): "Talking German: Othering Strategies in Public and Everyday Discourses." In: International Communication Gazette, Vol. 63, No. 4, pp. 351-363

Semmerling, Tim Jon (2006): "Evil" Arabs in American Popular Film: Orientalist Fear. Austin

Shaheen, Jack G. (2001): Reel Bad Arabs: How Hollywood Vilifies a People. New York

Shaheen, Jack G. (1984): The TV Arab. Bowling Green, OH

Simon, Reeva S. (1989): The Middle East in Crime Fiction: Mysteries, Spy Novels, and Thrillers From 1916 to the 1980s. New York

Stapp, Katherine (2005): "U.S.: Surging Ethnic Media Speak in Many Tongues, But Get Few Ads." IPS-Inter Press Service, June 8

Steet, Linda (2000). Veils and Daggers: A Century of National Geographic's Representation of the Arab World. Philadelphia, PA

Suleiman, Michael W. (1989): "America and the Arabs: Negative Images and the Feasibility of Dialogue." In: Arab Studies Quarterly, Vol. 11, Nos. 2&3 (Spring/Summer), pp. 251-269

Suleiman, Michael W. (1999a): "Islam, Muslims and Arabs in America: The other of the other of the other..." In: Journal of Muslim Minority Affairs, Vol. 19, No. 1, pp. 33-47

Suleiman, Michael W., ed. (1999b): Arabs in America: Building a New Future. Philadelphia. PA

Terry, Janice J. (1985): Mistaken Identity: Arab Stereotypes in Popular Writing. Washington, DC: American-Arab Affairs Council.

Waugh, Earle H./Abu-Laban, Baha/Qureshi, Regula B., eds. (1983): The Muslim Community in North America. Edmonton, Canada

Weston, Mary Ann (2003): "Post 9/11 Arab American Coverage Avoids Stereotypes." In: Newspaper Research Journal, Vol. 24, No. 1, pp. 92-106

Weston, Mary Ann/Dunsky, Marda (2002): "One Culture, Two Frameworks: U.S. Media Coverage of Arabs at Home and Abroad". In: The Journal of Islamic Law and Culture, Vol. 7, No. 1 (Spring/Summer), pp. 129-164

Youssef, Mervat (2005): "The Story of 'Us': Negotiating National Identity on Opinion Pages in Times of Crisis." Paper presented at Midwest Association for Public Opinion Research, Chicago, November 18-19

Zeller, Tom Jr. (2006): "No Koran in Congress, Fewer Muslims to America?" In: New York Times, December 20 (article available at http://thelede.blogs.nytimes.com/2006/12/20/no-koran-in-congress/; accessed June 8, 2007)

8.   Appendix A: Lyrics to *A-hab, The A-rab*

This song by Composer Ray Stevens was No. 5 on Billboard's top 40 list in 1962.

A-hab, The A-rab

Let me tell you 'bout A-hab The A-rab
The Sheik of the burning sand
He had emeralds and rubies just dripping off 'a him
And a ring on every finger of his hands
He wore a big ol' turban wrapped around his head
And a scimitar by his side
And every evening about midnight
He'd jump on his camel named Clyde...and ride

(SPOKEN) Silently through the night to the sultan's tent where he would secretly meet up with Fatima of the Seven Veils, swingingest grade "A" number one U.S. choice dancer in the Sultan's whole harem, 'cause, heh, him and her had a thing going. You know, and they'd been carrying on for some time now behind the Sultan's back and you could hear him talk to his camel as he rode out across the dunes, his voice would cut through the still night desert air and he'd say (imitate Arabian speech) which is arabic for, "stop, Clyde!" and Clyde would say, (imitate camel voice). Which is camel for, "What the heck did he say anyway?"

Well....
He brought that camel to a screeching halt
At the rear of Fatima's tent jumped off Clyde,
Snuck around the corner and into the tent he went
There he saw Fatima laying on a Zebra skin rug
Wearing rings on her fingers and bells on her toes
And a bone in her nose ho, ho.

(SPOKEN) There she was friends lying there in all her radiant beauty. Eating on a raisin, grape, apricot, pomegranate, bowl of chitterlings, two bananas, three Hershey bars, sipping on a "R C" Co-Cola listening to her transistor, watching the Grand Ole Opry on the tube reading the Mad magazine while she sung, "Does your chewing gum lose its flavor?" and Ahab walked up to her and he said, (imitate Arabian speech) which is arabic for, "Let's twist again like we did last summer, baby." (laughter) You know what I mean!

Whew! She looked up at him from off the rug, give him one of the
sly looks, she said, (coy, girlish laugh) "Crazy baby".

'Round and around and around and around...etc.
And that's the story 'bout Ahab the Arab
The Sheik of the Burnin' sand
Ahab the Arab
The swinging Sheik of the burnin' sand

(Source: http://www.raystevens.com/SongLyrics/AhabLyrics.html;
accessed June 8, 2007)

9.   Appendix B: Organizations Promoting Arab Interests[7]

9.1   Association of Arab-American University Graduates (AAUG)
http://www.aaug-asq.org/about_the_aaug.htm

*Mission Statement: To develop, foster, and promote educational and cultural information
and activities on the Arab World and the Arab-American community.*

The Association of Arab-American University Graduates is a membership
organization and its programs include an annual conference, cultural events,
summer study visits to the Middle East, publishing a journal, the Arab Studies
Quarterly, as well as books on the Arab world and Arab-American community.
The AAUG also provides a network for members and people who are
interested in furthering the aims of the Association, as stated in the mission
statement.

Academics such as Edward Said and Ibrahim Abu-Lughod were among
the founders of the AAUG in the late 1960s and 1970s. The need for academics of their caliber and depth are still needed to bridge the immense
information gap between the Arab world and the American people. The
AAUG continues to network and publish works by young Arab-American gra-
duate students, relying on membership dues for income. The strength and
commitment of the members new and old alike – is a testimony to its vibrant
educational exchanges and discussions. Objectives:

-       To publish and provide accurate, scientific, cultural and educational
        information about the Arab World and the Arab-American community

---

7   (Information collected from Websites; all sites accessed June 8, 2007).

- To build bridges of mutual respect and understanding between the Arabic-speaking and American peoples

- To create networks for Arab-American professionals, academics and students

- To present the Arab and Arab-American cultural arts in their various forms to American audiences (U.S. and Canada)

- To assist in the growth and development of the Arab World by providing the professional services and skills of its membership when needed

The history of the Association of Arab-American University Graduates is the history of a profound and irreversible intellectual and personal awakening of Arab-Americans to the critical issues affecting their original homeland and the powerful role of the United States in shaping the forms and the consequences of those issues. It is a history also of the events in the Arab world and their impact on the status and rights of Arab-Americans.

The June 1967 war changed the Arab-American community by jolting many of second and third-generation Arab-Americans and causing a highly hostile attitude toward Arab-origin individuals in the U.S. and Canada. In a book about the early years of the association, The First Decade, an overview of early AAUG history, describes the feelings of depression, anxiety, guilt and despair and helplessness that engulfed the community. The earlier immigrants began to understand the reasons for the hostility directed against them and became more active in understanding that part of the world that was now so much to affect their lives in their American environment. The June 1967 war acted as a catalyst for the older and newer Arab-Americans to realize and emphasize their common cultural and linguistic heritage.

9.2   The Arab Community Center for Economic and Social Services (ACCESS)
http://www.accesscommunity.org/site/PageServer?pagename=ACCESS_History2

The Arab Community Center for Economic and Social Services began operating out of a storefront in Dearborn's south end in 1971. It was truly amazing – people volunteering their time to serve the community. ACCESS' beginnings are humble, and we have made such great progress in the past 36 years...

The 1960s was an extremely volatile time both politically and socially, and this volatility deeply affected the Arab-American community. The burgeoning Dearborn Arab community was developing an identity, and it was in the midst of this a small group of dedicated and concerned people came together determined to provide assistance for immigrants in any way we could. We saw the daily struggles many Arabs who immigrated to the United States faced – the linguistic, cultural, and social barriers – and we knew we had to do something.

ACCESS was literally a labor of love; it was completely staffed by volunteers assisting those who had trouble with English fill out applications, complete their tax forms, translation, and anything else they needed. In 1970, George Khoury (a current lifetime member of ACCESS' Board of Directors) was elected our first board president.

9.3   National Association of Arab Americans (NAAA)
http://www.cafearabica.com/organizations/org12/orgnaaa.html

The National Association of Arab Americans is a foreign policy lobbying group dedicated to the formulation and implementation of an objective and nonpartisan U.S. foreign policy agenda in the Middle East. Founded in 1972, NAAA works to strengthen U.S. relations with Arab countries and to promote an evenhanded American policy based on justice and peace for all parties in the Middle East. The premier Arab-American political organization, NAAA serves as a spearhead for the community's lobbying activities in Washington, D.C. and is the only such organization registered with Congress.

9.4   American-Arab Anti-Discrimination Committee (ADC)
http://www.adc.org/index.php?id=125

Mission: The American-Arab Anti-Discrimination Committee (ADC) is a civil rights organization committed to defending the rights of people of Arab descent and promoting their rich cultural heritage.

ADC, which is non-sectarian & non-partisan, is the largest Arab-American grassroots organization in the United States. It was founded in 1980 by former U.S. Senator James Abourezk and has chapters nationwide.

ADC's Advisory Committee is made up of an impressive group of people that include: Muhammad Ali, Her Majesty Queen Noor, U.S. Congressmen John Conyers (D-MI), Darrell Issa (R-CA), & Nick Joe Rahall (D-WV), as well as the Honorable Paul Findley, Clovis Maksoud, Casey Kasem, Archbishop Philip Saliba and others.

ADC is at the forefront in combating defamation and negative stereotyping of Arab Americans in the media and wherever else it is practiced. In doing so, it acts as an organized framework through which Arab Americans can channel their efforts toward unified, collective and effective advocacy; by promoting a more balanced U.S. Middle East policy and serving as a reliable source for the news media and educators. By promoting cultural events and participating in community activities, ADC has made great strides in correcting anti-Arab stereotypes and humanizing the image of the Arab people. In all these efforts, ADC coordinates closely with other civil rights and human rights organizations on issues of common concern. Through its Department of Legal Services, ADC offers counseling in cases of discrimination and defamation and selected impact litigation in the areas of immigration. Additional information on the ADC at http://www.adc.org/index.php?id=119

The American-Arab Anti-Discrimination Committee is committed to:

- Empowering Arab Americans;

- Defending the civil rights of all people of Arab heritage in the United States;

- Promoting civic participation;

- Encouraging a balanced U.S. foreign policy in the Middle East and;

- Supporting freedom and development in the Arab World.

Now more than ever, the Arab-American community needs a powerful, effective national and local organization to defend its interests. ADC is that organization. ADC was founded in 1980 by former U.S. Senator James Abourezk.

Svetlana Serebryakova

Issues of Migration in Newspapers of the Stavropol' Area

Interethnic as well as interregional relationships have long been of great importance for the socio-economic and cultural live of the Stavropol' area, which due to its geographical position was named gateway to the Caucasus in the 19th century already (the city was founded as a fortress in 1777).

It was L.D. Trotsky who described the Caucasus as a gigantic ethnographic museum. This also applies to the North Caucasus with its numerous people of different cultures, races and religions living together on a relatively small territory. Here, economic and political conditions caused extensive migration after the breakup of the USSR.

Geographically, the Stavropol' area lies in the South of Russia (Southern Federal District), and belongs to the North Caucasian region. It is the most Southern Russian-speaking area, further South are – as part of the Russian Federation (RF) – the North Caucasian Republics of North Ossetia, Kabardino-Balkariya, Ingushetia, Dagestan, Karachaevo-Cherkessiya, Chechnya, most of which share borders with the Stavropol' Area.

2,723,900 people lived in the Stavropol' area in 2004. Since 1989 the population increased by 13%. Looking at population statistics you find the Stavropol' area on rank 16 in the Russian Federation, and on rank 3 in the Southern Federal District.

Russians, Armenians, and Ukrainians have the largest share in the population that has long been consisting of more than 100 different nations (for comparison: in the Russian Federation you find 152 different nations). A stable immigration from North Caucasian regions is being named in unison as determining factor for the increasing multiethnicity of the population in the Stavropol' area since the 1990s.

The first inflow of migrants from the 1980s to the turn of the century resulted from the independence of the Caucasian Republics. People mainly came as Russian refugees from Trans- and North Caucasian Republics. Only during the last seven years migrants came as members of the North- and Trans-Caucasian nations, which lead to an increasingly diverse population in the Stavropol' area.

The Stavropol' area today is among the top five administrative areas of the Russian Federation where among 1,000 inhabitants the population growth due to migration is more than twofold the average Russian population growth.

The inflow of migrants contributes to an increase of real estate prices, a more aggravated competition on the labor market, decreasing standards of living, a tightening of social conflicts and problems – mainly with regard to job training and health care –, an intensification of nationalistic and separatistic tendencies, as well as to a rising crime rate.

Social infrastructure is not laid-out for this increase in population (Khoperskaya/Kharchenko 2005, p. 49). This explains why administration officials as well as the average population in the area values migration as a social occurrence with a negative connotation. Migration in all its manifestations is being named almost in unison as one of the main reasons for ethnic tensions in Southern Russia, mostly in consequence of political conflicts, terrorism and inconsequent official migration policy. Characteristical for the ethnopolitical processes in the North Caucasus is their inconsistent dynamics, and further socio-economical and ethnic stratification.

Generally speaking it can be stated that the socio-psychological adaptation of refugees in our region is difficult, due to objective as well as subjective drawbacks. Problems of adaptation and integration of migrants are essential questions for the Stavropol' area, and as such they are a constant subject of discussion on different societal levels. A federal program "South of Russia" has been elaborated, containing different actions and measures aiming at the reduction of negative impacts of migration and the regions warranty of socio-political and economic stability. Among other things, the media is supposed to be supported in its objective discussion of migration issues and conflicts. A non-governmental organization "Danish Council of Refugees" has been working on an "Integration"-project in the Southern Federal District for years. According to surveys, problems of migration and refugees and their mutual relationships with the residing population, remains to be one of the most prevailing problems of the socio-political and economic life in the Stavropol' area – on different levels regularly discussed in the regional mass media as well. Problems of the socio-psychological adaptation of refugees, the idea of a positive interethnic and intercultural dialogue and the idea of tolerance are important topics not only in the newspapers of the Southern Federal District and the district capital, but also in the city- and county-issues.

Qualitatively and quantitatively, the branched system of district-, city-, and county-media has changed in the 1990s: today about 200 different newspapers and magazines are being published, among them news and entertainment newspapers, for general as well as for special interest, for purchase as well as for free. etc.

Popular are the regional issues of the federal newspapers: "Argumenty i fakty. Severnyi kavkaz", "Komsomol'skaya pravda na severnom kavkaze", "Moskovskii komsomolets – kavkaz". Since 1990 the evening newspaper of the district capital "Vechernii Stavropol'" plays an important role – with a constantly increasing readership. The newspaper "Stavropol'skie gubernskie vedomosti" is again being published (since 1992), and so is "Pyatigorskaya pravda" (since 1995). The newspaper "Rodina" (KPRF, Communist Party of the Russian Federation) represents the party press. On the sector of private media there are mainly weekly newspapers – with the exception of two daily newspapers. Highest circulations in the Stavropol' area can be found among the weekly advertisement-papers on the news-sector: "Ekstra-biznes", "Telekur'er", "Kavkazkaja nedel'ya", the daily district newspaper "Stavropol'skaya pravda", the city newspapers "Vechernii Stavropol'", "Pyatigorskaya pravda", the county newspapers "Rassvet" (Turkmensky County), "Blagodarnenskie vesti" (Blagodarnensky County), "Primanychskie stepi" (Apanasenkovsky County).

Matters of general social importance are subject of journalistic interest mainly in the general newspapers of the majority – special interest media looks at the respective subject matter from its special interest point of view. Accordingly, our sample to study the characteristics of journalistic description of migration processes and issues consists of regional-, city- and county-newspapers – different levels of media reporting, where different attitudes towards the subject matter can be observed.

Traditional and conservative is the coverage of issues of migration in county newspapers: Being published with 4-8 pages (3 of which contain journalistic material, the others advertisements, TV program etc.) once or twice a week, those publications aim at close contact to their readers, supplying them with information on local issues of their county. In doing so they focus on the activities of communal authorities, reporting on their sanctions and measures taken in order to solve migration-related problems.

A news report in the county-newspaper "Levokum'e" (April 7th, 2007) can be seen as an example: "On Migration and Security Measures" it says in the headline of the article, reporting on a meeting of the county council of economic and social security that discussed processes of migration in the Levokumsky County. In his article the journalist discusses several key issues related to migration: its uncontrolled development, its evocation of socio-economic and ecological chance in the Levokumsky County:

> The newcomers do not make an effort to get to know existing traditions, customs and conventions of the residing population, their behavior oftentimes attests to their depreciative relationship to the residing population. Should not the migrants be thankful to the residing population, that a higher educational level in new living conditions is being granted to them, and that they get the opportunity to be proficient in the use of the national language.

From there it can be concluded that certain efforts of assimilation are expected of migrants. In general, media content regarding their traditions, religion, and culture is being verbalized in a positive way.

County-newspapers also publish official statements of the public administration. These are oftentimes official greetings on public holidays. Representatives of the different administrative offices repeatedly declare the need for peace and friendship among the different Caucasian nations – even though they hardly ever mention the matter of migration in their official speeches and greetings, as our analysis shows.

Another characteristic of the county press is related to its traditional focus on personality, a focus on the people that are of special importance and interest for the development and history of the county – to be read in emotional portraits and life stories.

(Mostly successful) migrants and refugees can be among the "heroes" in these emotional reports as well, because their fate is unique, dramatic and interesting. They are being portrayed as people who subdued their fate, successfully reassembling their life in a new place and under new conditions. Without question, this kind of reporting can be seen as an important contribution of county-journalists to the building of a positive migrant image: the media is qualified to affect their readers emotions, evoking sympathy for their heroes. But in the total amount of material, this kind of publication makes up for a very little part.

Regional and city-press declares the intercultural dialogue of members of al nationalities to be of great importance, and it also sees public dialogue on a national level to be of great importance for the integration of the respective migrant groups. But our analysis shows regional as well as city press not to pay a great deal of attention to issues and problems of migration, even though the subject matter is not avoided. But informative and analytical reports on migration issues can be found on this level – indicating that journalists and newspaper offices have realized the topicality and importance of migration matters. The newspapers "Stavropol'skaya pravda", "Stavropol'skie gubernskie vedomosti", "Otkrytaya dlia vsekh i kazhdogo" often publish information and comments on migration-related conflicts. Most frequently migrants themselves and members of the authorities represent the parties of the dispute. This is along the lines of press guidelines to defend the average citizen in his or her dispute with administration officials. Where the former is often portrayed as hard-working and decent, the latter in many cases is depicted as mercenary.

You may take the article "Disguised Schemes" as an example: Reporting on current issues of city planning in Stavropol, the city newspaper "Otkrytaya dlia vsekh i kazhdogo" gives the floor to a refugee, telling of his law suit with "russian bureaucracy" – a preamble tells of his fate, his escape with children and parents from Grosny, and his first difficult years of adjustment to life in Stavropol' ("Otkrytaya dlia vsekh i kazhdogo" 2007, No. 21, p. 10).

On the other hand, media often diagnoses migrant problems, and the oftentimes problematic character of migration processes in the Stavropol' area, especially in the Eastern rural districts with more and more Dagestan settlements. In these cases, journalists seek for scientific comment and sociological evaluation of the migration development, asking regionally well-known political scientists, sociologists, and experts in the field of conflict studies. Concluding it can be stated that the regional-, as well as city- and county-press have a different attitude towards issues of migration – differences that result from different journalistic policies and a varied readership. Where county- and city-newspapers concentrate on single events or the story of one single person, they often report in news, advertisements, accounts of different social programmes, and letters to the editor, on migration issues from a positive point of view. Journalists avoid a discriminatory vocabulary and negative stereotypes.

In the Eastern counties of the Stavropol' area, sharing borders with the North Caucasian Republics, oftentimes unbalanced and negative material is being published, sometimes leading to a deepening of conflicts.

County newspapers inform a large readership about migration-related occurrences, about tendencies of integration policies – oftentimes in the context of federaly policy. In doing so, they prefer analytical news and interviews to report on the issue.

Letters to the editor are one more source of information on the subject. Regularly being published, refugees and migrants have themselves a share in the statements on problems of integration into the receiving society.

A survey that has been conducted among journalists by researchers from the faculty of history and theory of journalism at Stavropol' State University, shows that journalists are aware of the importance of the issue, as well as of their own responsibility when journalistically dealing with the respective subject matter. Sometimes this awareness leads to an omission of migration issues in reporting, in order to, as one journalist put it, "bring no harm".

All in all, the print media of the Stavropol' area acknowledges the potential for conflict going along with migration processes, especially in the Southern parts of the Russian Federation. But still, media content with positive tendencies prevails, thus encouraging positive associations and attitudes among citizens. In the process, tolerance and multicultural integration are keywords, positively shaping the main concept of interethnic relations and of non-controversial, intercultural communication in the North Caucasus.

References

Khoperskaya, L.L./Kharchenko V.A. (2005): Lokal'nye mezhetnicheskie konflikty na Yuge Rossii: 2000-2005. Rostov-na-Donu

"Disguised Schemes", in: Otkrytaya dlia vsekh i kazhdogo (2007), No.21, p. 10

"On Migration and Security Measures", in: "Levokum'e" (2007) April 7th

Worst Case and Best Practice in European and North American Media Integration: What Can We Learn from One Another?

Round Table Discussion

Participants

Prof. Dr. Heinz Bonfadelli (University of Zürich)
Prof. Dr. Rainer Geißler (Siegen University)
Prof. Dr. Leen d'Haenens (Radbouw University Nijmegen)
Souley Hassane (University of Poitiers)
Dr. Petra Herczeg (University of Vienna)
Prof. Dr. Horst Pöttker (University of Dortmund)
Prof. Dr. Kenneth Starck (Zayed University, United Arab Emirates)

Chair

Augie Fleras (University of Waterloo, Canada)

Augie Fleras

> *Good afternoon to everyone and welcome to this final session that will be a round-table colloquium.*
>
> *The theme of the conference is to see what media and journalists need to do in order to make minorities and migrants feel at home. I think, that we use that terminology is quite interesting, because it goes beyond abstractions like just integration or inclusion, but brings it really down to the fundamental issue – of making migrants feel at home – in terms of reaching out, in terms of inviting in, and in terms of inquiring: where are experiences of discriminatory barriers and what could be done to modify or eliminate these barriers? What kind of indicators do we have with feeling at home? We like to think that feeling at home means that your sense of belonging is as much to your country as to the one that you left behind; that your sense of identity is as great as the one that you left behind. So the notion of indicators – what constitutes this concept of integration in general and feeling at home more specifically? – is an important one.*

In the appendix of my paper, at page 23, I've reproduced a paraphrase of what the European Commission has defined as a working set of criteria for what constitutes integration. What I liked about it is that it seems to very much reinforce this notion of a two-way process in terms of "You adjust, we adapt. We adjust, you adapt". It seems that the news media is one of the more important sources in terms of making migrants feel at home.

The second theme is the idea of what kind of practices are likely to discourage migrants from feeling at home? What kind of structures, what kind of mind-sets? Many of these have been discussed in the sessions and papers we had today.

Finally, and I suppose it's a theme that is more specifically aimed at this afternoon session, is this notion of what can we learn from others. What are the best practices that we can absorb from other jurisdictions, from other places? One of the terms is: What can we learn from North American societies, which we regard as classic immigration societies who have had to deal with the challenges of immigration for generations? We [as North American Societies] like to think that we finally developed models that more or less work. Now the interesting issue is whether or not these models have legs. In other words: They may work well in a classic immigration society, but they may not necessarily work well in countries that historically have been emigrant societies – or as Mark J. Miller and Stephen Castles point out, that are regarded as complete societies. That kind of collective mind-set could be an obstacle in terms of creating the kind of responsiveness, accessability and the kind of equity that we normally associate as part of an inclusive society.

So, with this warm preamble I'll turn over to the other members of the panel or the colloquium.

Horst Pöttker

I want to answer your questions: What can media do to make migrants feel at home? And what are the barriers for migrants to feel at home that are made by the media?

It was a very important finding for me that local German newspapers before the First World War did not take any notice of the Polish minority. So, I think the answer to the first and the second question is: The worst case is that the mainstream media don't take any notice of the migrants and the minorities. I think it is a very deep reason for migrants *not* to feel at home in a country, when they don't have any access to the public discourse. And if the media don't take any notice of them, there is no chance to get into the public discourse. This is a very important point. Very often we start the discussion and say: well, there are negative stereotypes, the minorities are portrayed in a negative way, they are only criminals, and so on. But this is the second step. It is not really the worst case; the worst case is that migrants are not mentioned in the media at all.

Petra Herczeg

There seem to be different problems on different levels. If we see the structural level, the media producers have to see the migrants as a very important audience, which has economic power. So they have to see that they have to produce for these people, to broadcast to these people. This is a relevant group in society, so they have to be recognized.

On the content level, I think that in a democracy there is not only a question of quantitative variety, but also of qualitative variety. These two things thave to be combined to make sure that it would be good for the society to have more reportings about migrants.

Leen d'Haenens

I'd just like to add on this last point. The Dutch anthropologist Shadid had a good theoretical perspective. He said we should go beyond the "us/them"-perspective, we should try to adopt a so-called third perspective, that brings in also the diversity and the perspective of the other combined with your own. So that it can lead towards bridges between so-called ethnic media workers and the mainstream media workers. I think it's very important to have a tool for journalists, a source where you can look for experts of other origins than the mainstream origins, with all kinds of expertises.

Souley Hassane

First point: the experience of France. The problem in our country is that the place of minorities in the media can be compared with their place in the economy. I think that the situation of the minorities in the mainstream media in France is the translation of their own social situation. Another problem is the representation of minorities in the mainstream media. In 2004, France adapted a law for the representation of all minorities in the mainstream media. The real problem of France, and probably of all these countries, is the implementation. To implement the law, to implement the good practice.

Kenneth Starck

The media, I think, have to be very pro-active in terms of identifying as many segments of the community as possible and making sure that extra steps are taken to provide them with a voice. And the extra steps may be in terms of hiring people who have special language abilities or special intercultural abilities to be able to reflect a story.

These groups often do not know how the system operates. Language could be a problem, cultural barriers are a problem, and as a result, I think, the media have to go this extra mile if they are really discharging their responsibility to their communities. Having said that, I've worked as a journalist. I know the real world out there, and unfortunately the kind of idealism that my comments reflect and that some of the other comments are pretty far from reality. Because of some factors that already have been mentioned: the competition, the profit factors, the advertising. If a group of people doesn't have the economic ability to respond to advertising, then it's all likely that this group is not going to get very serious coverage in the media. I despair a little bit, insofar as the US commercial media are concerned.

It seems to me that we have to find some other model that bridges the public, the populist if you will, with – let's say – some aspects of the commercial. This may mean some kind of special government subsidy, or something that makes it at least viable financially for the media to go this extra mile.

Heinz Bonfadelli

Another point is to have more journalists with a migrant background. For instance, we just finished a representative journalists survey. In the private broadcast media in Switzerland there is a share of five per cent of journalists with a migrant background. And in the United States, about 15 per cent of the journalists seem to have a migrant background in a way.

When we talk about journalism in general, I think, what we try in Switzerland is to build partnerships with institutions in Switzerland that are educating journalists. And until now there is no module or educational unit dealing with intercultural communication or, for instance, discussing the examples that you're presenting with the new journalists. So I think education in journalism and more journalists – these are two important points to the question of what can be done.

Rainer Geißler

I have another approach to your question: I tried to compare the countries presented here. The criteria of comparison are your criteria: How do migrants feel? Do they feel at home in these countries? And a second criterion: How many and intensive ethnic conflicts are in these countries? These two criteria are combined by another. And if I say it very briefly – worst case and best practice – I think, best practice is Canada, worst case is France. I don't dare to evaluate the USA. Perhaps the Central European countries: there's not much difference between them, a similar situation in Switzerland and in Austria and in the Netherlands. Perhaps in the Netherlands it has been a little bit more complicated for the last two or three years than in other countries. In this ranking, the media play only a very limited role. I think, they reflect the situation in the country.

In Canada, we have a traditional multiculturalism, which is, in my opinion, the best practice to manage this diversity. Once I've heard a slogan which is typical of Canada. They say to migrants: "You're welcome to join us." In Germany, they don't say that. They say: "You're welcome to work here. If we don't need you, please go home." That's the guest-worker-ideology. And I think this guest-worker-ideology is dominant in Germany, and perhaps also in Switzerland and in Austria. Within this ideology the migrants don't feel at home. And this situation is reflected in the media. I think, in the Canadian media migrants are well-represented and ethnic media are no problem. In our countries they are more misrepresented and ethnic media perhaps are problems.

From the audience

What do the French say in your opinion? What do the French say to the immigrants? The Canadians say "You're welcome".

Rainer Geißler

I think a big mistake was made in France when the Arab migrants came in the 1950's and 60's. They were concentrated in certain areas with socio-economic disadvantages. It's a socio-ecomomic problem they had, which now provokes these conflicts; conflicts we don't have in Germany. This concentration policy created ethnic ghettos, Arab ghettos or black ghettos. And if they are concentrated in these ghettos and not included in society, one day they will explode. They exploded two years ago.

223

Souley Hassane

I want to say that the greatest problem in France is our relation between ethnic minorities and the mainstream media. As I see it, it's a combination of an economic situation and a political situation in which the minorities don't have a real place. If you consider the French Law against discrimination – a very good law. But the real problem of France is the implementation of this law. It is not a problem of language, because – immigrants for example – most of them are French, they speak French very well, and they respect the law. But the real problem is that they don't have equal opportunities like other citizens. That's why sometimes the suburbs of France and the people who live in the suburbs of France, they consider themselves as "under-citizens".

This ideology is very real; it's in the culture of the mainstream media and the journalists who are making the media. For example, during the riots of 2005, the mainstream media hired people who live in the suburbs to report from there. We were not in war, but they hired people who live there. They could not go there to interview people. The journalists who are in Paris cannot go ten kilometers away from Paris to make a report! Why? We are not on a warfield. We are in France. The problem is the culture of journalism. When you take the majority of French journalists, they come from the same class, the same cultural and social class. Their function in writing the papers is a translation of their own social position.

That's why I say it's necessary to inject, to push diversity into journalism. It may be colour, because the mainstream is very uncoloured. It's necessary, it's a symbolic revolution.

Augie Fleras

Just in relation to Rainer's comment: I do appreciate your positive attitude towards Canada. It's possible that we may have the most workable multicultural model. I use that term delibaretely, workable, that doesn't mean that it's best or perfect, but it's workable. And part of its workability (if there is such a word) is that it doesn't focus on diversity or ethnicity or "celebrate differences" and so on. Canada's multicultural model is very clearly focused on integration, inclusion, removing the discrimatory barriers. The idea is to incorporate all the new Canadians into society by the way of making them feel comfortable about themselves in making that transition. I suppose the underlying logic to official multiculturalism in Cananda is the notion that we treat everyone the same in Canada, regardless of your difference, and we do this as a matter of course. But we will also treat you differently if necessary, in order to surmount certain obstacles in society. So it's that kind of Ying-Yang between uniformity and diversity. The commonality proceeds, but the exception, the difference is workable if necessary. That's the theory; the practice is much more different.

Now, just a comment: I think that this kind of multicultural model can also be applied to the news media and to journalism. This notion, this idea that the content should not be about extremism or sensationalism or about ethnic exotica but in fact should focus on the responsibility that the news media have towards inclusion and integration. Which means that they have to very seriously rethink some of the news values that are associated with what constitutes newsworthiness – which brings me to the point that Ken and Leen made. I agree with you that a world in which we undermine this distinction between "us" and "them" and create a "we" is in fact an ideal world. But as Ken pointed out, there are certain ideals within the news media that are very difficult to implement in the 21st century. That notion of newsworthiness is based precisely on an us-them dichotomy, the notion of protagonists. So this medium of the negative continuity tries to frame the world in terms of conflicts – which of course makes it very difficult to achieve a "we", because it's the "us" and "them" that constitutes a core, if not THE core news value. Without conflict, you have no news. I think most people live in that scheme.

Leen d'Haenens

I agree with this and it's also a matter of extending the "we". And there is a market for that, if you get more members of your society to read your news. We know this from our research about youngsters. The Turks and the Moroccan youngsters, especially the Moroccans, experience a lot of hunger for Dutch news – so there is a market in the market logic. If you look at a certain event from a broader perspective you can have it really much more overall on the news agenda – because you reach different kinds of readers. A certain topic may be out of the news after a week, although the Turks are still looking for more news. So it's just a matter of broadness. You know – and you mentioned it too, Heinz, yesterday – that the Turkish and Moroccan youngsters are experiencing much more news hunger in general than their Swiss counterparts. So there's a market for you as a newsmaker.

I wonder about what you were saying about Canada and the Canadian model: Of course, as you said, Canada has a conditional immigration policy: In order to become a new Canadian you have to respond to a certain profile – agewise, languagewise, in professional terms also, right?

Augie Fleras

I'm not quite sure what you mean by that.

Leen d'Haenens

I mean, it's a conditional policy, and that's why also in Europe conditions are developed now. Look at the Netherlands and the change: it's more complex now, since five years ago. Before that, there was no entry condition whatsoever. Now there are a few conditions in terms of knowledge of the language. And Canada has had it from the start. I wonder how ready the Canadians are or will be for a news presenter wearing a veil now.

From the audience

Would you be ready?

Augie Fleras

Would I be ready? Of course. Again, I wonder how important it is what we see in public, in terms of news casting. I suppose we could open it up for debate. Because these are just the faces of people who are mechanically delivering the news. I'm much more interested in what is the social construction involved in terms of creating the news, regardless of who presents it, which seems to be a much more important issue with respect to how news items are framed, how they are placed within the news cast itself. And, you know, as a sociologist, I think I came to acknowledge some of the structural difficulties in making these kinds of changes. What we have is really a form of systemic bias towards news casting as negativity, which is deemed to be normal. It's not like a systematic bias, which one can see as an abnormality that can be isolated and removed with the right kind of attitude and action. It's systematically embedded and it truly does require a transformative change. But I think a woman with a veil on the news cast really would be more of a cosmetic change.

I don't know if somebody has heard of it, because apparently it was no international success, but we have the show "Little Mosque on the Prairie", a CBC special. The show has attracted enormous attention because it does feature Muslims who are trying to adjust themselves in a small prairie town. And as you can appreciate, the humour arises from the fish-out-of-water context, both for the white residents who are completely baffled by what is going on, as well as the Muslims who have to cope with the idiosyncrasies of that.

It would strike me that it would be a fairly short step to have a woman with a veil doing the news cast, especially now that "Little Mosque on the Prairie" has made the way. That's like the easy part. The tougher part is, get the media to move away from "us vs. them" and to think of news as "we".

From the audience

Regarding this ranking of Rainer Geißler, there's one remark I'd like to make, linking it with what Augie Fleras said about the immigration societies. There, of course, this acceptance by the population was built into the system. Canada was open, largely; therefore immigration was the norm for centuries. And in the United States, it was the same. All Americans, the sole exception may be the Native Americans, were descendants of immigrants and aware of it. And even if they didn't like the late comers – the protestants didn't like the Irish, the Irish didn't like the Germans, the Germans didn't like the South-East Europeans, the South-East Europeans didn't like the Asians, okay. But they took them all in; that was the norm. Whereas in Europe they didn't have this ideology. I think this is very much an elite discourse, which is typical of Europe: You have an elite discourse, then maybe you hold a referendum and then the Dutch and the French, just like with the European Constitution, say "no". Then you say: "Well, what do we do?" And you go around it. The consensus in the German society, in Swiss society, in Dutch society is missing. So the elites don't know what to do because the population hasn't been born into it. In Canada, in America, there's much criticism – "So many Hispanics" – but there's by and large a consensus "We are an immigrant country". This consensus has now arrived in the elites. The German elites say: "Yes, we are a country of immigration." But that's only the elites. The population says: "Well, we're not overly happy about it." So that's the problem. Because, of course, these are the constituents, this is the mass of the media audience. So it is a media problem, but it is also a democracy problem. The majority of the population is not very much pro-immigration – unlike in the U.S., unlike in Canada. Which I think explains, to a certain degree, why North Americans do better in such a ranking.

Augie Fleras

I would like to point out that we mainly use the term "immigrant society" not only in a descriptive sense to indicate that there are, let's say, 250,000 new Canadians. And note that the term we use is "New Canadians": They are Canadians, or we assume that they are going to be Canadians. But there is also a kind of prescriptive component to being an immigrant society, in so far as you have to fulfil certain criteria to become an immigrant society.

First, there are laws and regulations that are made to regulate the intake – so that the new Canadians we get tend to be pre-selected in terms of they are liberal in value, they are well-equipped in terms of skills, and they tend to be legal. They come through normal channels, which is not a luxury that a number of European countries face, with open and increasingly borderless borders. So, first there is a set of laws in place, and second, there is an extensive post-immigration settlement service package. So that immigration is not just coming into the country, it's also being serviced in terms of access to whatever is required to settle down, to fit in and to move up. And it's quite extensive, because the immigration process is seen as extending beyond arrival at "Piercing Airport" in Toronto.

Thirdly, immigrants tend to be seen as assets to society. Not everyone would agree with that and the government works hard to remind us that in an ageing economy we need immigrants, that they are good for society and that they provide us with a lot of benefits. Not the least of which is the idea of sustained economic development. 262,000 immigrants per year require food, shelter, start-up costs in terms of transportation and so on – a remarkable boost to the economy. And the service offered is seen as a basis for a kind of long-term sustained growth.

So there are these three components of an immigrant society, and all of them work together to create a kind of accommodativeness that makes both multiculturalism and immigration safe options for Canada.

From the audience

You didn't quite answer my question, I'm afraid. It's very short: You said immigrants are useful, very good. But if the population isn't persuaded and the majority actually doesn't buy it – you said some don't buy it, but if the majority actually doesn't buy it – what do you do? The majority in Germany is still sceptical, I would say: And they say: "Migrants, are they useful? Rather no!" What do you do?

Augie Fleras

Step up the government propaganda. Crank it up until they don't hear anything else except a humanistic version of 1984.

Horst Pöttker

I think there should be added one criterion for what is an immigrant society. And there is also the question what is a non-immigrant society, of course. I think, it's not only a question of the objective criteria – how is the share of immigrants and so on – but also a question of self-definition. I think, a non-immigrant society is a society where it is accepted that for integration or for the being of a societal whole, cultural homogenity is necessary. But an immigrant society is a society with a self-definition where cultural homogenity is not necessary for integration. Cultural differences are not only legal but they are accepted.

The question of integration is a question beyond the question of cultural homogenity. I think this a very important difference. A non-immigrant society is a cultural nation. You have to speak good English, not only English, but good English, to give a sign that you are belonging to the society. And you can see this difference also, let's say, between the British society and the North American societies, Canada and the US. From the very beginning, almost all of them were immigrants – except the Native Americans. And I think, this is very important that from the very beginning you have no definition of your nation as a cultural nation – as a nation of people, "all the same colour, all the same religion, the same language" and so on.

Heinz Bonfadelli

Just a short remark about the American Society. They are discussing now illegal immigration from Mexico. I think President Bush wants to build a fence – so even in the United States it's a dilemma.

Rainer Geißler

Augie, I like very much your three criteria for an immigration country. And I think the Central European countries are 50 years beyond Canada. Canada is an immigration country since the 60's or 70's. Germany makes its first tentative steps to begin to be an immigration country. Still we are "Deutschland", that means the "country of the Germans", and not yet an immigration country. For one or two years now, we have the first act of immigration to manage who comes in. We have the first steps. For three or four years, we have been discussing the concept of integration, how to manage the diversity. And it's a very controversial discussion, not multicultural like in Canada. It has just been said that our elite accepts that we need immigrants. That's only a part of the elite.

And in the last years they stopped migration. There's no immigration and emigration that was balanced. There was not one person who came to Germany. We had a loss of population.

Now we made the first steps and perhaps, I hope, that in half a century we will have made some progress, but I think not to a multicultural society, because we have another history. We don't have this immigration history, Horst explained. We have other conditions. There are structural differences between the classic immigration countries, North America or Australia or New Zealand, and those modern immigration countries that now need immigration for demographic reasons.

Kenneth Starck

It may well be that there is some kind of timeline of development or activation that takes place here. This might be a starting point: Whether the land is relatively open and being settled versus a society that has already been settled. But nonetheless it may be that the timeline is still in effect. One of the reasons why I think this is the reference to French newspapers not having reporters who are able to go into a war-like zone for coverage. Because I remember, back in the 1960's in the United States, the Los Angeles Times was covering the Watts riots – those of you who are interested in history will know that – and there was not a black reporter at the Los Angeles Times at all. They did find an African American who was working in the classified advertising section and they persuaded him to go into the area and telephone back to the news desk what was taking place. Now, in the United States that occured almost 50 years ago and that was, I think, a water-shed event in terms of integrating, in this case, African Americans into society. Because coming from that was something called the Kerner Commission Report which made a very close analysis of the media handling of minority groups in the society, especially the African Americans. And it made some dramatic recommendations which ultimately were picked up by many institutions in society, including most especially journalism and mass media schools. As well as professional journalism associations who suddenly recognized that they had to set up special programmes to bring minorities into the recording pool of talent. And I think this had a very positive effect subsequently. It certainly hasn't solved all the problems by any means, but anyway: the point is that it may be possible over time that these various things have to recure in different societies and different times.

Augie Fleras

That brings us back to the first question – the notion of what we can do to make minorities feel at home, what the media can do to make minorities feel at home. And of course, the notion of journalists of colour, of credibility and accessability strikes me as one useful practice. It would be nice to push it a step further and have gatekeepers and editors who take the news and reformat it in a way that reflects the realities of diversity – that's still another hurdle that needs to be taken.

It strikes me that, with few exceptions, the panel has monopolized the conversation – so perhaps if anyone from the audience ...

From the audience

I feel, you cannot feel at home in a class society when you are belonging to the lowest class. And that doesn't depend on the media. So a comparison between Canada and France seems very inappropriate because you have to think that this is also the heritage of colonialism France has to deal with now. It is also a problem of hopes, maybe illusions, of people who are coming to France. You have the whole Mediterranean which is full of people who want to come to Europe with a lot of hopes. And the people in the countries where they want to go to, don't want to fulfill any hope because they fear they have too much problems on their own. And in this field you cannot blame the media. You can describe the situation, but I fear that the media are more a mirror of society than able to change it.

Rainer Geißler

I agree. I will explain it with an observation from Germany. I explained before that in Germany the elites, and also the population, are changing their opinion, becoming more open to immigration and integration. And we can see that there are only a few studies which compare the situation in 2006 to the 1990s for instance. A student in Siegen made a comparison of the local newspapers and looked: are they also more open to immigrants and immigration? And the negativity is not totally gone, but they are more open. That means that newspapers reflect the change of opinion of the elites and the population. Policies change, and the newspapers change with them. And also the discussion about journalists with a migrant background – that's totally new, and without this change of opinion, I would say, that wouldn't have happened. Media reflect the changes or situations within the society and within politics.

Heinz Bonfadelli

I think, we altogether see the problem. It's complicated, and there are different levels. I showed you the data on the school level. That shows how children from migrant families don't have equal chances at school – what about the language, their first language at school? Are they allowed to use their own language at school or do they get lessons at school? So I think the school system is very important as well.

We talked about the media system and now we focused on the level of journalists, but then we have the level of media organizations and media outlets. You know, minority media are quite small, and we have an increasing commercialization of the media system. And normally, the big media market is where you can make money. We see small markets in Switzerland in the Alpine region, for instance, where there is not enough money to have local radio stations in rural areas. But in Switzerland we have a system where in those small rural areas local radio stations get subsidies. So I think here again, on this structural level of media financing, there are options and the government can put money into it and do more for a pluralistic media landscape.

From the audience

Dr. Hassane mentioned it yesterday, Augie Fleras mentioned it now. I think there's too much emphasis on this behind-the-camera aspect. That may be important. But especially regarding media effects, I would say the symbolic value of this black French anchorman on French prime time news is very important. And I would say even such non-creative roles as being actors in TV series are very important for representation, for how these people see themselves even if they don't write the script. The symbolic value of seeing a black person, reading the news in perfect French to the French mainstream audience, is very high. I would say that even if you write some more or less hostile texts about what happens in the Banlieues, the symbolic value is the most important one in the effect field. I would give this as a little hint to Augie, and I would stress this "before the camera" more than behind.

Leen d'Haenens

I read people want to see themselves.

Augie Fleras

Didn't you argue against the symbolic value of something this morning?

From the audience

If a news pronouncer in France would come up and say: "This is the evening news. We are in France all multicultural. Now the news." That's not enough. You must have something real. In Russia it was very much like this. I have many books at home about Stavropol for example. 200 pages, and on the first page: "In Stavropol there live 150 nationalities. Now on to the real topics." That's not enough. *(Laughter)* It's true, I can show it to you, but it's in Russian. That was less than symbolic, that was only affirmative about being "a multicultural nation". But in the rest of the book there were no minorities. All Russians. I would say that was pseudo-symbolic.

Petra Herczeg

Yes, I also think that we need symbols to create a better image of migrants. You can only create a new image via communication campaigns and a lot of communication. You have to speak to the population and we see that there's a very big difference between the opinions in the heads of the politicians and a lot of journalists. They are in favour of intercultural communication. But if you ask the people "How do you think about intercultural communication?", no one is in favour of intercultural communication. Perhaps because they made some bad experiences, because they are living in houses with a lot of foreigners, they are too loud and so on. This means we need a long time to change the minds and this has to be a big topic to the European Union to make image campaigns for example, to show that migration is a positive thing in our society and that we need migration.

Horst Pöttker

We are still working on the question what the media should do that people feel at home in a country. And I want to come back to this question, because I think there is a possible misunderstanding how it should be answered. Perhaps people might think migrants feel at home only if they are portrayed very good, as the better guys. That Journalists should not be allowed to say that Turkish people are criminal and such things. I think this is very dangerous because if the migrants are portrayed as better guys – and not as normal guys, as we all are – then what will happen when it comes to the point that in reality they are only normal guys and no better guys? That must lead to a special disappointment and I think this is very dangerous, too. So I think the best practice is not to portray them in a very good and friendly way, but in a way which shows that they can have all roles which are possible in a normal society.

Leen d'Haenens

Journalists should avoid extremism then, too positive and too negative portrayal.

Petra Herczeg

I think too, journalists are not the better people. And I think it is a case of fair reporting. It is better to show both sides. No one is the perfect good guy, and no one is the perfect bad guy.

From the audience

I would say that journalists should reflect reality. That's the most important point to me. We're not politicians, we don't have to create a picture of how migrants are. The only job we have to do is to show what reality is like. And another comment: I agree with you that the representation of migrants in the media is very important. So the topic of "having journalists with a migrant background" is the most important issue to me. But it's only one function, the other is the broader perspective on reality, which you mentioned – to me it is not a broader perspective but the only correct perspective on reality. Those people live in our society; they shape society, so this must be reflected in the media. I give you an example: Whenever I hear the term "German taxpayers" in our radionews, I phone the newseditor, because it's incorrect. We have taxpayers *in* Germany, we don't have German taxpayers. And I think journalists with migrant backgrounds help to remind us that we have sometimes an ethnic perspective and don't realize this. This is why migrant journalists are important in our business.

Augie Fleras

I would like to comment on the notion that the primary role of the news media or journalists is to report reality. Think about a hypothetical situation. As an investigative reporter you collect a story on a daycare in the inner city. A positive story about children getting a head start involving minorities. The other investigative reporter collects a story on drug dealing among gangs within the inner city. Both reporters present the story to the editor. I wonder which one will get published. Both are reality. But one reality is a little bit more angled than the other. I really wonder what we can do to change these newsvalues. In the past, America had some companies that started up "good news newspapers". Newspapers that only have good news. They didn't last long. But one has to admire the courage for just presenting good news.

But even reporting stories exclusively dealing with gangs and drugs and guns and so on would have less of an impact if there were neutralizing devices in society outside, where there were positive role models. So that people would see that these stories in the news are simply isolated incidents, that there are people of colour in positions of power, in positions of authority and so on. We need to talk about comprehensive change, which can also be a cowardly way, because comprehensive change is so difficult to achieve that it's like using a platitude, knowing well that the platitude will never be real.

Kenneth Starck

This question of making migrants feel at home, for some reason, has kind of annoyed me. Because I try to figure out what usually plays a role that a migrant feels at home. And I suspected in many cases it may drive him away, because they left home to begin with. It seems to me, if they come to our homeland, our homeland, then it is for some rationale, there are some reasons and it is not necessary to make them feel as though they're back home again. Otherwise they can just go back. It seems to me that we are going to be talking about a hope, a future, an expectation for family, for the children, an educational equality and so forth.

Heinz Bonfadelli

I would add a second level. I think journalism is not only to represent reality but it needs a reflective; I call this meta-journalism. I think it is important to add a level of reflection to the coverage. Especially in the commercial electronic media in Switzerland we have lots of very young journalists, with low wages and with a low level of education. And I think, here it's necessary to have more education to bring in this kind of level of reflection. For instance, we did observations in local TV-stations and there was an incident that happened in a Swiss court: some young guys from Morocco had sex with some young girls and they caught these young people. Then there is one camera team, they get the story, they have to go out just straight to the location. Without any possibility to, say, do some thinking about the backgrounds. They just go, film, take statements, lift the micro to school boys and these school boys tell things. So I think one thing is commercialization, is having no time for background thinking, for doing it on a deeper level, and no time to bring in some reflection.

Leen d'Haenens

What about the allusion of self-censorship? Look at the Netherlands after the murder of Theo van Gogh. Two months after the crisis itself you can see that there's a lot of framing on who's responsible for this. The conflict is framed heavily there. And if you look at the year 2005, you see there is much less framing going on. So what could be the reason for that rational phenomenon? Could it be that journalists are afraid or have become afraid of opinion, of polarising – are they self-censoring themselves? Because there is this whole conflict of freedom of expression and offending people. They want to keep away from van Gogh's practice as a journalist. So now we have this portraying in a very neutral fashion. And I have the impression that for the French reporters, opinion matters much more than just coverage and transmitting the information.

Souley Hassane

I think the real problem in France, you can say, is a cultural, an ideological problem. It is not only the mainstream media. Because when I hear a politician, who declares publicly, he is against Muslims or Arabs or Blacks, the consequence is that he pushes the media to produce the information, because the media need this information. The politicians understand that sometimes it is useful for them to produce a negative public discourse about minorities. Because they always want to be on the media. The function of this discourse in the public space is the creation of opinion. And I think there is negative dynamic of producing information on minorities between politicians and the mainstream media. I think it is a bad practice in France to use the minority, the negative opinion on minorities as an instrument of politics. I think that they can contribute to make the migrants feel at home by avoiding this manner which considers the minorites as instruments of the production of a political opinion.

Augie Fleras

I have to admit that Kenneth's probing comment, on what we mean by making people feel "at home", might be an interesting one to play through in terms of your own person's experiences. When you go and live in someone else's home on a visit, what does actually make you feel at home? Admittedly, there will be a variety of responses, but it's quite possible that there are certain communalities in terms of obeying the rules of the house but still having enough free space to move around in. That could be something that each one of us could think personally and see whether he wants it to be applied to the first question. In terms of worst practices we are heading to share some that seem to have emerged from the sessions or from your personal experiences. Horst mentioned that a worse practice will be just to shift stereotypes from the bad guys to the good guys and create, you know, all kinds of unrealistic expectations.

Horst Pöttker

Yes, but in the beginning I also mentioned another kind of worst case. And this is not to take notice of the minorities – not to take notice of the fact, that there are people who are not Christians but Muslims, who are not white but coloured, who have another language, and so on. I think it is the first and very important step to take notice. Even if it is a criticism and negative notice, it's better than not to take notice at all. I learned this from my historical material about the Polish minority in Germany before World War I. But you also know this from your personal relationships, to your relatives and to your wife and your children and so on – not to take notice of the other is the worst case.

Augie Fleras

Just in response to your comment. I mean, would you say that, prior to the First World War, German presses actually did see themselves as exclusively ethnic presses? With the result, that they made no bones about the fact that if we are white, ethnic press, we're not interested in you. We are only interested in ourselves or we are only interested in you when you provoke or create problems. That notion of the mainstream media as ethnic media provides us with plausible answers why the media don't do what one will assume to be the right and responsible thing to do, but that they invisibilize minorities unless there is a crisis or a catastrophe.

From the audience

I think that in this case, like Horst mentioned in his paper, there was a dialogue of silence. You had the Polish papers with completely no reports about Germans, as far as they could: not to buy in German shops, not to read German newspapers, not to marry Germans, not to take any notice of Germans. So it was a dialogue between two who didn't want to talk. I would say, one should take this kind of worst-case scenario of ignoring each other. I am now reading a Turkish newspaper and I would say we can compare this Turkish newspaper, for example, to the Polish papers of the late 19th century and early 20th century. This huge Turkish paper produces a European edition, half of which is produced in Frankfurt. That's 20 pages every day from Frankfurt and 20 other pages from Istanbul. The Germans hardly ever occur. If they occur, they occur only insofar as they interact with Turks, positively and negatively. But it doesn't appear if Angela Merkel announces that welfare will go down, or train fares will go up, or electricity bills will rise, although this is very important for the Turks. Normal life in Germany doesn't appear at all in these 20 pages. So they are restricted to their own ethnic community.

Rainer Geißler

But nobody of the Germans knows that they don't appear. It's totally irrelevant. That's not the right comparison. Because no one reads these Turkish newspapers in Germany and so I don't know that I...

From the audience

The Turkish minority reads them. Horst has talked about the Polish newspapers for the Polish minority, in Polish, written in Germany. The Poles couldn't learn about the Germans either. They didn't write about their German co-citizens in the same city, with which they were interacting everyday. The German papers didn't write about the Poles, the Polish papers didn't write about the Germans. And the modern Turkish press here, available in Germany, produced here for the Turks, in Turkish, doesn't write about the Germans, if it's avoidable. Let's say there's a huge football match in Germany, with two million people watching on television, including half a million Turks. They would not report it, because there is no Turkish involvement. That's not dialogical, because the German media report on Turks – very negatively, but they don't ignore them. But the German elites are in power, they pass the laws. And about these laws, which affect the Turks who live here, you don't learn anything in the Turkish papers in Germany. For 50 years they haven't learned anything about this in these papers.

Rainer Geißler

Perhaps one sentence I would add to Horst's: Ignoring the immigrants is not the worst case, but insulting the immigrants. Mentioning them, but insulting them. Negative pictures are worse than ignoring them.

Horst Pöttker

I don't think so, Rainer. Kenneth and I are in the same boat in this case, because we are journalism educators and we think about what is the task of journalism – it is to create public. To make things visible. And even if it is a negative visibility, it is better than no visibility.

Heinz Bonfadelli

I want to add a point from communication researchers. 60 to 70 percent of the daily articles are generated by public relation sources. The question of the sources is important as well. Normally you have, say, organizations with money, which can afford to produce texts. And I think the minority organizations should as well have the chance or should be motivated to produce more news. Not only for daily media but as well for a channel of special-interest media. Here you have lots of texts that are subsidized and paid by industry, by interest groups and here, I think, one could influence a little bit more or pay a little bit more to have more sources, more input into the media system, coming from minority organizations.

Souley Hassane

I want to tell you something about a bad practice. First, for me, this is a binary vision of the mainstream media and journalists. This binary vision you can see everywhere in the French mainstream, for example about the suburbs: Bad? Good? Devil? God? This is, I think, the worst part. It's the worst practice. If we want to change the image of minorities, I think it is necessary to educate the journalists to produce information without this binary vision. Because a binary vision creates binary practise, and binary practise creates binary papers. Another important aspect is the relations between journalists, businessmen, politicians. I think that these are corrupted relations. I don't say corrupted by money, but by ideology. Because if journalists started to be in the suburbs, they could also adopt the view of the suburbs.

Kenneth Starck

I can add something about the danger of indifference with a little anecdote: Elie Wiesel often asks his audience what is the opposite of love. When I first heard him say that I thought it was hate, which seems to be logical. But that's not the answer. It's indifference, not giving a care at all, that's the worst practice. But coming back to the question: I used to belong to the organization of news ombudsmen and I was an ombudsman for a news organization for a while. I have written some columns in respondence to readers who were objecting to things, as they pertained to nationalities and ethnic groups and so forth: reporters confusing different nationalities or ethnic groups, for example, referring to them as part of a certain sector or group, when they weren't. You know, they just happened to have a funny hat or something like this and the reporters drew an immediate conclusion. Occasionally we would get complaints about that. But also about crime reporting: reference to nationality or the ethnic origin of someone who committed a crime. Simply asking the question, is it relevant to identify an individual in that way? Often it is not. It may be on occasion, but there should be a rationale for inclusion of that information. The website of ONO, the organization of news ombudsmen, will list different topics that news ombudsmen around the world have written about. And, I believe, there is one dealing with ethnicity reporting, which will provide again a list of practices, maybe not the worst, but pretty bad practices.

Petra Herczeg

I think the worst practice in Austria is that the population expects assimilation of the migrants and there's no discussion in the public about the meaning of the words "assimilation" and "integration". There has to be more information about these topics and about these basic words: what do they mean? They're mixed up all the time. And that's the fault of the journalists. Therefore, I think it is necessary to have more education for journalists on this field.

From the audience

I just want to add what Horst Pöttker has said about taking notice. It's not only important to take notice but it's, in doing so, important to take a minute and think about who you ask, who you make your source for the article and who you give a voice in the article that you write. I can give a little example from Dortmund. There is a discussion about a mosque being built or not being built, and in relation to that there have been demonstrations and also discussions in the newspapers about how migrants feel living in Dortmund and whether they arrived here and feel at home or not. And the journalist who wrote this article asked representatives of the church, representatives of the local government and of the trade unions – but no migrants themselves. Members of the church said that the migrants of the second generation feel a little better, but they didn't get the chance themselves to have a voice in this article. I think this is a good example how journalists sometimes should take a while and think who they ask.

From the audience

In a study that is part of our research project "Media Integration of Ethnic Minorities in Germany, the U.S., and Canada" we're asking journalists here in Dortmund two sets of questions. First we ask: What are minority organizations doing in the field of public relations? Are they sending in material? If they are sending in material, what are you doing with it? Are you taking it into account like the other? If you have language problems, do you put that special input into it, so you can print it or do you throw it away, or what do you do with it? And the journalists all say that they hardly send anything. But if they do, we do make a special effort. They seem very sincere. But at the same time, something else is also true. I asked them: and you, have you ever contacted any ethnic minority on your own? "Well, maybe." In what case? Then they admit "well, I can't remember." Some outright said "no". I've asked some 40 journalists now and I had one or two who had an example. And in these cases, it weren't even minority organizations. This was another context; they had personal connections to someone, whom they could phone on a private line. The barrier seems to be high. The public relations are bad and the journalists are also afraid, so to speak, to ask those people most concerned.

From the audience

One of the worst practices in journalism is not to ask why in a serious way. If you ask why, everything gets better.

Augie Fleras

We are getting very close to four o'clock and I think that four o'clock is a great time to end the proceedings of our assembly. Just one question remains to be responded. What can we learn from other media, from other countries or more specificly, what can your European media learn from experiences in the classic countries of immigration in North America? And if you recall, that in this morning presentation, it was quite revelatory for me to study ethnic aboriginal media in Canada and to come away with the absolute other conviction. It strikes me that the confusion of ethnic media can only collectively move the yardsticks forward in terms of creating a process by which new Canadians can make the transition into Canada at a pace and a degree that they feel comfortable with, not having to be customized or standardized to "one size fits all". Does someone like to have the last word for this afternoon?

Horst Pöttker

A very short last word. I think what European and especially German journalists can learn from the classic North American immigration societies is to contribute to a self-definition and a self-understanding of society in which cultural homogenity is not necessary for integration. I think this is a very important point. If you look at things and if you cover events from this perspective, then you can contribute to integration as a journalist.

Augie Fleras

It is true. I have to agree with you that we managed to find a model in which you can live together with differences. But in order to do that you have to have a vision. You have to have a vision that everyone buys into. And if you have that vision, then these differences become supporting, become inclusive, become non-threatening. So "yes" to diversity and diversity with a coverage. Rainer, the final word goes to you as the organizer.

Rainer Geißler

Yes, the programme gives me the last word. And I will use it, but only for a very few remarks. We had a conference concerning central basic problems of every immigration society, the classical ones, and the modern ones in Europe. We discussed and listened for two days. Yesterday evening I expressed my thanks to our speakers and I express them again, especially to Augie as the chairman of the last session and also to the chairwoman, who has left already. But at a conference, speakers, chairmen and chairwomen need an audience who listens to them and who discusses with them. I thank all participants for their interesting contributions.

People in the limelight need also people in the darkness, the invisible helpers. They have to remain in the background although they are the backbone of such a conference. They organize it, they manage it, they provide food, a wonderful lunch today, they take care of the electronics, so that PowerPoint works, they do a lot of things, which are done invisibly. I express my thanks to Angelika Schomann. (Applause) I have mentioned it several times. The last conference was in Siegen, this conference is in Dortmund and the Dortmund team did a very good job, many thanks. And many thanks also to the Siegen team, who were helpers with a secondary status at this conference – I thank you all. I wish everybody a nice journey home. Those who use the plane are the lucky ones. Those who have to use the car are the unlucky ones, because Angelika told me: traffic jams everywhere, because of the beginning of holidays in North Rhine Westfalia today. And the weather also caused a lot of problems on the motorways. Nevertheless, have a good journey home and I bid you, as the programme says, farewell. Not only farewell but also adieu, au revoir, auf Wiedersehen, tschüss!

The Authors

Horst Pöttker, Prof. Dr., is professor at the Institute of Journalism at the University of Dortmund. Currently he serves as dean of the Department of Cultural Studies. His teaching and research interests include media and migration, journalism history and theory, the language and style of journalistic genres, public ethics and research methods.

Rainer Geißler, Prof. Dr., is professor of Sociology at Siegen University. Main research areas include social structure/social inequality, migration and integration, sociology of mass communication, sociology of education/ socialization.

Sonja Weber-Menges, Dr., is research assistant at the Department of Sociology (Prof. Dr. Rainer Geißler) of Siegen University and works at the research project "Media Integration of Ethnic Minorities". Research areas include social structure, social inequality, migration and media.

Heinz Bonfadelli, Prof. Dr., is professor at the Institute for Mass Communication and Media Research, University of Zurich, Switzerland since 1994. His research interests include uses and effects of mass media, the knowledge gap and digital divide; mass media and youth, reading behaviour of children and adolescents, media and migration.

Petra Herczeg, Dr., works as assistant at the Institute of Communication Studies, University of Vienna, since 2001. Since 2002 she also works as a freelance radio-journalist for the cultural programme Ö1 of the Austrian broadcasting Company (ORF). Research interests include multilingualism and childhood in the communication society, journalism, ethnic minorities and media.

Leen d'Haenens, Prof. Dr., teaches as associate professor at the Radboud University Nijmegen and the Catholic University of Leuven. She also was guest lecturer on issues such as media policy, media and minorities, media convergence and media ethics, and Canadian studies at several international Universities.

Souley Hassane, Dr., is post-doctoral fellow at the University of Poitiers, CNRS Research Laboratory: "Migrinter", in the Minority Media Programme.

Augie Fleras, Prof. Ph.D., is professor at the Department of Sociology, University of Waterloo, Waterloo Ontario, Canada. His research focusses on ethnic minorities in Canada.

Kenneth Starck, Prof. Ph.D., is a former journalist and current dean of the Zayed University College of Communication and Media Sciences in Dubai. Before joining Zayed, he was professor at the University of Iowa School of Journalism and Mass Communication where he served as director for 17 years. His interests center on role of the media in society, including media freedom and responsibility.

Svetlana Serebryakova, Prof. Dr., is professor and chair of the Theory and Practice of Translation Department at Stavropol State University. Her research interests include linguistcs, semantics, and the language of mass media.